# Law and Finance after the Financial Crisis

The 2008 financial crisis has become one of the defining features of the twenty-first century's first decade. The series of events that unfolded in the aftermath of the crisis has exposed major structural flaws in many of the financial systems around the globe, triggering a global call for legal and regulatory reforms to address the problems that have been uncovered.

This book deals with a neglected angle of the 2008 financial crisis, looking in depth at the implicit effects of the crisis on the UK financial market. The book considers new trends in finance that have emerged or proliferated since the crisis, as well as the challenges faced by some older practices in the UK financial markets. After providing a reflective account of the history of law and creditors in the UK, the book examines the impact of the 2008 financial crisis on one of the old practices in the UK financial market – that is, ethical finance. The book then goes on to investigate the proliferation of certain forms of financing that have recently become very visible parts of the UK financial market's structure, such as high-cost, short-term lending and peer-to-peer lending. It provides legal and economic accounts of some of these forms of alternative lending, charting their developments and current status, and critically assessing their impact on the UK financial market. Also examined are the ongoing funding difficulties faced by small and medium enterprises (SMEs) and the suitability of the UK current legal framework to support these institutions. The book goes on to look at the viability and safety of some other post-crisis trends, such as banks' use of contingent convertible bonds (Cocos) to improve their resilience.

**Abdul Karim Aldohni** is a Senior Lecturer in Finance Law at Newcastle University, UK.

## Routledge Research in Finance and Banking Law

Available:

**European Prudential Banking Regulation and Supervision**
The Legal Dimension
*Larisa Dragomir*

**International Secured Transactions Law**
Facilitation of Credit and International Conventions and Instruments
*Orkun Akseli*

**The Legal and Regulatory Aspects of Islamic Banking**
A Comparative Look at the United Kingdom and Malaysia
*Abdul Karim Aldohni*

**Banking Secrecy and Offshore Financial Centres**
Money Laundering and Offshore Banking
*Mary Alice Young*

**Fiduciary Law and Responsible Investing**
In Nature's Trust
*Benjamin J. Richardson*

**Redefining the Market-State Relationship**
Responses to the Financial Crisis and the Future of Regulation
*Ioannis Glinavos*

**Financial Stability and Prudential Regulation**
A Comparative Approach to the UK, US, Canada, Australia and Germany
*Alison Lui*

**Law and Finance after the Financial Crisis**
The Untold Stories of the UK Financial Market
*Abdul Karim Aldohni*

Forthcoming:

**Competition Law and Financial Services**
*David Harrison*

**Institutional Structure of Financial Regulation**
Theories and International Experiences
*Robin Hui Huang and Dirk Schoenmaker*

**Microfinance and Financial Inclusion**
The Challenge of Regulating Alternative Forms of Finance
*Eugenia Macchiavello*

**Banking and Society**
Mapping Financial Regulation and Social Justice for the 21st Century
*Gary Wilson and Sarah Wilson*

# Law and Finance after the Financial Crisis

## The Untold Stories of the UK Financial Market

**Edited by Abdul Karim Aldohni**

Routledge
Taylor & Francis Group
LONDON AND NEW YORK

First published 2017 by Routledge

2 Park Square, Milton Park, Abingdon, Oxfordshire OX14 4RN
52 Vanderbilt Avenue, New York, NY 10017

*Routledge is an imprint of the Taylor & Francis Group, an informa business*

First issued in paperback 2018



*British Library Cataloguing in Publication Data*
A catalogue record for this book is available from the British Library

*Library of Congress Cataloging in Publication Data*
A catalog record for this book has been requested

ISBN: 978-1-138-93636-2 (hbk)
ISBN: 978-0-367-07549-1 (pbk)

Typeset in ITC Galliard by
Servis Filmsetting Ltd, Stockport, Cheshire

# Contents

# Notes on contributors

**Orkun Akseli** is Senior Lecturer in Commercial Law at Durham University Law School, UK, where he teaches company law, commercial law, international banking law and international commercial dispute resolution. He was Co-Director of the Institute of Commercial and Corporate Law at Durham University between 2012 and 2013. He has law degrees from Turkey, the United States and the UK. His monograph *International Secured Transactions Law: Facilitation of Credit, International Conventions and Instruments* was published by Routledge in 2011. He has edited *Financial Regulation in Crisis? The Role of Law and the Failure of Northern Rock* (with J. Gray, Edward Elgar, 2011); *Availability of Credit and Secured Transactions in a Time of Crisis* (Cambridge University Press, 2013); *Experiencing the Unfair Commercial Practices Directive* (with W. Van Boom and A. Garde, Ashgate, 2014); *Secured Transactions Law Reform: Principles, Policies and Practice* (with L. Gullifer, under contract with Hart Publishing, 2015); and *International and Comparative Secured Transactions Law* (with S. Bazinas, under contract with Hart Publishing, 2015). He has published on secured transactions and harmonisation of law, financial regulation, arbitration and sale of goods. He practised law in Turkey and acted as arbitrator/consultant in international arbitrations. He is a member of the Turkish Bar, the Chartered Institute of Arbitrators and the European Law Institute.

**Abdul Karim Aldohni** is Senior Lecturer in Finance Law at Newcastle Law School, Newcastle University, UK. He is the author of *The Legal and Regulatory Aspects of Islamic Banking: A Comparative Look at the UK and Malaysia* (Routledge, 2011) and *The Law of Islamic Capital Markets in the UK and EU* (under contract with Edward Elgar, 2017). He also published a student text *Foundations of Islamic Banking and Finance* (Kent: *ifs* School of Finance, 2010). In 2009 he was awarded a one-year Research Fellowship of the Institute of Financial Services/Henry Grunfeld Foundation.

**TT Arvind** is Professor of Law at Newcastle Law School, Newcastle University. He is the author of *The Law of Obligations: A New Realist Approach* (Cambridge University Press, forthcoming) and the editor of *Tort Law and the Legislature: Common Law, Statute, and the Dynamics of Legal Change* (with Jenny Steele,

Hart, 2012). He was awarded the ICLQ Young Scholar Prize in 2011 and the Society of Legal Scholars Best Paper Prize in 2010.

**Ulrich Atz** is the Head of Statistics at the Open Data Institute (ODI), where he does research, training and consultancy for open data. He has over seven years' practical experience of interpreting data and blends modern statistical techniques with storytelling. Before joining the ODI, Ulrich worked in the market research industry identifying commercial insights in seven-digit research projects. He holds a Diploma in Economics from the University of Mannheim and an MSc in Social Research Methods from the London School of Economics.

**David Bholat** is Senior Analyst in the Advanced Analytics Division at the Bank of England. A former Fulbright fellow at the London School of Economics and Political Science, he graduated with highest honours from Georgetown's School of Foreign Service. He later received his PhD from the University of Chicago.

**Gabriel Adeoluwa Onagoruwa (Adeolu)** is a lawyer at the London office of the international law firm of White & Case LLP. He is qualified to practise law in the United Kingdom and in Nigeria. He commenced his professional career with Templars, one of the foremost full service commercial firms in Lagos, Nigeria and has worked with the international consultancy firm of KPMG Services in Nigeria. He obtained his LLB degree from the University of Ibadan, Nigeria graduating with a First Class Honours. He holds an LLM and a PhD in law from the University of Cambridge. He is a recipient of numerous international laurels and awards. He is widely published in reputable international journals and has honoured several speaking engagements. He is a member of the International Bar Association, the Nigerian Bar and the Law Society of England and Wales.

**Nicholas Ryder** is a Professor in Financial Crime in the Department of Law, at the University of the West of England. He joined the University of the West of England in September 2004 after holding posts at Swansea University and the University of Glamorgan. His principal areas of teaching and research are white collar crime. He has published over 60 articles within prestigious journals and has contributed towards many conference papers. He has published four monographs including *The Financial War on Terror: a review of counter-terrorist financing strategies since 2001* (Routledge, 2015), *The Financial Crisis and White Collar Crime: The perfect storm?* (Edward Elgar, 2014), *Money Laundering – an Endless Cycle? A comparative analysis of the anti-money laundering policies in the USA, UK, Australia and Canada* (Routledge Cavendish, 2012) and *Financial Crime in the 21st Century – Law and Policy* (Edward Elgar, 2011). He has also published two textbooks: *The Law Relating to Financial Crime in the United Kingdom* (Ashgate, 2013), *Commercial Law: Principles and Policy* (Cambridge University Press, 2012) and an edited collection *Fighting Financial Crime in the Global Economic Crisis* (Routledge, 2014). Nicholas is the series founder and editor of Routledge's *The Law Relating to Financial Crime* and co-series editor of *Risky Groups and Control* for Palgrave MacMillan. His research has been sponsored by the Economic and Social Research Council, the City of London Police Force, ICT Wilmington Risk & Compliance, Universities South West, France Telecom Group and the European Social Fund.

# 1 Introduction

## Providing a different narrative: the 2008 financial crisis and the UK financial market

*Abdul Karim Aldohni*

### How the 2008 financial crisis changed the UK financial market

The 2008 financial crisis is one of the most defining features of the twenty-first-century's first decade. The series of events that was unfolded in the aftermath exposed major structural flaws in many of the financial governance systems around the globe. This triggered global calls for legal and regulatory changes in order to address the problems that were uncovered by the crisis. Therefore, the financial era that followed the 2008 financial crash has had a dominant theme – that is, regulatory reforms. In this regard, some major collective actions were taken at the international level to deal with the uncovered regulatory defaults. The Basel Committee on banking supervision introduced Basel III, which is 'a comprehensive set of reform measures' that aims to improve banks' management, governance and ability to absorb shocks; and to strengthen banks' transparency and disclosure'.[1] Further, at the domestic level, countries such as the UK, which host major international financial markets, were very swift to take on the regulatory challenge and reassure investors not only of their ability to stabilise their financial markets but also their commitment to improve their resilience.

In the UK, the Banking (Special Provisions) Act 2008 was introduced to deal with the failing banks, providing short-term emergency measures for up to 12 months. The 2008 Act enabled UK-incorporated banks and building societies to be taken into public ownership, provided a framework to compensate shareholders and included some further provisions to empower the Treasury.[2] Following the expiry of this emergency legislation, the Banking Act 2009 came into force. The 2009 Act established a Special Resolution Regime – a permanent framework

1 See Bank for International Settlement <http://www.bis.org/bcbs/basel3.htm> accessed 25 April 2016.

2 The Treasury was enabled to make an order to transfer the securities issued by, or property, rights or liabilities belonging to, an authorised deposit-taker; to amend relevant building society legislation that might otherwise prevent equivalent government action; to provide scope for flexibility with respect to unintended tax consequences and other measures like the 'extinguishment of subscription rights'. See Banking (Special Provisions) Act 2008 <http://services.parliament.uk/bills/2007-08/bankingspecialprovisions.html> accessed 25 April 2016.

that provides UK financial authorities with tools to deal with failing UK banks and building societies.[3]

Despite the radical regulatory changes that were introduced by the Banking Acts 2008 and 2009, it can be suggested that the beginning of a new regulatory era for the banking and financial sector in the UK was effectively marked by the breaking-up of the Financial Services Authority (FSA), which came into force on 1 April 2013. Under the new regime the FSA has been replaced by two regulatory bodies, the Prudential Regulatory Authority (PRA) and Financial Conduct Authority (FCA). This signifies the return of prudential regulatory responsibilities[4] to the Bank of England ('the Bank') since the PRA is established as a subsidiary of the Bank.[5] Despite its significance, the restructure of the regulatory authorities was not the only vital part of the UK national reform agenda. Further important changes to the legal and regulatory framework of the financial sector were introduced. They aimed at supporting the newly established authorities and promoting stability in the UK banking and financial market. For example, the Financial Services Act 2012 (FSA 2012) amended the Financial Services Market Act 2000 in order to accommodate the newly allocated powers of the FCA and the PRA. The FSA 2012 also established an independent Financial Policy Committee (FPC) at the Bank. The FPC is tasked with a primary objective to reduce systemic risk and protect the financial system resilience. Therefore its mandate includes 'identifying, monitoring and taking action to remove or reduce systemic risks with a view to protecting and enhancing the resilience of the UK financial system'.[6] The FPC also has a secondary objective to provide the required support of the government's economic policy.[7]

Additionally, the government established the Independent Commission on Banking (ICB) in 2010 to review and make recommendations in order to promote the UK banking system. The ICB final report in 2011 recommended certain reforms to ensure a more stable and competitive banking sector in the UK. Many of the final report's recommendations and other provisions, including those on ring fencing, were implemented by the Financial Services (Banking Reform) Act 2013. The notion of ring fencing stemmed from the regulator's determination to protect depositors (individuals and small businesses) and, consequently, tax-

3 See UK, Bank of England 'Resolution' <http://www.bankofengland.co.uk/FINANCIAL STABILITY/Pages/role/risk_reduction/srr/default.aspx> accessed 25 April 2016.

4 The scope of the PRA prudential supervision of investment firms should focus on those likely to cause systemic risk directly through their disorderly failure. See HM Treasury, 'A New Approach to Financial Regulation: Securing Stability, Protecting Consumer' (Cm 8268, January 2012) para 3.20; Andrew Bailey, 'The Prudential Regulation Authority' (2012) Q4 *Bank of England Quarterly Bulletin* <http://www.bankofengland.co.uk/publications/Documents/quarterlybulletin/qb120405pre.pdf> accessed 1 August 2016.

5 HM Treasury, 'A New Approach to Financial Regulation: Judgment, Focus and Stability' (Cm 7874, July 2010) para 3.29.

6 The Bank of England, 'Financial Policy Committee' <http://www.bankofengland.co.uk/financial stability/pages/fpc/default.aspx> accessed 25 April 2016.

7 The Bank of England, 'Financial Policy Committee' <http://www.bankofengland.co.uk/financial stability/pages/fpc/default.aspx> accessed 25 April 2016.

payers from banks' exposure to the securities markets. Deposit takers, primarily retail banks, are prohibited from dealing in investment as principal.[8] This means that they are not allowed to buy, sell, subscribe for or underwrite designated investments (for example shares, debentures, alternative debentures, life policies, options) as principal.[9] By setting a ring fence around these deposits, a clear line is being drawn between 'the high street and the trading floor'.[10]

At first glance, these regulatory changes might seem as the only recognisable major effects that the 2008 financial crisis has had on the UK financial market. This view is understandable and expected given the clear and direct links that these regulatory changes have with the events unfolded by the 2008 financial crisis. For instance, the failure of the FSA to foresee the problems with the soundness and safety of the banking system before they were exposed by the 2008 financial crisis has led to the creation of a separate regulator, the PRA, to perform effective prudential supervision; while supervising the business conduct is now conducted by another regulator, the FCA. Another example, the loss of depositors' money which was invested in highly speculative and complicated securities, has led to the enforcement of ring fencing in order to protect retail banks deposits.

However, a careful look into the UK financial market post 2008 reveals more implicit effects that the crisis had on the market and which exceed the obvious regulatory ones. These implicit or indirect effects probably have subtle links with the 2008 crisis but they are by no means less important than the regulatory ones. For a start, the landscape of the UK financial market itself has changed over the last few years with the disappearance of some of the market's main regional players (such as Northern Rock in the north east of England, which was fully nationalised and then sold to Virgin Money),[11] and the break-up of some of its large banking institutions (Lloyds TSB).

More importantly, the financial shock that the UK market experienced in 2008 has primarily impacted on credit flow as banks became either scared or were financially incapable of lending. Therefore, the market suffered from a sharply bipolar division of easy/reckless lending pre 2008 and hardly any lending post 2008. This shift from one extreme to another created a credit gap in the market, which many viewed as a serious problem while others saw an opportunity. New trends, such as peer-to-peer lending and crowdfunding, which emerged not long before 2008, started to gain significance in the UK market after 2008. They provide a service that the shrinking banking sector has become less able to offer and

8 FSMA 2000, s 142A, as amended by Financial Services (Banking Reform) Act 2013, s 4.

9 See the definition of 'dealing in investments as principal' and the definition of 'designated investment' in the *FCA Handbook*, Glossary (D) <https://www.handbook.fca.org.uk/handbook/glossary/G264.html?page=8&page-size=1000> and <https://www.handbook.fca.org.uk/handbook/glossary/G282.html> accessed 25 April 2016.

10 HM Treasury, '2010 to 2015 government policy: bank regulation' (Policy Paper, HM Treasury and Department for Business, Innovation and Skills 2015) <https://www.gov.uk/government/policies/creating-stronger-and-safer-banks> accessed 25 April 2016.

11 S Goff, 'Last Traces of Northern Rock Name Vanish', *Financial Times* (12 September 2012).

they benefit from new platforms that the new digital technology made available for their business. To a certain extent the same can be said about high cost short term credit providers, whose proliferation, although long established in the UK market, post 2008 can be attributed to the same factors that peer-to-peer lenders benefited from (i.e. the shortage in the credit supply and the use of online platforms to reach wider groups of customers).

These alternative forms of lending, which have become very visible parts of the UK financial market's structure, are not the only new emerging trends post 2008. In the last few years a relatively new type of hybrid bonds, known as contingent convertible capital instruments (Cocos), have been widely considered as an essential instrument to improve banks' resilience. Banks have been increasingly using Cocos to promote the resilience of their capital structure as these instruments convert into a capital cushion at time of sever financial stress. Cocos are a new financial innovation that is designed to avoid the shortcomings of pre 2008 crisis hybrid bonds.

Moreover, the UK financial market's landscape was not only shaped by the emergence of new trends post 2008 but also by the failure of some of the old practices in this market. The ethical finance sector, for instance, has been an integrated part of the UK market for hundreds of years yet the inability of some its institutions to withstand the ethical challenges of the 2008 events has undermined its credibility. Finally, the strain that the 2008 crisis put on credit supply has had a reverberating impact across the business sector. Small and medium enterprises (SMEs) are specifically affected by the reduction of funding available in the UK financial market. These institutions are particularly vulnerable at a time of economic crisis yet they play a central role in social renewal and economic recovery and growth.

It can be suggested that the above identified issues share a number of common features: first, they stem from new conditions imposed – one way or another – by the financial meltdown of 2008; second, they deepen our understanding of the financial crisis; and finally, they influence our perception of the post-2008 UK financial market. For these reasons they are no less important than the legal and regulatory changes, which are the obvious manifestation of how the crisis of 2008 changed the UK financial market.

## About this book

This collection of essays is neither designed nor aims to provide any analysis or assessment for the legal and regulatory changes that took place in the UK financial market in the wake of the 2008 crisis. This subject has been widely addressed by an extensive volume of the published literature since 2008.

Instead, this book deals with a neglected angle in the narrative of the 2008 financial crisis, which is no less important than the legal and regulatory reforms that followed the 2008 crisis. This collection of essays, therefore, provides an in-depth insight into, what can be arguably described as, the implicit effects of the 2008 crash on the UK financial market.

It is important to note from the outset that this book does not claim to deal with all the implicit effects that the 2008 financial crisis has had on the UK financial market. Rather, it identifies a selection of the 2008 crisis by-products and provides an extensive analysis of their nature and legal context.

To achieve its objective the book clearly identifies two threads that run through its chapters and map on to its central objective. The first thread focuses on the rising new trends in the UK financial market post 2008. The second thread, which complements the first, reflects on the strain the crisis put on some of the older practices in the UK financial market and examines the market's relationship with some aspects of the business sector post 2008.

## Book structure

Given that the main objective of this edited collection is to examine the implicit manifestations of the 2008 financial crisis in the UK financial market, it is important to provide a reflective account of the 2008 financial crisis in the UK context. Chapter 2 examines the 2008 financial crisis from a unique perspective. Instead of focusing on the questionable financial practices in the run-up to the crisis, which have been widely addressed by an extensive body of the published literature since 2008, the chapter traces its origins to the shift in the nature of debt. Through the use of the history lens the chapter documents the nature of this shift and the enduring role it has played in making debt a destabilising influence on the economy. The chapter highlights the replacement of the relational understanding of debt by a more commodified understanding. It argues that the key lesson that the history of the construction of debt offers is that regulatory systems that fail to remember the fictional character of the commodified understanding of debt are inevitably unlikely to promote stability.

After providing a reflective account of the 2008 financial crisis in the UK context from a historic perspective, the book investigates some of the new trends that have emerged or proliferated as implicit effects of the crisis. Chapter 3 examines one of these new financial trends in the UK market, namely peer-to-peer lending platforms. By using loan-level data and empirical research (interviews), the chapter provides an insight into the evolution of this business and its turning point which was marked by the crisis. The chapter explains why borrowers and lenders participate in the peer-to-peer market highlighting some of the innovative features that this new form of finance is providing. It also speculates about the impact that peer-to-peer lenders may have on the conventional banking sector in the near future.

Chapter 4 deals with another rising financial trend at the retail financial level, that is high cost short term credit providers. The chapter charts the evolution of the consumer credit market in the UK in order to contextualise the proliferation of the high cost short term credit sector post 2008. It illustrates how the rapid expansion of the consumer credit market resulted in continuing record levels of consumer debt and increasing evidence of irresponsible lending practices with particular reference to the high cost short term credit sector post 2008. The chapter analyses the UK legal and regulatory approach in dealing with this phenomenon. It provides a damning critique of the regulation and the ineffective legislative framework that offered little or no protection to consumers. It also charts the legal and regulatory developments that have taken place since 2008 in this respect.

Chapter 5 is also an integral part of the first thread – emerging new trends – of this edited collection as it analyses another implicit effect of the 2008 crisis on the UK financial market. The chapter focuses on a new instrument, namely convertible contingent capital instruments (Cocos), which, post 2008, have become widely used by banks to improve their resilience. The chapter provides a detailed account of the context in which these instruments are being used through addressing the nature and function of regulatory bank capital. It also examines the nature of Cocos as ideal complements for equity by considering the arguments in favour and against their adoption as part of the framework for regulatory capital requirements. The chapter touches upon some of the regulatory aspects of these instruments within the UK financial market.

As highlighted earlier, the second thread in this book's argument concerns the challenge that was brought about by the crisis to the credibility of some of the older practices in the UK financial market and also entails the strain that the crisis put on this market's relationship with some aspects of the business sector post 2008. In this regard Chapter 6 brings particular focus to the topic of ethical finance given its historic roots in the UK financial market. In the wake of the 2008 crisis many argued that the financial business culture needs to be changed and that ethical finance could have an important role to play. On the other hand, one of the main ethical banks in the UK market, Co-operative Bank, has failed to withstand the test of the 2008 financial crisis. The near collapse of the Co-operative Bank in 2013 uncovered that the bank was involved in some questionable practices that contradicted its ethical agenda. Therefore, this chapter questions the viability of the concept of ethical finance in theory and in practice. The chapter brings special focus to the experience of the Co-operative Bank in the UK. It further examines the possible and realistic steps that are needed to promote the effectiveness of ethical finance as part of the solution to the contamination problem in the business culture of the UK financial sector.

This edited collection continues to peruse its central theme concerning the implicit effects of the 2008 crisis by exploring how it impacted on certain aspects of the business sector, which is an essential part of the second thread of the book's argument.

Chapter 7 particularly focuses on one of the main key impacts that the 2008 crisis has had on the UK business sector, that is the shortage of funding for SMEs. The chapter highlights the importance of SMEs in the process of economic recovery in the UK and examines their vulnerable positon at this current stage. It investigates the problem of limited access to finance from a legal and regulatory perspective and provides an in-depth critical legal analysis of how this problem can be addressed.

Chapter 8 reflects on the two threads of the book's argument in order to provide a holistic assessment, from a non-regulatory perspective, of how the 2008 financial crisis has changed the UK financial market. It also critically evaluates whether that change was for the better or the worse.

# 2 Law, creditors and crises: the untold story of debt

*TT Arvind*

## Introduction: the transformation of debt

Three financial crises involving the state stand out in the history of English law, in each case because of the significant consequences that the steps taken in response to the crisis had on the development of the legal system. The first was the crisis faced by King John in the early thirteenth century, as a result of the expense of the war in France and the dramatic reduction in national revenue occasioned by the loss of Normandy. The second was the crisis faced by King Charles I in the middle of the seventeenth century, once again caused by the inability to raise sufficient revenue to meet the expense of wars on the Continent. The third was the crisis faced in the late seventeenth century by King William III and Queen Mary, also as a result of the expense of wars on the Continent.

The revenue-raising measures taken in response to all three crises had important constitutional dimensions. The first produced Magna Carta, the second produced the Civil War and the English Revolution, and the third was at the time seen as potentially posing a grave threat to the constitutional settlement created by the Glorious Revolution. Yet while the first two continue to be seen as key moments in the evolution of the English constitution, the primary legacy of the third is today seen as having been on the law of companies, in the form of the South Sea Bubble to which it gave rise and the Bubble Act[1] that imposed restrictions on the creation and operation of joint-stock companies.

At the heart of this difference in the consequences of the three, and the manner in which they have come to be embodied in the popular perception, was a shift in the way in which debt was approached and understood. This shift began shortly before the South Sea Bubble and has continued to reverberate in the legal system to the present day. The purpose of this chapter is to document the nature of this shift, and the enduring role it has played in making debt a destabilising influence on the economy. The 2008 financial crisis was not the first time debt played such a role, as Reinhart and Rogoff showed in their history of financial crises,[2] and

1 6 Geo I, c 18.

2 CM Reinhart and KS Rogoff, *This Time is Different: Eight Centuries of Financial Folly* (Princeton University Press, 2009).

it will not be the last. But the propensity of debt to cause crises is nevertheless peculiar. Stripped to its essentials, debt is simply one way of procuring purchasing power, much like income, gifts or inheritance. Other ways of procuring purchasing power do not cause crises. A country with a high level of income is generally seen to be doing well, and few would speak of a country having 'excessive' income[3] – or, for that matter, excessive gifts, or the excessive sale of assets.[4] Nor do we commonly hear of 'income' crises or 'gift' crises or 'inheritance' crises. While the distributional aspects of income and inheritance may be seen as economically problematic, their aggregate levels are not. With debt, the precise opposite is true.

Why, then, of all the means by which purchasing power may be acquired, is debt and debt alone seen as being a source of economic crisis and instability? History suggests that this is not merely a matter of perception: debt truly does have destabilising effects. The story of an economy with high aggregate levels of indebtedness has rarely ended happily, unlike the story of economies with high aggregate levels of income. What makes debt exceptional among ways of acquiring purchasing power? All that distinguishes debt, seemingly, is that it involves a continuing obligation of repayment between debtor and creditor, which other modes of obtaining purchasing power do not. But contractual obligations are not usually seen as posing systemic threats to an economy, and even the simultaneous occurrence of a large number of breaches of contract does not usually have the effect that a simultaneous default on a large number of debts does. What is it about this obligation – the legal relationship of debtor and creditor – that makes it such a prominent source of economic risk and economic instability?

That is the question this chapter seeks to answer through a historical study of how law has approached the nature of debt and the relationship between debtor and creditor. As we will see in the course of this chapter, the history of the legal understanding of the relationship between creditors and debtors is one of rupture rather than continuity. Prior to the eighteenth century, debt was not particularly different in legal terms from other modes of acquiring purchasing power. It involved a legally enforceable obligation, but so did the right to collect income; and debt-based instruments frequently took forms such as annuities that blurred the distinction between debt and income. Equally, an important theme in the legal understanding of debt was the idea that taking on debt was an expression of individual *need*, to which society had a religious and moral obligation to

3 While high inflation or low productivity can be seen as being economically problematic, in both macro- and micro-economics the problem is not attributed to the high level of income per se. It is, instead, attributed to broader factors relating to the health of the underlying economy, for example the mismatch between the supply of money and production (in relation to inflation) or the failure to improve the efficiency with which goods and services are produced (in relation to productivity). High levels of income unaffected by such factors are rarely seen as contributing to economic or financial crises.

4 Note that I refer to *aggregate* levels of inheritance and income in an economy, which are seen as being economically unproblematic, rather than to *how evenly* that income or those inherited assets are distributed among the various persons in that economy, about which opinion is more divided.

respond. The clearest manifestations of this were the Usury Laws, which initially prohibited, and subsequently tightly regulated, the charging of interest on debts.

The financial revolution of the eighteenth century saw a decisive shift away from this understanding of debt. Its result was the gradual erosion of the traditional picture of debt, which we may broadly call a *relational* understanding, in that it saw debt as a legal relationship between debtor and creditor, and its replacement by a more *commodified* understanding, which transformed debt into a commodity capable of being traded on a market, with an existence independent of whatever may have been the social relationship between the original debtor and creditor. This shift had a twofold effect. First, it moved the legal system away from a need-based understanding of debt to one which saw the taking on of debt as no different from the acquisition of any other commodity, and hence primarily as a matter of contract rather than social relations. One consequence was a shift in perception of responsibility for debt from creditor to debtor. Second, because it had no parallel in relation to other means of acquiring purchasing power, it resulted in a growing divergence between debt and these other forms, with debt in particular assuming legal forms that are far more complex, and capable of far more manipulation, than income, gifts or the other means by which purchasing power may be acquired.

But history provides us not just with an understanding of *how* and *why* the shift occurred, but also of the *consequences* of the shift. The 2008 financial crisis itself provides an excellent example both of the complexity of the debt-based structures that a commodified understanding facilitates, and of the role of this complexity in causing crisis. As we will see, it is the commodified character of debt that lets it affect the broader economy as no other way of acquiring purchasing power, and no other type of contract, can. If we take a closer look at the 2008 crisis, we can see this complexity manifested in the interaction between at least three different types of debt that were implicated in this crisis. Critically, although different aetiological accounts of the crisis chose to highlight the role of different types of debt in bringing about the crisis, their actual roles in producing and exacerbating the crisis were closely intertwined; and they all ultimately arose out of the same underlying instances of borrowing. At the most basic level, the crisis involved debt incurred by individual borrowers to institutional creditors. The most obvious example, although not the only one, was the 'sub-prime' mortgage borrowing that formed the basis of the complex securitised products that played such a major role in bringing about the crisis. The inability of individual debtors (mortgagors) to pay their creditors (the banks) led, in turn, to the originators of the securitised products (usually special purpose vehicles (SPVs)) being unable to pay the amounts due to their creditors, namely the investors in those products. Second, and following on from this, the crisis involved debt owed by financial institutions, including inter-bank borrowing and borrowing on international money markets, but also including money owed to retail depositors. It was the collapse of counterparties' confidence in the creditworthiness of financial institutions, and of depositors' trust in the ability of banks to repay their deposit, that prompted the run on Northern Rock, the collapse of Lehman Brothers and Bear

Stearns, and the government-sponsored bailouts and takeovers of virtually every significant financial institution in the Western world. Third, and as a direct consequence of the second, the crisis involved government debt and, more specifically, the dramatic consequences for certain governments of a loss of market confidence in their ability to continue to service their debts. This aspect of the crisis was particularly pronounced in the Eurozone, and while a history of fiscal irresponsibility may well have played a part in bringing about a crisis of confidence, the immediate prompt was the need to bail out large financial institutions.

Much has been written about the irresponsible practices of borrowers, the financial industry, and governments that led to each of these three types of debt producing the collapses of confidence that ultimately reached crisis proportions. The purpose of this chapter is not to rehash that discussion, but rather to argue that a deeper, and less-noticed, factor is the disappearance from the legal and regulatory framework of the relational dimensions of debt. Debt is a *fictitious* commodity, not a true one,[5] and the key lesson which the history of the construction of this legal fiction offers is that a regulatory system that ceases to remember the fictional character of the commodified understanding of debt is inevitably likely to promote instability.

## The problem of finance

The story this chapter seeks to tell begins in 1688, with the ascension of King William III and Queen Mary to the English throne following the Glorious Revolution. William's interests did not lie in England as much as they lay in the Continent, and he came to the throne intending to use English revenues to fund the expensive European wars in which he was involved.

The problem of finding money to fund a foreign war was, of course, not new. Yet William faced constitutional constraints which had not hampered his predecessors in quite the same way. Past monarchs had raised funds through a combination of taxation and extortion. Charles I's use of the prerogative to demand ship money is, of course, notorious. The relationship between Magna Carta and King John's financial exactions is no less striking, although it has played a lesser role in popular understandings of the meaning of that document. Magna Carta was to a very significant extent the product of a sovereign funding crisis. John's campaigns on the Continent were expensive, and the expense came at a time when his income was under pressure following the loss of Normandy and the not-insubstantial income it generated. He resorted to a range of near-despotic measures to raise revenues, ranging from confiscating estates to raising court fees to such a high degree as to make access to justice nearly unaffordable.[6] Quite apart from the individual hardship this caused, the vast withdrawal of money from the economy brought about by John's taxation and hoarding of money

5 The understanding of a fictitious commodity this chapter uses is derived from the work of Karl Polanyi. See the discussion at p 24 below.

6 RV Turner, *Magna Carta* (Longman, 2003) chs 1, 2.

resulted in widespread deflation,[7] causing enormous hardship. The hardship only just stopped short of a full-blown economic crisis because of the simultaneous expansion of commerce and trade, and the growth of fairs, which provided a very significant stimulus to the economy.[8] Its effects were real, and many of the celebrated provisions of Magna Carta, including the promise not to sell or deny justice, were direct responses to the extortionate character of John's revenue-raising measures.

Such routes were not open to William III. Parliament after the Glorious Revolution was not in a mood to admit any broad claim in relation to the scope of the royal prerogative, particularly when it pertained to the monarch's revenue-raising powers. Extortion, as the Stuarts and generations of earlier monarchs had done, was no longer a viable way of raising revenue. Equally, the Whig oligarchy that effectively controlled Parliament after 1688 was unwilling to raise taxes much further than the level at which they stood, which was seen as already being at the outer limit of what could be borne. The inevitable result was that if revenue had to be raised, it had to be raised by borrowing.

Royal borrowing was, of course, not unknown – indeed, in England it went back at least to the Plantagenets. The ability to borrow the very large sums of money required for William's European wars was, however, limited by the fact that the character of debt and credit at that time was still overwhelmingly relational. The relational character of debt had a two-fold limiting effect on William's ability to use debt as the primary source of the finance of the magnitude he required. First, it led to a situation where borrowing took a very limited range of forms, which lacked the flexibility William would have required to raise the sums he needed. Second, it meant that borrowing was on the King's personal credit and was often granted in circumstances bordering on extortion. The result was that raising substantial sums from a broader range of persons entailed a second task, namely restoring and upholding faith in the public credit.

Overcoming these problems was not straightforward, and one of the most enduring impacts of the Financial Revolution arises from the manner in which it did so. To put it in somewhat anachronistic terms, the Financial Revolution resolved these issues by creating a derelationalised form of debt and, in particular, through the emergence, and eventual rise to dominance, of a *commodified* understanding of debt in the course of the financial revolution.

## Dimensions of relationality

The assertion that has just been made requires some explanation. What, specifically, does it mean to characterise debt in early modern England as 'relational', and how does it differ from a 'commodified' understanding? The nature of the

7 JL Bolton, 'The English Economy in the Early Thirteenth Century' in SD Church (ed.), *King John: New Interpretations* (Boydell, 1999).

8 J Masschaele, 'The English Economy in the Age of Magna Carta' in JS Loengard (ed.), *Magna Carta and the England of King John* (Boydell, 2010).

claims made by modern relational theories of private law, and of the sections of feminist theories that are in sympathy with them,[9] has led relationality to be associated with care, trust and co-operation; but relationality as an analytical concept does not necessarily entail any of these elements. The theory of relationality, in essence, does no more than assert the relevance of *social* relations, and the expectations arising out of those relations, to the study of *legal* and *economic* relations.[10] It asserts, to put it differently, that the practical working of legal and economic relations depends in significant part on the nature of the social relations in the community within which the legal and economic relations subsist.

It is in that sense that I use the phrase in this chapter. The relational character of debt in early modern England gave it three distinctive features that distinguish it sharply from the way in which debt is perceived in the present day. Two of these, from a modern perspective, will generally be regarded as positive, even if some of their specific consequences were not, and they are likely to have had a stabilising influence on society in their contemporary setting. These are the primacy of the social aspect of debt relations, and the idea that debt was a manifestation of an underlying need that other members of the community had some level of obligation to satisfy (even if the obligation was not a very strong one). The third feature or dimension of relationality, in contrast, strikes the modern eye as obviously negative, and in its contemporary setting played an equally obviously destabilising role. This was the role of social and political power in shaping the practical working of the relations between debtor and creditor. In this section, we will examine how each of these three dimensions of relationality affected debt in early modern England, pointing out in the process how they differ from the commodified understanding of debt that characterises modern society.

The first two can be dealt with together. In relational terms, debt is simply an incident of social relations, part of the inevitable web of obligations that are incurred and discharged in the course of everyday co-existence. Debt, in this sense, is a manifestation of mutual dependence, in particular the mutual dependence of people on each other for satisfying their needs. Debt is a mode of mutual dependence that pertains specifically to the satisfaction of needs that depend on having purchasing power.

In a fascinating study of debt relations among common folk in early modern

9 J Steele, 'Duty of Care and Ethic of Care: Irreconcilable Difference?' in J Richardson and E Rackley (eds), *Feminist Perspectives on Tort Law* (Routledge, 2012).

10 IR MacNeil, 'Reflections on Relational Contract Theory after a Neo-classical Seminar' in D Campbell, H Collins and J Wightman (eds), *Implicit Dimensions of Contract: Discrete, Relational and Network Contracts* (Hart, 2003). The basic point is not fundamentally different from what Polanyi termed 'embeddedness': the phenomenon by which (according to him) economic relations are necessarily embedded in social relations, and markets are necessarily embedded in other social institutions: K Polanyi, 'The Economy as an Instituted Process' in C Arensberg, K Polanyi and HW Pearson (eds), *Trade and Market in the Early Empires: Economies in History and Theory* (Free Press, 1957).

England, Muldrew has shown that this is precisely how debt functioned at an everyday level.[11] As his account shows, debt relations were common and widespread, but they did not represent borrowing in the sense we would understand today. Instead, much of the debt that appears to have been owed between people, as far as we can gather from the evidence of wills and account books, is in connection with perfectly ordinary transactions. It appears to have been common practice for people to maintain ledgers of the money they owed to and were owed by different people, with the balances set off and the outstanding sums paid on a day of reckoning. The main forms that debt took in early modern England, in other words, were deferred payments or advanced payments of the sort that one might arrange with tradesmen, shopkeepers and other suppliers. Muldrew's research suggests that forgiveness of debts was also relatively common, and seems to have been a consequence of the fact that debt and credit were deeply embedded in social relations. This does not mean that individuals were necessarily happy to forego debts that were due to them. Nevertheless, the possibility that debt might have to be forgiven was seen as being implicit in the relations between debtor and creditor.

The primacy of social relations, and the needs-based understanding of debt, had two consequences in terms of the way in which the law approached debt. Because a debt was seen as primarily being a relationship between two people, it was not assignable in early modern English law. Property that was not real could either be a chose in possession, or a chose in action – a mere right of action against another party that was only enforceable through bringing legal proceedings (unlike a chose in possession where, as the name suggests, interests were enforceable by actual possession of the object). It was a long-established rule at common law that choses in action were not assignable, a rule which was affirmed and extended by Lord Coke in *Lampet's Case*[12] to encompass any future interest. After *Slade's case*[13] in 1602, debts were enforceable at common law both through the independent action of debt and the action of assumpsit, which was the ordinary action brought to enforce contracts. They were thus choses in action, and a contract to sell or trade a debt thus had no legal effect: the debt remained owed by the debtor to the original creditor rather than to the assignee, and an assignee had no legal right to sue on the debt.

Some exceptions were made to this by inheritance from the Law Merchant, most notably an exception for bills of exchange where the common law, after initial resistance in the seventeenth century, eventually came to recognise assignment by negotiation.[14] But these were construed narrowly, and debts that did not fall within them were not assignable. In *Clerke v Martin*,[15] for example, Holt CJ held that a promissory note was not transferable by negotiation because it

11 C Muldrew, *The Economy of Obligation: The Culture of Credit and Social Relations in Early Modern England* (Macmillan, 1998).

12 (1612) 10 Co Rep 46b, 77 ER 994.

13 (1602) 4 Co Rep 92b.

14 See e.g. *Buller v Crips* (1703) 6 Mod 29, 87 ER 793 (KB).

15 (1702) 2 Ld Raym 758, 92 ER 6 (KB).

was not a bill of exchange and hence did not fall within the exception created by the Law Merchant. The debt it represented was therefore non-transferrable. The decision was quickly overturned in 1704 by statute,[16] but the broader reluctance of the courts to recognise the assignability of debts remained unchanged.[17] At the heart of this lay a clear view that the proper nature of debt was contractual (and, hence, relational), from which the courts were unwilling to depart however much merchant practice might benefit from their doing so.[18] A debt was, in essence, a promise to do something, and was therefore a contract. The only legal interest created by a contract was a right to bring an action to recover if it was breached (unlike a chose in possession, where the legal interests extended to physical possession). Any assignment of a chose in action was treated as maintenance if it was gratuitous, or as champerty if it was done for profit, both of which rendered the transaction void at common law.[19]

Simultaneously, the relationality that was seen as being an inherent part of debt also played a significant role in the justification behind the usury laws, and in early seventeenth-century debates about lowering the maximum rate of interest. The charging of interest upon loans had been prohibited for much of the mediaeval period both at common law and by statute,[20] due to the Catholic teaching that it was sinful to charge interest.[21] Following the Reformation, interest was initially legalised by statute in 1545, but was subject to a cap of 10 per cent.[22] The legalisation was controversial, and the statute was repealed in 1552,[23] before being legalised in 1571 with the same cap of 10 per cent.[24] The courts' attitude towards interest, however, remained grudging rather than enthusiastic. In *Sanderson v Palmer*,[25] the Court of King's Bench acknowledged that practice since the statute had given the charging of interest the strength of usage by statute, and impeaching it would be a great impediment to trade and commerce. However, Sir John Lea, the Chief Justice, qualified the court's statement that a person was free to charge interest within the statutory cap by saying that he might do so if he 'wished to endanger his conscience', and one of the other judges was reported as

16 3 & 4 Ann, c 9.

17 For a fuller discussion of the case, see JS Rogers, *The Early History of the Law of Bills and Notes: A Study of the Origins of Anglo-American Commercial Law* (Cambridge University Press, 1995) 178ff.

18 On this point, see J Baker, 'The Law Merchant as a Source of Law' in W Swadling and G Jones (eds), *The Search for Principle: Essays for Lord Goff of Chieveley* (Oxford University Press, 1999) 79.

19 'Maintenance' was (and remains) the legal term for a situation where a person provides financial or material support to a litigation, despite having no interest in it. Champerty specifically covers situations where a person does so for profit. While champerty and maintenance continue to render transactions void at law, they now have far narrower meanings than they did in early modern law.

20 3 Henry VII, c 5. The statute specifically prohibited the practice of 'dry exchange', which was a fictitious contract commonly used to avoid the usury laws at the time (1488) when it was passed.

21 On the relationship between religion and the usury laws more generally, see N Jones, *God and the Moneylenders: Usury and the Law in Early Modern England* (Blackwell, 1989).

22 37 Henry VIII, c 9.

23 5&6 Edw VI, c 20.

24 13 Eliz, c 8.

25 [1721] Palm 291 (KB), also reported as *Saunderson v Warner* (1622) 2 Rolle 239.

speaking scathingly of 'horrible, divelish, damnable usury', which even heathens possessed of natural reason condemned.[26]

Unsurprisingly, then, the trend through the course of the seventeenth century was to seek to abate the charging of interest. The ceiling on interest was lowered first to 8 per cent in 1624,[27] and then to 6 per cent in 1660.[28] A recurrent theme in the debates that surrounded the passage of these statutes was the importance of borrowing in meeting needs. Two needs, in particular, were prominent in the debate. The first was manufacturers' need for capital. Lower rates of interest, it was argued, would give more manufacturers access to the capital they needed, and would do so more cheaply, hence making English manufactured products more competitive.[29] The second was the need of the poor. Poverty, it was asserted, was always worse where interest was higher. Contrasts were commonly drawn between the condition of the poor in countries with high and low levels of interest. In Ireland and Spain, both naturally fertile countries, the inhabitants were said to be 'poor, ill fed and clad' because interest rates were 10 to 12 per cent. In contrast, in Italy and Holland, interest rates were much lower at 3 per cent, and the people in general were said to have a much higher standard of life even though their lands were less fertile.[30]

The two dimensions we have just examined fit with the traditional understanding of relationality as a broadly positive notion. This does not hold of the third dimension of relationality, namely the role of power. Power, at first glance, might seem contrary to the general association of relationality with co-operation and trust. If one's subject is a society or community characterised by care and trust, then a relational analysis will indeed lead to care and trust having primacy. If, however, one's society is characterised by power imbalances, and by the willingness of the powerful to exercise their power ruthlessly, then relationality can be a vehicle of injustice as easily as it can be a vehicle of greater care, trust and co-operation.

The drawbacks of this third dimension of relationality had a strong influence on the emergence of new, derelationalised approaches to debt during the Financial Revolution. The problem of power had a particular resonance in the late seventeenth century because its effect had been particularly baneful in the very near past in the context of sovereign debt.[31] As far back as the Angevin period, monarchs had established the habit of confiscating the estates of unfortunate nobles, who then had to shower the sovereign with lavish gifts or loans to restore themselves to his favour. By the time of the later Stuarts, however, rulers had honed the art of extorting loans to a degree of perfection. The dealings of Charles II with the East India Company after the Restoration serve as a good

26 [1721] Palm 291, 292.

27 21 Jac I, c 17.

28 12 Car II, c 13.

29 T Culpeper, *A Discourse Shewing The Many Advantages Which will Accrue to this Kingdom by the Abatement of Usury* (Thomas Leach, 1668) 10–15.

30 RC, *A Letter to a Friend Concerning Usury* (London, 1690) 23.

31 Although, as this section has also shown, the position in relation to private debt was very different.

illustration. The business of the East India Company depended on the continued validity of the charter it had originally been granted by James I. Charles II and his treasurer Lord Danby used this to demand a series of payments from the East India Company, amounting in total to well over £300,000. Some were 'repayable' through a remission of customs duties, but others were non-repayable 'voluntary presents'.[32]

It was not just large corporations like the East India Company, or the City of London, whose debt relations with the Crown were potentially affected by power. This was starkly demonstrated by the incident that has come to be known as the Stop of the Exchequer, which took place in the reign of Charles II. In 1672, Charles II was facing a shortage of funds to supply the naval fleet.[33] To meet the immediate financing problem, an Order in Council was issued suspending all payments from the Exchequer on certain types of warrants, all of which related to debts owed by the Crown. The suspension was to last only one year, but its effect was chaotic. All eight of Charles II's principal creditors went bankrupt. Several died in debtor's prison, and others found their goods and assets seized. In at least two cases, the bankruptcy of the creditors caused such problem for *their* creditors that Private Acts of Parliament were needed to sort out the problem. And the repercussions ran even further. Some of the creditors were bankers who had invested funds on deposit, whose depositors then in turn lost their money.[34] Horsefield has estimated that, in total, nearly 2,500 individuals were affected, including widows and orphans who are likely to have been left destitute.[35] A suit was dismissed on the basis of Crown immunity, with Lord Somer justifying his decision on the basis that the King must have the sole power to order the course of payments of money in his own coffers. To do otherwise would be to take from him 'the judgment of public necessities'.[36] Resolving the matter ultimately required a vote of the full House of Lords on a writ of error, followed by statute, but even so the creditors only received a small portion of what they were owed.

It is, therefore, important not to romanticise the relational period in the long history of debt. While there is much that, on its face, might appear attractive in the relational treatment of debt and credit, it also had its weaknesses. Although these became particularly evident in the context of sovereign credit, they were by no means unique to it. It is against this background that we must understand the legal and social derelationalisation of debt that accompanied the Financial Revolution.

32 GO Nichols, 'English Government Borrowing, 1660–1688' (1971) 10 *Journal of British Studies* 83, 85–8.

33 A concise summary of the circumstances of the stop is set out in A Browning, 'The Stop of the Exchequer' (1930) 14 *History* 333.

34 For a contemporary account, see T Turnor, *The Case of the Bankers and their Creditors* (London, 1675).

35 JK Horsefield, 'The Stop of the Exchequer Revisited' (1982) 35 *Economic History Review NS* 511, 526–7.

36 *The Case of the Bankers* (1696) 14 State Trials 1, 105.

## The logic of derelationalisation

The commodified form of debt that emerged from the period of the Financial Revolution differs fundamentally from the earlier, relational debt in two principal ways. Commodified debt, unlike relational debt, treats the debt as a thing that has an existence independent of the underlying social relationship, and is thus capable of remaining unaffected by the distribution of power that is immanent in the underlying social relationship between the debtor and the creditor. More fundamentally, the commodified account distinguishes itself by seeing debt as something that is capable of being provided and harnessed to the common good through an appropriately constituted market of borrowers and suppliers of credit, in precisely the same way as any other commodity.

It is the emergence of this second idea in the late seventeenth century that marks the most radical break with debt's more relational past. The key conceptual shift that characterised the post-revolutionary period was the birth of the idea that, as with commodities, credit can be manufactured and supplied in sufficient quantities to meet demand. To contemporary writers, the ability to produce credit to meet demand, unlike money per se, which cannot be so produced, meant that credit had the potential to unlock the economy's full hidden potential, which would otherwise remain untapped for want of specie-money. In a world of competitive trading, a nation whose economy is characterised by an abundance of credit would therefore be one whose trade would prosper, to the benefit of its manufacturers and merchants. The rapid growth of market-based credit would, therefore, confer benefits upon the public generally. And, as long as the process remained safely in the hands of an effective entrepreneur or manager, the production of credit could and would proceed without deleterious effects to the health of the economy.

The writings of commentators and public figures associated with the Whig party, who were the strongest champions of the new credit-based economy, provide us with clear insight into this way of thought. The writings of Daniel Defoe provide a good, and representative, example. Defoe is today perhaps best known for his works of fiction, but in his own time he was also a prominent commentator on the political questions of the day, and put out a periodical under the title *A Review of the State of the British Nation.* Britain, he wrote in 1710, had only been able to fight and win the wars in which it had lately been engaged because of credit. Had it relied on money simpliciter, it simply would not have been able to afford what credit let it buy:

> CREDIT is at present the Soul of this Nations Greatness, and by which we have been enabled to carry on a War, the Expence of which, all the Specie in the Nation could not have supported, nor all the Circulation of Money have supplied.[37]

37 D Defoe, *A Review of the State of the British Nation*, vol VII no 48, 15 July 1710, reprinted in *Defoe's Review* (facsimile book 17) 186.

Defoe's argument, in essence, was that credit was a far more effective way of acquiring purchasing power than other modes, such as trade, because it was capable of generating purchasing power in contexts where these other modes could not. Credit, as he put it a fortnight later, had 'turn'd nothing into something, Coin'd Paper into Metal, and stampt a Value upon what had no Value before'.[38] And this did not just apply to war and public credit, but also to trade, where private credit could transform the fortunes of 'the meanest Shop-Keeper, Country Woll-Comber, or petty Chapmen'.[39] Seen in its context, there is substance to Defoe's views. Money, in his time, consisted of specie, that is to say, of coins minted from gold and silver, and there could therefore only be a limited quantity of money in circulation at any point of time. Creating more money would have required the acquisition of more gold or silver to mint more coins; but credit could, seemingly, produce purchasing power without requiring any greater quantity of money.

This was, of course, a dramatic shift in how debt was seen, and it is this shift that I have sought to characterise as a shift from the view of debt as a relationship to one that saw it as a market commodity. The question of why the view of debt as a relationship came to be displaced by this new vision of debt as a market commodity is a complex one, which cannot easily be answered in the course of this chapter. Nevertheless, the shift in sovereign debt in the period between the Glorious Revolution in 1688 and the South Sea Bubble in 1721 provides an excellent lens through which to trace the progressive emergence of this conception, as well as the effects it had on the stability of the economy.

The predominance of relationality in debt relations in the sense we discussed in the previous section was not confined to commoners. Much of the debt incurred by Charles II also took precisely this form. Although direct loans in the modern sense were not entirely unknown, much sovereign borrowing and repayment before the Glorious Revolution took place in forms that were much more closely akin to the informal systems of credit that prevailed in everyday life. The biggest source of Charles II's indebtedness came from advance spending, under which he spent in advance of the revenue being earned.[40] To put it differently, he spent money which his treasury did not currently hold, but which it would get through taxes and other revenue payments that were certain to come in at an ascertainable point of time. One way of closing this temporal gap was to use credit in the form of deferred payments, of precisely the same type that an ordinary individual of that time might have relied on in his dealings with his suppliers. This was not infrequently used when borrowing from companies, such as the East India Company, where loans were not directly repaid but were

38 D Defoe, *A Review of the State of the British Nation*, vol VII no 55, 1 August 1710, reprinted in *Defoe's Review* (facsimile book 17) 215.

39 D Defoe, *A Review of the State of the British Nation*, vol VII no 57, 5 August 1710, reprinted in *Defoe's Review* (facsimile book 17) 221.

40 See A Feaveryear, *The Pound Sterling: A History of English Money* (2nd edn, Oxford University Press, 1963) 110.

instead gradually set off by granting the Company exemption from a particular tax or duty.[41]

Monarchs, however, also used more complex techniques involving the exotic instruments of the day, such as tally sticks and exchequer bonds. The essence of the borrowing, regardless of the instrument used, was that the monarch granted the right to a specific future revenue to a person who advanced him goods or money. Under this system, the Crown gave the creditor from whom it had accepted money a token, traditionally a tally stick, which entitled that creditor to a particular sum of money from a particular revenue stream.[42] This was not so much borrowing in the modern sense as it was a way for the Crown to realise revenues that it knew it would receive but had not yet received. It was, nevertheless, wholly relational. The number of persons involved was very small, and the form in which royal debts were incurred and repaid demonstrates their close links with the systems we have just examined in relation to debt held or owed by common folk and, hence, their shared roots in relational debt.

The Financial Revolution by itself did not change this. Many of the early innovations brought in by the Financial Revolution took the form of instruments that were relational. A common way of raising revenue was through the sale of annuities, under which the proceeds from a particular revenue source – for example, a tax – were applied to pay an annuity to the persons who advanced money to the Crown.[43] The move from this relational starting point to a market-commodity form of debt can be traced in three steps, none of which by themselves were definitive, but each of which provided the basis for a subsequent move.

The first step derelationalised debt by explicitly seeking to widen the pool of creditors, and by facilitating the manufacture of credit which, as noted above, is the key characteristic of debt as a commodity. This occurred in the reign of Charles II, with the innovations in credit created by Sir George Downing. Downing's principal aim was to liberate Charles from his dependence on a small number of bankers for credit, by getting the investing public to lend.[44] To this end, he fashioned a new payment instrument, the repayment order.[45] A repayment order was a document that gave the holder the right to receive payment from a particular revenue stream, according to an order of priority stated on the order itself. Critically, drawing on merchant practice, payment orders were made assignable through endorsement.[46] Even if a debt could not be assigned at common law, therefore, the repayment order gave assignees the ability to demand, and receive, payment from the Exchequer.

The repayment order was very successful, and the pressure of wartime finance led to the extension of the system to a new instrument, called fiduciary

41 Nichols (n 32) 86.

42 Feaveryear (n 40) 110.

43 PGM Dickson, *The Financial Revolution in England: A Study in the Development of Public Credit 1688–1756* (Macmillan, 1967) 39–46.

44 Nichols (n 32) 97.

45 Ibid 98.

46 Ibid.

orders.[47] These orders resembled repayment orders, but differed in one material circumstance. A repayment order was issued after a sum of money, the loan, had been paid in by a creditor. A fiduciary order, in contrast, was simply a promise to pay, unconnected to the actual receipt of money. Heads of department were given the ability to use them at their discretion, and, given the exigencies of wartime, a number of them used the orders to pay suppliers. The scale at which these orders were issued meant that they quickly exceeded what could reasonably be repaid. It was at these orders that the Stop of the Exchequer (discussed at p 17 above) was primarily targeted.[48] If repayment orders represented the emergence of assignability, then fiduciary orders represented the pure production of credit, 'turning nothing into something'.

The second step in the development of debt into a market-commodity was the emergence of the ability to repackage and subdivide the income earned from debt. By the end of the seventeenth century, when the New East India Company was briefly created as a rival to the old, it was possible to speak of the company having a 'Fund of Credit', constituted by the special revenues that had been sold to it by the government, which it could use as the basis on which to issue notes and bonds to the public.[49]

Measured in terms of the availability of credit to the government, these measures had succeeded wildly. In 1719, just over three decades after William III's arrival in England, the national debt amounted to around £50 million held by over 40,000 individuals[50] – a staggering change from the £1 million that it amounted to before 1688, or even the £19 million in 1697.[51] In political terms, however, all was far from well. The project of credit was largely a Whig project, and it was meeting with growing Tory opposition (especially since the financiers were mostly Whigs).[52] There was fear of the power that financiers (or the 'monied interest' as they were commonly called by contemporary commentators) would gain over the conduct of government, and a nearly equal fear of the amount of power the Crown would get over financiers due to their financial dependence on investments (which, as the East India Company's experience in the time of Charles II demonstrates, was not unwarranted).[53] In 1711, a Tory ministry was returned under Robert Harley and Henry St John, who set to work to tame the monied interest. This marked the start of the third phase in the development of debt into a market-commodity. The result was the first iteration of the South

47 Ibid 99.

48 Feaveryear (n 40) 111.

49 Dickson (n 43) 93.

50 Ibid 96.

51 S Quinn, 'The Glorious Revolution's Effect on English Private Finance: A Microhistory 1680–1705' (2001) 61 *Journal of Economic History* 593.

52 Dickson (n 43) 15–35.

53 For the broader intellectual context of these debates, and their relationship to the themes of 'wealth' and 'virtue' that dominated political thought in that period, see JGA Pocock, *The Machiavellian Moment: Florentine Political Thought and the Atlantic Republican Tradition* (2nd edn, Princeton University Press, 2003) 423–61.

Sea Scheme, whose second iteration would produce the infamous South Sea Bubble. At its core, the idea was both simple and attractive. The government could get the short-term national debt off its balance sheet by transferring it to the South Sea Company, who would receive the government's payments on the debt. The holders of the debt would receive shares in the Company in exchange for agreeing to transfer their portion of the debt to the Company. By combining the returns on the debt with the returns from its trading activities, the Company would provide the government's former creditors a better return than they could have achieved on the debt itself. The government would see its risk reduce, and the Company would also provide a Tory counterweight to the overwhelmingly Whig-leaning financial industry.

Much has been written about the unravelling of this scheme after the 1719 attempt to transfer the long-term debt to the South Sea Company, and it is not my purpose to add to that body of work.[54] The point to which I seek to draw attention, rather, is the close relationship between the South Sea Scheme and the emergence and growth of commodified debt. From the schemes we have examined in this section as having followed from derelationalisation, it was only a short step to the South Sea Scheme, where it was debt that was sold rather than revenues, and where the general public were the target rather than wealthy individuals. The element of manufacturing credit, and drawing the public in as investors, widened the supply of debt and the circle of buyers of debt in the market. In the South Sea Scheme, we see this come together with what was, in effect, an early instance of securitisation: the privatisation of the manufacture of credit, thus widening not just its demand but also its supply. From this perspective, what arguably matters most about the inflation and subsequent bursting of the South Sea Bubble is what it tells us about the *limits* of the derelationalised conception of debt. A fundamental characteristic of commodities is that they are capable of being controlled, modified and transformed, and their productive use and social value dramatically increased, in the hands of a skilled entrepreneurial manager. This idea of control and entrepreneurial management was, as we have seen, foundational to the thinking that underlay the Financial Revolution, and it lay at the heart of the South Sea Scheme. The failure of the scheme, and of many similar schemes, thus points to a fundamental flaw in the underlying assumptions as to what entrepreneurial management of debt is capable of.

From a contemporary point of view, the sloughing off of a burdensome obligation, and the conversion of that burdensome obligation into one that was both less burdensome and offered a higher yield, represented a radically new phase in the unfolding story of debt. The mixing of expensive difficult-to-service debt with other types of income to create a new payment instrument that, in theory, could yield a higher return for a lower cost represents a type of alchemy that is entirely too familiar to us, in this era of AAA-rated sub-prime securities. The South Sea Scheme, however, represents the first instance of such an attempt,

54 The most recent treatment is contained in R Dale, *The First Crash: Lessons from the South Sea Bubble* (Princeton University Press, 2004).

and the genealogy of the scheme that has been presented here shows how such an idea was born. As with many intellectual revolutions, it is only intelligible in the light of its context, the problems that the individuals involved were trying to solve, and the slow, incremental evolution that borrowing had undergone in the previous three decades. The intellectual shift it represented in the conceptualisation of debt, however, was far-reaching, and continues to have effects to the present day.

## Conclusion: the limits of non-relational debt

This chapter has thus far shown how the concept of debt underwent a remarkable transformation in the early modern period, from being a predominantly relational concept to something far more akin to a commodity. This shift had several other consequences. In legal terms, it led directly to the emergence of the framework that makes complex financial products possible. The law soon abandoned its earlier opposition to the assignability of debt. Equity devised its own ways of permitting an assignee of a debt to maintain an action upon that debt in Chancery, initially only for suits upon bonds,[55] but subsequently for all debts.[56] This ultimately also came to encompass permitting the assignee to maintain a suit in the name of the original creditor if the debt was only actionable at common law. As the eighteenth century gave way to the nineteenth century, the social, commercial and legal consequences of the failure to pay debts grew ever more serious, and the situation of indebted persons more precarious.[57] The enforcement of debts grew stricter, culminating in the creation of new jury-less courts in the nineteenth century, with efficient and quicker procedures to deal with petty debts.[58] By the late nineteenth century, it was perfectly normal for shareholders to be bankrupted to satisfy creditors: even if in reality both were common victims of directorial misconduct, it was the company that was the debtor and shareholders with partly paid shares had to satisfy those.[59] The usury laws were eventually repealed and caps on interest lifted, on the basis that individuals had to be free to pay the market price and to structure their contracts in any way the market permitted.

Aspects of derelationalisation had already begun to worry commentators at the time of the Financial Revolution, including those like Defoe who were generally favourably disposed to the new forms of credit then emerging. Defoe was, in particular, worried by the erosion of the mutuality that characterised relational

55 *Fashion v Atwood* (1680) 2 Cha Cas 6, 38.

56 *Mitchell v Eades* (1700) Pre Cha 125.

57 Julian Hoppit, *Risk and Failure in English Business 1700–1800* (Cambridge University Press, 1987).

58 MC Finn, *The Character of Credit: Personal Debt in English Culture 1740–1914* (Cambridge University Press, 2003).

59 A particularly egregious example was the aftermath of the collapse of the Royal British Bank, discussed in P Johnson, *Making the Market: Victorian Origins of Corporate Capitalism* (Cambridge University Press, 2010) 133–5.

debt. Writing in his *Review* in 1706, he pointed to the adverse impact this had on social relations:

> Debtors abuse Creditors, and Creditors starve and murther their Debtors; Compassion flies from human Nature in the Course of universal Commerce; and *Englishmen*, who in all other Cases are Men of Generosity, Tenderness, and more than common Compassions, are to their Debtors meer Lunaticks, Mad-men and Tyrants.[60]

The answer, he thought, lay in cultivating moderation and virtue. Credit was best approached 'full of application, sober, sensible and honest' by a man who 'has his Heart behind his Counter, whose Mistress is his Counting House, and his Pleasure is his Ledger'.[61] To one without these, credit would be a gulf, 'easie to fall into, hard to get out of'.[62]

The three centuries that have passed since then have convincingly demonstrated that the inculcation of virtue has not proved to be a feasible solution, and the propensity to cause instability noted by Defoe continues to stalk economies based on debt as a market commodity. Let us, then, return to the question with which this chapter began. Can the history of debt shed light on why debt, unlike other modes of acquiring purchasing power, appears to have this destabilising character?

The tentative answer which this chapter advances is that the cause lies in certain tensions that are inherent in the character of debt-as-commodity. Polanyi pointed out that capital and debt were both fictitious commodities, not true ones, and that the limits of the fictitious representation had to be recognised in a sensible political order.[63] Fictitious commodities were treated as if they could be dealt with through a price-setting and self-regulating market. However, Polanyi argued, fictitious commodities could not sustainably be so treated because they were not actually produced for consumption. The examples Polanyi gave were land and labour, neither of which can be created to meet demand in the way widgets can, and neither of which were therefore true commodities.

Polanyi associated the limitations of fictitious commodities with the impossibility of dealing with them through a self-regulating market. In economics the essence of a commodity is indeed its tradability on a market. But to the legal mind, there are other features that distinguish commodities and that are of greater prominence. The first is their fungibility. A person who contracts for the purchase of 10 tonnes of pepper does not, unless otherwise agreed, contract

60 D Defoe, *A Review of the State of the British Nation*, vol III no 92, 1 August 1706, reprinted in *Defoe's Review* (facsimile book 7) 365.

61 D Defoe, *A Review of the State of the British Nation*, vol VII no 57, 5 August 1710, reprinted in *Defoe's Review* (facsimile book 17) 222.

62 D Defoe, *A Review of the State of the British Nation*, vol III no 7, 15 January 1706, reprinted in *Defoe's Review* (facsimile book 7) 25.

63 K Polanyi, *The Great Transformation: The Political and Economic Origins of Our Time* (2nd paperback edn, Beacon Press, 2001) 71–80.

for the specific, identifiable set of peppercorns that were in the warehouse at the time he contracted. He contracts, instead, for peppercorns of a like description, because it is taken as a given that, unlike in relation to horses or cars, he does not care which specific peppercorn he gets as long as it has the properties he requires. The second is that commodities are largely instrumental, in that they are acquired for the purpose of being transformed or put to productive use. At the same time, they have a colourlessness, in that they are capable of being used in a range of ways, with the result that their acquisition as a matter of law is not tied to a particular intended use.[64] As such, the commodity is divorced from the purposes that might have prompted its creation, sale or acquisition.

Both these also hold true for how the legal and regulatory systems approach fictitious commodities. In relation to debt, we do not ask why the borrower is driven to borrow, nor do we ask how it is that the creditor can lend, nor why that borrower approached that creditor. The debt-as-commodity is detached from the social relationship in whose context it arises. When debt is commodified, it is desocialised and derelationalised, meaning that it is detached from the underlying questions (fundamental to the relational understanding of debt) of the purpose for which the debt was acquired, the factors driving the use by the borrower of the instrument of debt, why there was an underlying need for purchasing power, and the source of the funds that are being lent. For that matter, whether purchasing power is acquired through debt, or through income, is irrelevant in a commodified understanding: it is a matter of the acquirer's choice.

Commodified managerialism is thus, in essence, a claim that the *need* for purchasing power is no different from the *demand* for any other commodity and can, therefore, be met in the same way as the demand for any other commodity, namely through a market purchase. Equally, the *supply* of debt can be handled in the same way as the supply of any other commodity, namely through the endeavours of a creative, entrepreneurial class. There is no need to look at deeper factors – in particular, there is no need to address the *wants* that create the need for purchasing power. That it is precisely such an approach that underlies the modern regulatory framework surrounding debt should be self-evident. The regulatory framework for achieving stability in the financial system continues to focus primarily on regulating the supply of debt, in as much as it is concerned with the systemic risks posed by individual institutions and by lending in the economy as a whole. The focus on the supply side, rather than on the needs underlying the demand for debt, ties in with a derelationalised understanding of debt.

Debt in the modern sense is therefore a fictitious commodity version not of money or specie, but of need. Instead of focusing on understanding and meeting the needs of people in society (and of judging which bits of those needs should be met and in what way), the understanding of debt we have examined in this chapter puts the focus on constructing market-based structures of ever-increasing

64 The most obvious manifestation of this is seen in the rules on damages for the breach of a contract for the sale of goods, which almost never take into account the use to which the purchaser actually intended to put the goods in question, unless that purpose was incorporated into the contract.

elaborateness with the express aim of shifting attention away from those underlying needs by transforming them in a way that reduces them to a need for purchasing power, which we trust market entrepreneurship to provide. But is this true? Perhaps the best riposte to the claim that all types of needs for purchasing power can be treated on the same footing came from Adam Smith, in a passage in his *Wealth of Nations* where he gave the usury laws of his day qualified support. The effect of leaving interest rates to be set solely by the market, he said, would be that:

> the greater part of the money which was to be lent, would be lent to prodigals and projectors, who alone would be willing to give this high interest. . . . A great part of the capital of country would thus be kept out of the hands which were the most likely to make a profitable and advantageous use of it, and thrown into those which were most likely to waste and destroy it.[65]

In the light of what we now know about the events leading up to the 2008 financial crisis and, indeed, the events that followed, these words now seem prophetic. The reason too much debt destabilises is because it points to an absence of purchasing power, which is sought to be ameliorated through the expedient of creating purchasing power, but without any attempt to determine the destination of that purchasing power. That such a process is inherently unstable, and that alternate and more experientially grounded accounts can exist and have existed within historical memory, are the most important lessons history can teach. Until governments and regulators begin to appreciate the limits of the commodified account of debt, and get to grips with the real task of dealing with the needs that underlie the demand for greater purchasing power, the situation is unlikely to change.

65 A Smith, *An Inquiry into the Nature and Causes of the Wealth of Nations* (first published 1776; Oxford University Press, 1976) 357.

# 3 Peer-to-peer lending and financial innovation in the UK

*David Bholat and Ulrich Atz*[1]

For the real question is whether the brighter future is really always so distant. What if, on the contrary, it has been here for a long time already, and only our own blindness and weakness has prevented us from seeing it around us and within us, and kept us from developing it?

Václav Havel[2]

## Destructive creations, creative destruction

Since 2007 the world has grown accustomed to believing that we are experiencing a global economic crisis. Some distinguished economists such as Robert Gordon have even gone so far as to predict permanent stagnation.[3] Even if Gordon's pessimism is extreme, what has become commonplace is to claim that we are living in some sort of 'End Time'[4] characterised by the end of economic growth,[5] maybe even the end of capitalism.[6]

This pessimism has been acute among financial sector commentators because of numerous scandals and crises that have beset the industry. Former Federal Reserve Chairman Paul Volker captured the mood well when, in 2009, he famously quipped that the only useful financial innovation in the previous quarter century had been the invention of the ATM.[7] Volker's not-so-subtle suggestion

1 Views expressed are those of the authors and not necessarily those of the institutions with which they are affiliated. We thank Giles Andrews, Rhydian Lewis, Samir Desai, David Nicholson, Andrew Mullinger, Grant Alexander, Matt Everitt, John Gillespie, Stuart Coleman, Mark Robson, Paul Robinson, Christian Wong, Paolo Siciliani, Michael McAuley, Matthew Willison, Kevin Dowd and Abdul Karim Aldohni for making this chapter possible.

2 V Havel, *The Power of the Powerless: Citizens Against the State in Central-Eastern Europe* (Routledge, 2010) 86.

3 R Gordon, 'Is US Economic Growth Over? Faltering Innovations Confronts The Six Headwinds' (Working Paper No 18315, National Bureau of Economic Research, 2012).

4 S Žižek, *Living in the End Times* (Verso, 2011).

5 D Harvey, *Seventeen Contradictions and the End of Capitalism* (Profile, 2015).

6 J Rifkin, *Zero Marginal Cost Society: The Internet of Things, The Collaborative Commons and the Eclipse of Capitalism* (Palgrave Macmillan, 2014), and more recently P Mason, *Post Capitalism: A Guide to Our Future* (Allen Lane, 2015).

7 D Kansas and D Weidner, 'Volcker Praises the ATM, Blasts Finance Execs, Experts' *Wall Street*

was that many of the products and services marketed by financial firms in the run-up to the crisis had been 'fool's gold'.[8] Since Volker, some scholars have found empirical support that efficiency and innovation in finance has been disappointing and downward trending.[9]

However, what if we turn this conventional wisdom on its head? What if, to steal a sound-bite from Václav Havel, a brighter future is not far away but already here? If instead of secular stagnation and permanent crises, we are instead witnessing renaissance, financial innovations that may, to echo another great twentieth-century thinker Hannah Arendt, enhance our capacities to make new beginnings?[10]

This chapter makes that case. We argue that the post-crisis period has seen a wave of financial innovation, especially in the UK. New mechanisms for making payments have evolved and proliferated, such as contactless cards. New currencies have also been established, such as Bitcoin and the Brixton pound.[11] And most relevant to the focus of this chapter is the growth in sources of credit beyond banks. At the level of wholesale finance, the post-crisis period has seen the continued growth in the size of the shadow banking sector (Figure 3.1).[12] And at the level of retail finance, there has been a boom in the UK in short-term, often high-interest lending companies, both on the high street in the form of pawnshops, and online, the most famous being Wonga. However, this development at the retail finance level has been disconcerting to some commentators (see Chapter 4).

In this chapter we focus on one instance of new financial providers in the UK, namely *peer-to-peer (P2P) lending platforms.* These are websites where borrowers

*Journal* online (8 December 2009) <http://blogs.wsj.com/marketbeat/2009/12/08/volcker-praises-the-atm-blasts-finance-execs-experts/> accessed 25 April 2016.

8 G Tett, *Fool's Gold: How Unrestrained Greed Corrupted a Dream, Shattered Global Markets and Unleashed a Catastrophe* (Abacus, 2010).

9 At least in the United States: T Philippon, 'Has the US Finance Industry Become Less Efficient? On the Theory and Measurement of Financial Intermediation' (2015) 105(4) *American Economic Review* 1408.

10 H Arendt, *The Human Condition* (University of Chicago Press, 1999).

11 On local currencies like the Brixton pound, see M Naqvi and J Southgate, 'Banknotes, Local Currencies and Central Bank Objectives' (2013) Q4 *Bank of England Quarterly Bulletin* 317. As Naqvi and Southgate note, the value of local currencies in circulation is estimated to be less than £500,000 in circulation, compared to £50 billion worth of Bank notes in circulation (in 2014).

12 Perry Merhling and his co-authors have correctly compared the evolving financial system to the system that was in place in the late nineteenth century, when the City was dominated by three actors: the Bank of England, the discount houses and the commercial banks. See, P Merhling, Z Pozsar, J Sweeney and DH Neilson, 'Bagehot was a Shadow Banker: Shadow Banking, Central Banking and the Future of Global Finance' (5 November 2013) <http://papers.ssrn.com/sol3/papers.cfm?abstract_id=2232016> accessed 26 April 2016. Back then, the Bank did not deal directly with the commercial banks but did so through the intermediation of the discount houses. Similarly, the Bank's programme of Quantitative Easing (QE) involved, in the first instance, buying assets from non-banks such as insurers rather than from the banks themselves. See M Joyce, M Tong and R Woods, 'The United Kingdom's Quantitative Easing Policy: Design, Operation and Impact' (2011) Q3 *Bank of England Quarterly Bulletin* 200.

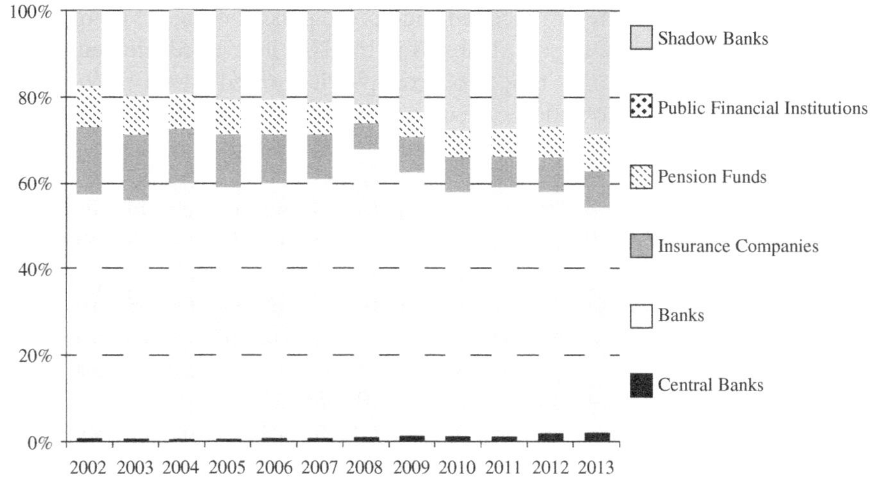


*Figure 3.1* Percentage of assets held by various financial subsectors in the UK

*Note*: The chart shows that the share of financial assets held by shadow banks such as hedge funds and money market mutual funds share has grown over time. The relative amount of public financial institutions is too small to be discernible in the chart.
*Source*: Financial Stability Board 2014.

can solicit funds from investors. Although the exact business model differs from platform to platform, and changes across time, they all roughly work as follows. The platforms act as a kind of broker between borrowers and lenders. Each borrower requests a sum of money – a loan. In most cases the loan requested by the borrower will be funded by multiple investors. So each loan comprises multiple loan agreements with each of the investors. This kind of syndicated lending means that P2P is a species of a larger genus of online 'crowdfunding' that involves individuals, or 'the crowd', pooling their contributions into a larger 'fund'.[13] Generally, the term of loans runs between 24 and 60 months, though loan agreements often can be sold before maturity in secondary markets operated by platforms. The platforms typically make their profits by charging various transaction fees at origination.

The core of this chapter is based on a report the authors wrote in 2013 which, at that time, provided the most comprehensive snapshot of the then £378 million

13 For a general overview of crowdfunding, see S Neiss, J Best and Z Cassady-Dorion, *Getting Started with Crowdfunding Investing in a Day for Dummies* (Wiley, 2012); and J Frutkin, *Equity Crowdfunding: Transforming Customers Into Loyal Owners* (Cricca Funding, LLC, 2013). While P2P lending are debt-based transactions, other crowdfunding models are donation-, reward- or equity-based. Donation-based crowdfunding involves individuals pooling their funds online and making a charitable contribution. Reward-based crowdfunding involves individuals pooling funds and prepaying for goods and services. Equity crowdfunding involves the online issuance of equity, usually in start-ups. See P Baeck, L Collins and B Zhang, 'Understanding alternative finance: The UK Alternative Finance Industry Report 2014' (Nesta, November 2014) 9.

P2P loan market.[14] Our report received widespread press coverage.[15] Using loan-level data from the three largest platforms in the UK, it revealed the geography of P2P lending for the first time. For example, it showed which regions and postcodes were net lenders and borrowers, and overall lending terms and prices. Among our key findings as of July 2013 were the following:

- Four regions lent more than they borrowed: London, the South East, the South West and the East of England. All four regions lie in the South of the UK.
- While there was substantially more lending in London and the South of the UK, borrowers were more evenly distributed across the country. Scotland, the North East and the North West of England had similar statistics for pound per person borrowed as in the South of the UK.
- Lending per person ranged from £1.4 to £11.8 for UK regions, whereas the range for borrowing only went from £3.90 to £7.30 per person.

Besides restating our original empirical results, this chapter provides further commentary on P2P lending not contained in our earlier report. For example, we explain the origins and factors responsible for the growth of P2P lending in the UK, including how platform entrepreneurs got the idea to start them.

Our description here is based on interviews conducted in 2015 with the current CEOs and/or co-founders of Funding Circle, RateSetter and Zopa. Our discussion may interest those seeking to understand economic entrepreneurship and financial innovation in general. Rather than depicting innovation as an exogenous shock, as many models in economics do, we show how the P2P lending idea arose endogenously, in the course of considered reflection by financial professionals on the foundations of the banking business. Our chapter also explains why borrowers and lenders participate in the P2P market, and speculates about the impact P2P lenders may have on the conventional banking sector in the near future.

In the context of the scholarly literature on P2P lending, we see our contribution in this chapter as three-fold.[16]

First, building on the pioneering work of Agrawal, Catalini and Goldfarb who investigated the geography of the US crowdfunding industry in 2011,[17]

14 Open Data Institute, 'Show me the Money: Opening up Big Data in Finance' (Open Data Institute, 2013). Parts of this chapter are taken from that report.

15 For example, the front page of the *Financial Times*. See E Moore, 'Digital Finance Lending Set to Hit £1 Billion', *Financial Times* (15 July 2013).

16 For general overviews of the academic P2P literature, see Burkhardt Funk, Alexander Bachmann, Alexander Becker, Daniel Buerckner, Michel Hilker, Frank Kock, Mark Lehmann and Phillip Tiburtius, 'Online Peer To Peer Lending – A Literature Review' (2011) 16(2) *Journal of Internet Banking & Commerce* 1; A Morse, 'Peer-to-Peer Crowdfunding: Information and the Potential for Disruption in Consumer Lending' (Working Paper No 20899, National Bureau of Economic Research, 2015); RB Bouncken, M Komorek and S Kraus, 'Crowdfunding: the current state of research' (2015) 14(3) *International Business & Economics Research Journal* 407.

17 AK Agrawal, C Catalini and A Goldfarb, 'The Geography of Crowdfunding' (Working Paper No 16820, National Bureau of Economic Research, 2011); AK Agrawal, C Catalini and A Goldfarb,

we provided the first map of the P2P lending market to the UK in 2013. Like Agrawal and his co-authors, we found that proximity plays little role in the investment decisions of lenders. By design, with Zopa and RateSetter, investors cannot make investments based on the geographical location of the borrower.

Second, our chapter lays stress on subjective factors, notably the motivations of lenders, borrowers and P2P operators in creating this new market.[18] These factors are often neglected relative to the emphasis typically placed on technology and other structural changes in the economy that have made P2P lending possible. But technology as such does not cause economic change. It is rather how technology is used, and this is determined by what matters to people.[19]

Finally, we flesh out the implications of P2P lending on the conventional banking sector. Here we sharpen observations made by early commentators in detailing which products and business strategies are most likely to be impacted.[20]

## P2P lending: the untold story

Online P2P lending began in 2005 with the public launch of Zopa in the UK. Like other types of financial innovation in modern history, from the overdraft to the creation of credit default swaps, the UK was precocious. Zopa was also the first P2P platform in the world. Although it is difficult to say with certainty why the UK is continually at the forefront of financial innovation, one explanation is economies of learning. This concept refers to the fact that economic efficiency and the capacity for innovation improves with experience. The implication is that early innovation is a basis for long-term competitive advantage. The consequence geographically is that innovation in particular industries is often clustered in specific parts of the world – IT in Silicon Valley, for example. In the case of the UK, its history as a financial centre may give it a comparative advantage in generating financial innovation.

The existence of economies of learning means that innovation should be conceived less as an exogenous shock and more as an embedded process. As we note below, this view of innovation corresponds with how innovators actually create new businesses. Like comparative advantage among countries, individual skill develops from learning in the course of doing.[21] Innovation is the fruit of

'Some Simple Economics of Crowdfunding' (Working Paper No 19133, National Bureau of Economic Research, 2013).

18 G Bruton, S Khavul, D Siegel and M Wright, 'New Financial Alternatives in Seeding Entrepreneurship: Microfinance, Crowdfunding, and Peer-to-Peer Innovations' (2015) 39(1) *Entrepreneurship: Theory & Practice* 9; L Einav, M Jenkins and J Levin, 'The impact of credit scoring on consumer lending' (2013) 44(2) *RAND Journal of Economics* 249.

19 For example, the Romans famously developed the steam engine but basically used it as a toy rather than to power industry. W Baumol, 'Entrepreneurship: Productive, Unproductive and Destructive' (1990) 98(5) *Journal of Political Economy* 893.

20 A Haldane, 'Banking may be on the Cusp of an Industrial Revolution', *Wired* (29 August 2013).

21 R Grant, *Contemporary Strategy Analysis* (Wiley, 2013) 123.

sustained reflection and involvement in existing commercial practice rather than a radical break from it.

When we interviewed Rhydian Lewis, CEO of RateSetter, and Andrew Mullinger, Global Head of Credit and Co-Founder of Funding Circle, both confirmed that Zopa provided the baseline business model that to a large degree inspired their own.[22] So understanding the origins of P2P lending to a large extent involves understanding the early origins of Zopa.

Before launching Zopa, its three founders – Richard Duval, James Alexander and David Nicholson – worked at Egg, an online bank created by Prudential in 1998. Egg was innovative on a number of fronts. For example, it introduced the UK's first end-to-end online application for credit cards, and created the UK's first online fund supermarket. The fact that Egg enjoyed early commercial success, despite exclusively interacting with its customers online, later instilled confidence in Zopa's founders in the potential of a purely online intermediary. Also, the fact that Duval, Alexander and Nicholson focused on unsecured personal loans while working at Egg goes a long way in explaining why it was in this asset class rather than others that P2P first developed.

Of the three founders, Nicholson is largely regarded as the father of the idea. As Giles Andrews, Executive Chairman of Zopa and, until recently, its CEO, told us: 'Zopa was Dave's idea'. When we interviewed Nicholson, we asked him to reflect on the sources of his idea:

> I was one of the strategy managers on the strategy team and one of the things I started thinking about, not particularly in a structured way, but just sort of a 'what if?' sort of way, was actually trying to get my head around what's a bank for, what does a bank really do and therefore what opportunities are there to think about how that could change and what's really important to a bank. Obviously banks do a huge number of things, but for a retail bank a lot of it's quite simple. It's about matching up deposits with loans and actually acting as an intermediary, between somebody with a deposit and somebody with a loan . . . But actually that sort of got me starting to think around, well, what if there are other places that could act as that intermediary? Why does it have to be a bank that sits in between depositors and people who are borrowing money?[23]

22 Lewis also mentioned Betfair, a company he worked at early in his career, as an important influence on his thinking about the P2P model. Betfair is an online gambling site started in the UK in 2000. Rather than punters betting against the bookmaker, as is conventional, Betfair allows them to bet against each. In other words, P2P betting.

23 The depiction of banks as intermediaries is not without its critics: Z Jakab and M Kumhoff, 'Banks are Not Intermediaries of Loanable Funds – and Why this Matters' (Bank of England Staff Working Paper No 529, Bank of England, 2015); D Bholat, 'Money, Bank Debt and Business Cycles: Between Economic Development and Financial Crises' in O Akseli (ed.), *The Availability of Credit and Secured Transactions in a Time of Crisis* (Cambridge University Press, 2013) 11–32.

Nicholson's recollection of the early part of the thought process that led him to conceive of P2P lending is notable. Rather than, in the first instance, trying to imagine the future of finance, Nicholson started by casting his mind back to the past and to first principles:

> I sort of was building a deeper understanding of what's really going on here and what's really going on in a bank and sort of reading a little bit about where banks came from and how banking has moved over the years and actually understanding that really, although a lot of stuff looks very complex, there's actually some pretty simple basic buildings blocks underneath. Then if you go back and look at those building blocks you understand why banks have been the institutions that have been capable of doing those because you wind back 100 or 200 years you didn't have any of the information or the systems or the technology that would enable anybody else to do that intermediary function.

Nicholson's deep, almost existential, reflections about what banks do led him to think of them as the intersection of 'two markets': a borrowers' market (loans) and a lenders' market (deposits). He and his colleagues at Egg spotted opportunities in both. In the debt market, they projected that a growing part of the population would become what they dubbed 'free formers' – contract workers not in full-time employment – who were creditworthy but unable to access credit from banks. In the credit market, they thought they could win over two groups. First, those who would see 'a social angle' and feel that by lending directly instead of indirectly they had 'some real connection to where their money would end up'. And second, that they could cater to savvy financiers who would see in P2P loans a new asset class through which to reduce risk by diversifying their portfolios.

Conceiving of banks as the union of two markets, Nicholson and his colleagues scoured the horizon for techniques that could enhance the functioning of both. In terms of the lending market, they envisioned it operating along the lines of an eBay auction, with lenders bidding to fund part or the whole of a loan requested by borrowers, with 'winning bids' going to those who offered the best terms (the lowest interest rate). On the debtors' side, their source of inspiration was the corporate bond market. In particular, they envisioned assigning individuals *public* credit ratings, just as corporations are assigned public grades by credit rating agencies.

Starting at Egg, and then later as part of a start-up consultancy called New Barns Studios, Duval, Alexander and Nicholson pitched the rudiments of the P2P concept to colleagues, but without much success. Setting out on their own in 2004 'on the back of a [small support] team and a PowerPoint presentation', they pitched their idea to various venture capitalists in the City. Although they were successful in their funding endeavours to launch Zopa in 2005, Nicholson described the early years of the company as 'very, very tough' because there were few interested lenders, a premature market, and because of the poor credit quality of those seeking funding.

The financial crisis starting in 2007 marked a turning point. On the credit supply side, new lenders entered the market, attracted by the higher rates (and risk) available from exposure to P2P assets, relative to those offered on conventional banking products.[24] And on the credit demand side, a wider and more creditworthy pool of potential borrowers appeared as banks deleveraged.[25] Zopa's new-found success encouraged the entrance of competitors. RateSetter, like Zopa, a P2P platform providing unsecured personal loans, launched in 2010. Funding Circle, the UK and the world's first P2P platform to fund business loans, started that same year.

## 'Show me the money': its background and rationale

One of the more innovative features of many UK P2P platforms is the extent of their data disclosure. While conventional banks' portfolios are often opaque,[26] those of the up-start P2P sector are often less so and, in some instances, 'open by default'.[27] For example, Funding Circle has made its data publicly available through its website on a loan-by-loan basis since it started trading in 2010.[28] The dataset is available for download and contains every loan Funding Circle has intermediated, whether outstanding or already paid off. It includes a wide range of information on these loans, which is regularly updated.

24 At the time we conducted our research there was also much discussion that the rate of return on P2P investments exceeded equity returns from investing in small companies. See J Moules, 'Peer Lending Beats Equity Returns', *Financial Times* (25 June 2013). It is also difficult for many ordinary individuals to have the opportunity to directly invest in small, early-stage enterprises via the equity market. This is because investment banks often distribute shares in newly listed companies to their existing network of high net worth individuals or fund manager clients.

25 In 2013 there was a great deal of concern that the demand for external investment by businesses exceeded supply, with SMEs facing particular difficulty. See Department for Business, Innovation and Skills, 'Boosting Finance Options for Business' (DBIS, March 2012). See also A Cosh, A Hughes, A Bullock and I Milner, 'SME Finance and Innovation in the Current Economic Crisis' (Centre for Business Research, University of Cambridge, 2009) and N Lee, H Sameen and L Martin, 'Credit and The Crisis: Access to Finance for Innovative Small Firms Since The Recession' (Big Innovation Centre, June 2013).

26 D Kohn, 'Enhancing Financial Stability: The Role of Transparency', Speech at the London School of Economics, 6 September 2011. Not surprisingly, greater transparency is a key part of post-crisis banking regulation. Thus the very first policy recommendation of the UK's Financial Policy Committee in June 2011 advised micro-prudential regulators to make public disclosure of sovereign and banking sector exposures by major UK banks a permanent part of their reporting framework: Bank of England, Record of the interim Financial Policy Committee meeting, June 2011. The importance of data disclosure is a regulatory lesson often learned following financial crises. For example, following the failure of the City of Glasgow Bank in the nineteenth century, Parliament passed the 1879 Companies Act mandating for the first time that banks publish their balance sheets. See B Koehler, *History of Financial Disasters, 1763–1995* Volume 2 (Routledge, 2006) 148.

27 See <https://theodi.org/blog/open-new-default> accessed 10 October 2015.

28 See also the highly granular data available for download from the largest American P2P platform Lending Club: <http://www.lendingclub.com/info/download-data.action> accessed 10 October 2015.

*Figure 3.2* Lending activities of the UK P2P market at a national level

*Note*: The map, or cartogram, on the right shows lending activity in regions. Darker areas are regions with higher gross lending volumes.

In 2013 we conducted research that built on Funding Circle's precedent with the inclusion of loan level data from RateSetter and Zopa. Our resulting research report, titled 'Show me the money', published their combined portfolios online on an anonymised basis – nearly 14 million loan contracts.[29] At the time, these three P2P platforms' portfolios constituted over 92 per cent of the UK market.[30] We then contracted with a third party firm named iconomical, who created an interactive visualisation showing the geography of UK P2P lending in our sample frame spanning from October 2010 to May 2013. Their dynamic visualisation allowed users to drill down and see the P2P market, as it was then, at different levels of geographical analysis. Figures 3.2 and 3.3 are snapshots of

29 See <http://smtm.labs.theodi.org/download/>. This was the first time financial data had been published with an open data certificate: https://certificates.theodi.org/> accessed 10 October 2015. Since much of the data pertained to individuals, we took the following steps to protect individual identities: (1) we published the data without full postcode or other direct identifiers; (2) we omitted all variables not relevant to the geographical focus of our study; and (3) we conducted a privacy impact assessment: <http://smtm.labs.theodi.org/privacy/> accessed 10 October 2015.

30 Comparison of the three platforms' combined loans to date against the whole of the UK P2P market (as at 19 June 2013). See for details <http://www.P2Pmoney.co.uk/companies.htm> accessed 10 October 2015.

*Figure 3.3* Borrowing activities of the UK P2P market at a national level

*Note*: The map on the right shows borrowing activity in regions. Darker areas are regions with higher gross borrowing volumes.

the visualisations at a national level. Figure 3.4 depicts a more granular cut of the data, showing the London region and, specifically, P2P lending activity in the EC postcode that comprises nearly the whole of the City of London.

We wanted our project to make three key contributions to academic and policy discussions happening at the time.

The first was to contribute to a growing economics literature exploiting massive micro-level datasets.[31] A key message of our project was that this sort of 'big data' are analytically tractable with the right statistical and visualisation tools.[32]

Second, we wanted our project to benefit consumers by giving them a more comprehensive picture of market prices to aid their financial decision-making.

Finally, we hoped that our project would encourage conventional banks to disclose similar data. And they did: following calls by the government at around the same time, they started disclosing postcode-level lending data.[33]

31 For example, G Jiménez, S Ongena, JL Peydró and J Saurina, 'Hazardous Times for Monetary Policy: What Do Twenty-Three Million Bank Loans Say About The Effects of Monetary Policy on Credit Risk-Taking?' (2014) 82(2) *Econometrica: Journal of the Econometric Society* 463.

32 D Bholat, 'Big Data and Central Banks' (2015) Q1 *Bank of England Quarterly Bulletin* 86.

33 Community Development Finance Association, 'Government commits to disclosure of Postcode Level Lending Data' (15 November 2012). See <http://responsiblefinance.org.uk/2012/11/

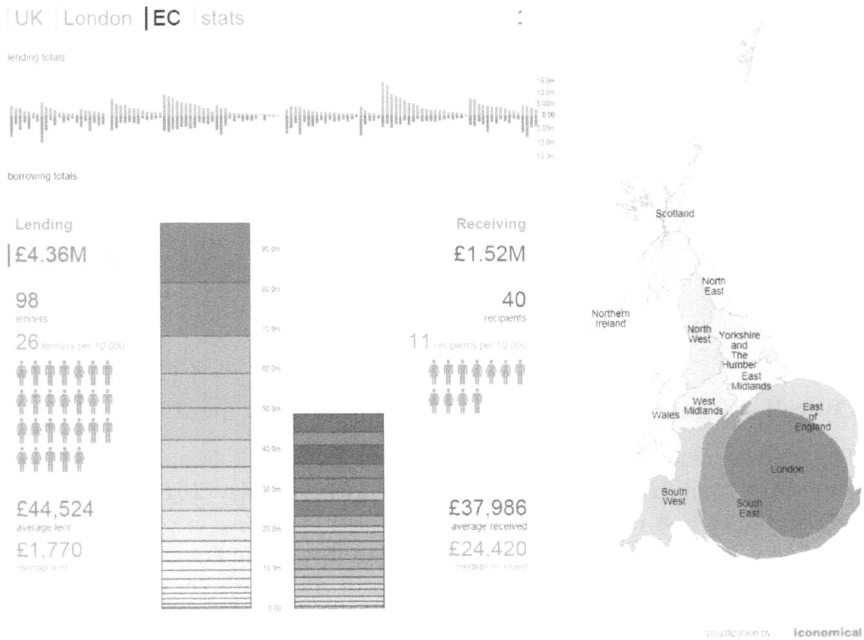


*Figure 3.4* P2P activity in EC postcode

*Note*: The stacked graph on the left allows users to discover regional details such as the average and median amounts lent and received. The bar graph at the top gives a high level overview of loans funded and received by postcode. As of May 2013 in the EC postcode, the median amount borrowed (received) was £24,000 but the postcode as a whole was a net creditor, lending £4.36 million against £1.52 million contracted as debt.

## The regional geography of P2P lending in the UK

Our research focused on the geography of lending for two reasons. First, there are longstanding concerns in the UK about a perceived 'North-South' divide along many dimensions including access to finance, with the North perceived to be at a disadvantage when compared to regions in the South, particularly London.[34] Hence we were interested in understanding to what extent, if at all, P2P platforms were bridging this perceived regional funding gap.

Our second reason for focusing on the geography of the market was more pragmatic. Although each of the three P2P platforms in our sample provided loan-level data with a number of attributes, these data attributes were not the

government-commits-to-disclosure-of-postcode-level-lending-data/> and <https://www.bba.org.uk/news/statistics/postcode-lending/> accessed 10 October 2015.

34 See, for example, D Smith, *North and South: Britain's Economic, Social and Political Divide* (Penguin, 1989); or more recently, 'The North of England: The Great Divide', *The Economist* (15 September 2012) <http://www.economist.com/node/21562938> accessed 26 April 2016.

same across platforms, in terms of their definition. For example, while all three P2P platforms documented the purpose of the loan, these descriptions were free text fields that varied across platforms and thus were not easily comparable.[35] Focusing on geography meant working with data that was already standardised in terms of postcode.

An important limitation of our study is that we did not focus on defaults and rates of recoveries because the industry was still in its infancy. Recently, some commentators, including Lord Adair Turner, have warned that P2P lenders may manifest significant losses in the near future.[36] No reliable inferences about the riskiness of the industry can be made on the basis of our study.[37] Our empirical results now follow.

## Overall statistics for nearly 14 million loan agreements

The data contained all loans intermediated by Zopa, Funding Circle and RateSetter over 32 months, from October 2010 to May 2013. This sample reflects the earliest date on which all three platforms were in operation, up to the date when we conducted our research. As this was the first time a combined analysis had been produced, we spent substantial effort harmonising the datasets.

The basic unit of analysis in the data was loan agreements rather than loans because of the nature of P2P lending. Each loan can be funded by many different lenders. Equally, lenders may subdivide their investment into loans to many different borrowers. In total there were 13,924,547 loan agreements in the combined dataset. We excluded an additional 20,916 loan part observations, 0.15 per cent of the sample. Most of the omissions were because the observation was missing the postcode, or the postcode was not valid. We also excluded loan agreements with postcodes from the Isle of Man (IM), the British Forces (BF), Guernsey (GY) and Jersey (JE), as these areas are not formally part of the UK mainland. The median amount for a loan part was £10. Once aggregated, the nearly 14 million loan agreements represented 59,851 distinct loans with an aggregate value of £378.3 million.

Table 3.1 presents measures of central tendency and dispersion in the data.[38] One feature we found is that lenders were more skewed towards granting large value loans than borrowers were to receive them. The salient difference in mean and median loan values, and the large standard deviation, suggests a few lenders lending large sums, while most borrowers were borrowing amounts between £3,000 and £6,000. This makes intuitive sense because lenders, with a surplus of

35 This example evidences why the financial industry needs to develop a common data classification system, as discussed in-depth in D Bholat, 'The Future of Central Bank Data' (2013) 14 *Journal of Banking Regulation* 185.

36 S Farrrell, 'Former City Regulator Warns of Potential Peer-To-Peer Lending Crisis', *The Guardian* (10 February 2016) <http://www.theguardian.com/money/2016/feb/10/former-city-regulator-warns-peer-to-peer-lending-lord-turner> accessed 26 April 2016.

37 One of the platforms also expressed concern about disclosing this information publicly.

38 All R code is available on GitHub: <https://github.com/theodi/R-projects/tree/master/peer-to-peer> accessed 10 October 2015.

*Table 3.1* Measures of central tendency and dispersion in our data

| | *Lender* | *Borrower* |
|---|---|---|
| Mean loan | £7,737 | £6,320 |
| Median loan | £1,290 | £4,160 |
| Standard deviation | £29,369 | £11,060 |

funds, have more financial freedom than borrowers, who have a deficit they are seeking to cover.

We identified 48,891 lenders and 59,851 borrowers in the data. These were estimates because we interpreted each loan ID and counterparty postcode to be distinct agents. However, there might have been cases where two different lenders lived in the same postcode or where the same person or company took out more than one loan.

## Geographic flows show that four regions were investing more than they borrowed

Each loan part in the dataset had a postcode for the lender and the borrower. Therefore we could calculate regional flows at different geographical levels. These were geographical flows *at origination*. We emphasise this point because certain P2P platforms have secondary markets that allow the original lender to sell their rights to the remaining repayments from the borrower to other investors. Thus the recipient of cash flows from a loan part at a later point in its lifecycle may not be the original lender. Since loan agreements often change hands, we focused on the original lenders' postcodes rather than where cash flows were flowing at the point in time when we conducted our study.

Table 3.2 aggregates postcode data at a regional level. Unsurprisingly, London was the biggest lender by value. It was also the second biggest borrowing region, with the South East first. We found that four regions were investing more than they borrowed: London, South East, South West and the East of England. All four regions are in the South of the UK.

It is important to bear in mind that the regional allocation of funds is *not* a deliberate decision made by investors for Zopa and Ratesetter. Therefore the resulting regional allocation of funds may reflect other variables.

We then combined the loan level P2P data with other available sources. For example, population estimates from the UK census for each region allowed us to normalise the regional figures by population. London still topped the lenders' list with £11.80 per person. But there was great regional diversity, especially in terms of lending per person. Lending per person ranged from £1.40 to £11.80. The regional range for borrowers went from £3.90 to £7.30 per person. In sum, there was substantially more lending in London and the South of the UK, while borrowers were more evenly distributed across the country. Our findings therefore suggest P2P platforms have been bridging the historically perceived regional funding gap.

*Table 3.2* Regional P2P statistics

| *Region* | *As lender* | *As borrower* | *Net* | *Population* | *Lending (£ p.p.)* | *Borrowing (£ p.p)* | *Net sum (£ p.p.)* |
|---|---|---|---|---|---|---|---|
| London | 96,535,000 | 48,725,000 | 47,810,000 | 8,204,000 | 11.8 | 5.9 | 5.8 |
| South East | 76,353,000 | 57,602,000 | 18,751,000 | 8,653,000 | 8.8 | 6.7 | 2.2 |
| South West | 41,144,000 | 32,076,000 | 9,068,000 | 5,301,000 | 7.8 | 6.1 | 1.7 |
| East of England | 37,243,000 | 29,748,000 | 7,495,000 | 5,862,000 | 6.4 | 5.1 | 1.3 |
| West Midlands | 21,207,000 | 29,978,000 | -8,771,000 | 5,609,000 | 3.8 | 5.3 | -1.6 |
| East Midlands | 15,665,000 | 25,239,000 | -9,574,000 | 4,537,000 | 3.5 | 5.6 | -2.1 |
| North West | 26,803,000 | 42,434,000 | -15,631,000 | 7,056,000 | 3.8 | 6 | -2.2 |
| Yorkshire and The Humber | 20,584,000 | 32,756,000 | -12,172,000 | 5,288,000 | 3.9 | 6.2 | -2.3 |
| Northern Ireland | 2,527,000 | 6,993,000 | -4,466,000 | 1,807,000 | 1.4 | 3.9 | -2.5 |
| Scotland | 19,219,000 | 33,108,000 | -13,889,000 | 5,255,000 | 3.7 | 6.3 | -2.6 |
| Wales | 12,880,000 | 22,355,000 | -9,475,000 | 3,064,000 | 4.2 | 7.3 | -3.1 |
| North East | 8,104,000 | 17,250,000 | -9,146,000 | 2,596,000 | 3.1 | 6.6 | -3.5 |

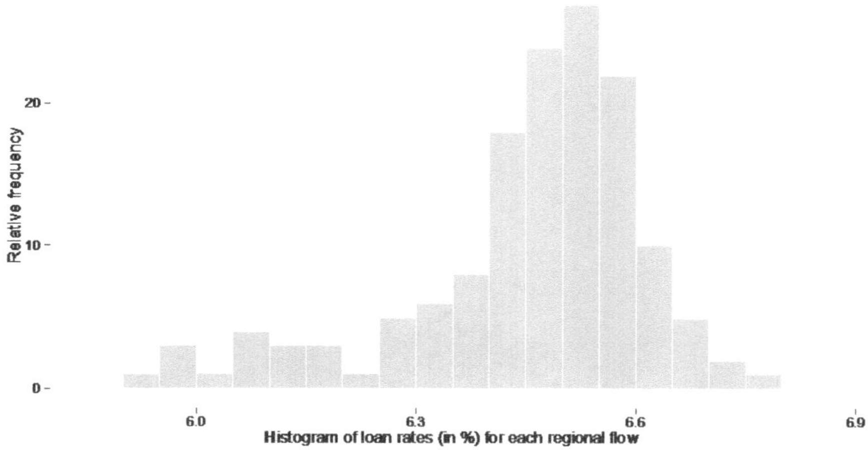


*Figure 3.5* Histogram of loan rates for each regional flow

*Note:* There are 12 regions in the UK and each lends to 11 others and itself. This creates 144 regional flows. The chart shows the distribution of loan rates across all 144 regional flows.

We found variation in loan terms between regions to be surprisingly low. On average, interest rates on the loans in our dataset were between 6.1 and 6.7 per cent and had a term of 37 to 41 months. We did not find any obvious pattern when it comes to the interest rates paid by borrowers. By contrast, the lowest rates received by lenders were in the East of England. This stems from the fact that, for whatever reason, the term of loans in the region was on average shorter than other parts of the UK. Figure 3.5 displays a histogram of loan rates for each of the regional flows. Figure 3.6 displays a histogram of the term length of the loans.

## Why and how P2P lending matters in the UK

The UK P2P market grew rapidly from practically nil before the financial crisis to over £500 million in cumulative gross lending as of May 2013 when we conducted our research.[39] Figures 3.7 and 3.8 are maps plotting the growth in lending and borrowing, from 1 October 2010 to 30 June 2011 (left hand panel) and 31 May 2013 (right hand panel). Growth has continued since. According to the Peer 2 Peer Finance Association, a trade body representing many of the largest P2P platforms in the UK including Zopa, RateSetter and Funding Circle, new gross lending facilitated by its members in Q2 2015 totalled £450 million. This brings the total lending intermediated by its member platforms from their origins to nearly £3 billion.[40]

39 See for details <http://www.P2Pmoney.co.uk/companies.htm> accessed 10 October 2015.

40 See <http://P2Pfa.info/data> accessed 26 April 2016. We exclude MarketInvoice from their headline figures because it is not in the P2P lending business.

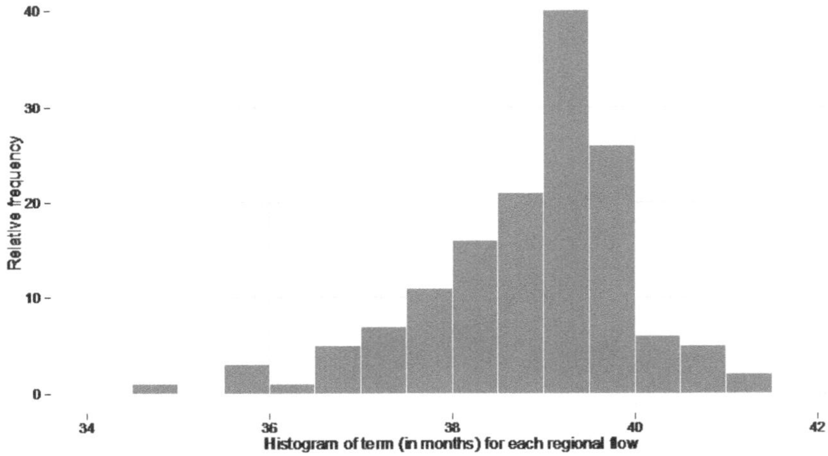


*Figure 3.6* Histogram of terms for each regional flow

*Note*: There are 12 regions in the UK and each lends to 11 others and itself. This creates 144 regional flows. The chart above shows the distribution of the average loan rates across all 144 regional flows.

The following explains the increased public prominence of P2P lending in the UK:

(1) the extraordinary growth rate of the market relative to the rate of net bank lending recently, and
(2) the direct and indirect support from the public sector and regulatory bodies.

Let us take these in turn. The first point to note is the growth rate of the sector. Nesta, a UK-based think-tank, has estimated that in recent years the growth rate of P2P lending has been in triple digits, while during the same period, *net* bank lending, that is, gross lending minus repayments, has been volatile and often negative.

Here the growth of P2P lending has been driven by supply and demand factors. On the supply side, when it comes to lending, some sector enthusiasts claim that the main drivers have been ideological. In the memorable rhetorical pitch of the crowd-funding platform BnkToTheFuture.com, 'Who gets funded? You decide'. No doubt that empowering promise, of giving individuals control over how their monies are invested, has resonance in some circles post-financial crisis.

However, results from a survey conducted by Nesta in 2014 suggest that the main motivation for lenders is pecuniary. When asked why they were participating in the P2P market, 82 per cent of surveyed lenders on peer-to-business lending sites ticked 'To make a Financial Return' as very important, while only 35 per cent ranked 'To have control over where my money goes' of similar significance.[41] Likewise, while 78 per cent of lenders supplying funds through P2P consumer lending sites cited the interest rate available as very important, just 35 per cent of those surveyed ranked 'Supporting an alternative to the big banks' of equal significance.[42] Shifting focus from supply to demand factors, the Nesta survey found that borrowers' main motivations were similar to lenders in being about the bottom-line rather than the pursuit of lofty ideals. For example, surveyed borrowers using P2P consumer lending sites ranked the interest rate available as their major motivation for participating in the market.[43]

A second factor responsible for the increased prominence of P2P lending in the UK is interest and encouragement from public sector and regulatory bodies. The UK Department for Business, Innovation and Skills and, latterly, its subsidiary, the British Business Bank, have invested nearly £200 million in P2P platforms, often by topping up the remaining unfunded portion of near-fully funded loans.[44] Such funding is not only financially but symbolically important. Arguably, it has boosted public confidence to participate in the market.[45]

Exactly the same can be said of the fact that the Financial Conduct Authority started to regulate the sector from 1 April 2014. Broadly speaking, the regulation sets minimum standards for the equity that P2P platforms must raise and maintain in order to operate. It also laid emphasis on platforms making honest disclosures about the risks to which investors are exposed.[46] Arguably P2P regulation, like regulation in general, has had the effect of 'crowding in' participants because it gives them the perception that markets are fair and orderly.[47] The announcement by the government that interest from P2P loans can be shielded from tax as part of tax-free individual saving accounts (ISAs) from 6 April 2016 is likely to further boost P2P business.[48]

41 P Baeck, L Collins and B Zhang, 'Understanding alternative finance: The UK Alternative Finance Industry Report 2014' (Nesta, November 2014) 34. That said, another 46% of surveyed lenders said that 'To have control over where my money goes' was important. Another 17% said 'To make a financial return' was important. Responses where the majority of those surveyed responded that the factor was neither important nor unimportant, or unimportant/very important included: supporting the SME sector; lending to industries 'I know/care about'; doing social or environmental good; lending to local businesses/enterprises; curiosity; supporting a friend or family members; to help increase housing stocks.

42 Ibid 44.

43 Ibid 55.

44 A Bounds, 'Government Interference Risks Distorting UK P2P Market', *Financial Times* (26 October 2014).

45 For an overview of related developments in the US, see K Stanberry, 'Crowdfunding and the Expansion of Access to Startup Capital' (2014) 5(12) *International Research Journal of Applied Finance* 1382.

46 Financial Conduct Authority, 'PS 14/4: The FCA's Regulatory Approach to Crowdfunding Over the Internet, and the Promotion of Non-Readily Realisable Securities by Other Media' <http://www.fca.org.uk/news/ps14-04-crowdfunding> accessed 26 April 2016.

47 M Friedman, *Capitalism and Freedom* (University of Chicago Press, 1962).

48 A new type of ISA will accept peer-to-peer investments from next year. See <http://www.thisismoney.co.uk/money/saving/article-3153630/New-kind-Isa-accept-peer-peer-investments-year.html> accessed 30 October 2015.

*Figure 3.7* Growth of P2P lending over time

*Note*: Dots represent lenders in postcodes. The greater number of dots on the map in 2013 (right hand side) gives visual evidence of the growth of the UK P2P lending market.

## The impact of P2P lending on conventional banks

Looking ahead we envision two key impacts of the P2P lending sector on the conventional banking sector:

(1) reduced rates on unsecured personal loans brought about by competition from P2P platforms, putting downward pressure on bank profitability in this product line; and
(2) further impetus and a model for banks as they shift their distribution channel from brick-and-mortar branches to internet and mobile services.

Although there is P2P lending to fund businesses and real estate, we think that consumer credit is the area where banks are most vulnerable to competition from online platforms. In part this is because it is the asset class in which P2P emerged and is most mature. For example, one striking fact to emerge from Nesta's survey of the industry is the difference in the credit profile of individual and business borrowers on P2P platforms. In the P2P market for personal loans, 59 per cent of respondents sought funding from banks at the same time they applied for a P2P loan, and 54 per cent were granted funding but chose to fund themselves via the platforms. By contrast, in the market for P2P business loans, 79 per cent sought

*Figure 3.8* Growth in P2P borrowing over time

*Note*: Dots represent borrowers in postcodes. The greater number of dots on the map in 2013 (right hand side) is visual evidence of the growth in borrowing in the UK P2P market.

funding from banks but only 22 per cent were granted it.[49] One interpretation of these results is that while banks and P2P platforms are operating with different credit models when it comes to business loans, P2P platforms are actually competing away some customers from banks in the unsecured personal loans space.

Looking ahead, unsecured personal loans are the market where P2P platforms are likely to continue to make inroads against banks. In contrast to the retail mortgage and deposit market, no British bank has a dominant position in consumer credit.[50] Also, British banks' unsecured lending is typically a small component of their overall balance sheet.

The results of this competition could be good for consumers, increasing the availability of unsecured personal credit while lowering its price. This would amplify recent trends. Over the past year, UK banks have increased their issuance of unsecured personal loans, and quoted interest rates on these have fallen sharply.[51] However, we caution that P2P platforms still trail banks by some distance

49 P Baeck, L Collins and B Zhang, 'Understanding alternative finance: The UK Alternative Finance Industry Report 2014' (Nesta, November 2014).

50 J Napier and D Lock (2014), 'Bank to the Future: UK Retail Banking' (2014) *Deutsche Bank Markets Research* 74.

51 Bank of England, 'Financial Stability Report' (Issue No 37, Bank of England, July 2015) 50.

in terms of their share of the unsecured personal loans market. For example, in Q4 2014, the net lending flow to individuals through P2P platforms was just over £70 million, while those from UK banks and building societies topped £2 billion.[52]

A second, long-term, less direct but still important impact we expect P2P lenders will have on banks is in how they interact with consumers. Over the last two decades banks have taken steps to move their customers online to reduce costs from operating a branch network. By some estimates, 30 to 40 per cent of retail banks costs in the UK come from running physical branches, even though footfall in them has been falling at 10 per cent per annum in recent years, possibly because younger generations are more comfortable doing business purely online.[53] This means that banks are likely to renew their push to transition their customer interaction from brick-and-mortars to internet browsers.[54] As this happens, we anticipate that banks will look to P2P platforms for inspiration in how to redesign their websites, as these are often noted for being slick and speedy because, for example, they incorporate videos, pictures and communication channels for investors to interact with borrowers.[55]

## Conclusion

Let us sum up the terrain we have covered in this chapter.

P2P lending – direct lending between lenders and borrowers online outside traditional financial intermediaries like banks – first emerged in the UK and the world with the launch of Zopa in 2005. In this chapter we have shown how P2P lending evolved in the UK based on interviews with the founders of three of the most significant UK platforms (Zopa, RateSetter and Funding Circle), with an eye toward understanding the sources of economic entrepreneurship. We also discussed the geography of lending and borrowing created through these platforms based on a quantitative analysis of nearly 14 million loan agreements. Finally, we offered some reflections on the reasons why P2P lending has risen to prominence, and speculated on the impact the sector may have on the conventional banking sector. Competition from the P2P sector may reduce the price for unsecured personal loans, and encourage banks to enhance their digital offer. This could benefit consumers.

In closing, we want to underscore a point we made at the beginning. An untold, or underemphasised, story of the UK financial sector since the crisis

52 Data sources are the Bank of England and the P2P Finance Association. The P2P figures may also include secured lending to individuals, and factoring and discounting. Both P2P and bank figures exclude student loans.

53 Napier and Lock (n 50) 106.

54 For example, in autumn 2014, the front page of London's *Evening Standard* announced the closing of 200 Lloyds branches and its renewed push to drive their business digitally. See <http://www.standard.co.uk/business/business-news/lloyds-to-cut-9000-jobs-and-close-150-branches-9822362.html> accessed 30 October 2015.

55 P Jeffrey and D Arnold, 'Disrupting Banking' (2014) 25(3) *Business Strategy Review* 10.

is that it has seen a wave of innovation. We do not echo the chorus of gloom merchants whose voices have rung loudest since the crisis. Instead we suspect that competition from the P2P sector will benefit consumers over the long term by reducing the price for unsecured personal loans, and encouraging banks to enhance their digital offer.

In this sense, nothing we are seeing is new or innovative. Instead, at a more abstracted level of analysis, we are simply witnessing the recurrence of innovation, entrepreneurship and economic change typical of market capitalism. The motor of change throughout these fluctuations is always the same: 'The consumer is king, is the real boss, and the manufacturer is done for if he does not outstrip his competitors in best serving customers'.[56] In the words of Funding Circle's Andrew Mullinger:

> I'm not sure we've actually had any innovation . . . We think that putting the customer at the forefront of what we're doing is advantageous over the long term of our business and if we focus on doing that we will win ultimately over the long term . . . I'm not sure it is innovation.

56 L Von Mises, *Liberty and Property* (Mises Institute, 1991) 20.

# 4 High cost short term credit in the new UK marketplace

*Nicholas Ryder*

## Introduction

This chapter examines the high cost short term credit sector that has long existed in the United Kingdom.[1] The chapter argues that the proliferation of this sector not only contributed towards the most recent financial crisis but has also become one of its main manifestations. The first part of the chapter illustrates how the rapid expansion of the consumer credit market resulted in continuing record levels of consumer debt, increasing evidence of irresponsible lending practices and the evolution of an ineffective legislative framework that offered little or no protection to consumers. The next section of the chapter judiciously considers the evolution of irresponsible lending practices in the UK and provides a damning critique of the regulation.

## The evolution of the consumer credit market

Since the introduction of the first credit card in 1966,[2] the groundbreaking recommendations of the Crowther Committee on Consumer Credit[3] and the introduction of the Consumer Credit Act 1974, consumers are able to access credit 24 hours a day, 365 days a year. The evolution of the credit market was hastened by the deregulation of consumer credit legislation in the 1980s and 1990s. This section of the chapter outlines how the deregulation of the consumer credit legislative framework resulted in an increase in the availability of 'convenient credit', which is defined as 'credit that is granted by the creditor with little or no reference to the credit worthiness of the debtor'.[4] This chapter identifies several problems that have arisen from access to 'convenient credit', which has resulted in a dramatic alteration in policy by successive governments towards

1 Hereinafter 'UK'.

2 The UK Cards Association, 'History of Cards' <http://www.theukcardsassociation.org.uk/history_of_cards/index.asp> accessed 26 October 2015.

3 Hereinafter 'Crowther Committee'.

4 See N Ryder and R Thomas, 'Convenient Credit and Consumer Protection – A Critical Review of the Responses of Labour and Coalition Governments' (2011) 33(1) *Journal of Social Welfare and Family Law* 85, 85.

promoting access to 'affordable credit'. Affordable credit contains five basic elements: access to loans that are simple and transparent; lenders that are sympathetic towards low-income consumers' circumstances; simple loan application procedures; small loans over a short period of time; and affordable repayments.[5] Access to the UK consumer credit market, which 'less than a century ago barely existed', has dramatically altered since the introduction of the Consumer Credit Act 1974.[6] Consumers are able to access credit over the World Wide Web, using their interactive television sets, and through telephone banking, retail outlets and mobile devices.[7] Initially, the increased use of credit products had a positive impact for consumers, a view originally made by the Crowther Committee, which concluded that 'on balance consumer credit is beneficial, since it makes a useful contribution to the living standards and social wellbeing of the majority of the British people'.[8] Similarly, Borrie commented that the benefits afforded by access to credit enabled consumers to pay for more expensive goods and services without having to accumulate the necessary savings.[9] This was a view supported by Scott and Black who noted that purchasing items on credit would enable the consumer to pay for 'major purchases . . . without the need for immediate payment'.[10] The Griffiths Commission stated that the 'credit markets have grown to their present size because the service they have provided have responded to consumer demands. The result has been that consumers have been able to enjoy a higher standard of living than would have been the case if these markets had not existed'.[11]

The consumer credit market has undergone a dramatic and continuing period of evolution since the 1970s when the government's legislative control over the sector was extremely restrictive.[12] Indeed, prior to the introduction of the Consumer Credit Act 1974, the then existing legislative framework consisted of the restrictive and unsuitable Pawnbrokers Acts 1872–1960,[13] the Moneylenders

5 National Consumer Council, 'Affordable Credit: a Model That Recognises Real Needs' (National Consumer Council, 2005) 1.

6 M Richards, P Palmer and M Bogdanovva, 'Irresponsible Lending? A Case Study of a UK Credit Industry Reform Initiative' (2008) 81(3) *Journal of Business Ethics* 499, 501 (hereinafter 'Richards et al').

7 See, for example, the excellent report of the National Association of Citizens' Advice Bureaux, 'Daylight Robbery – The CAB case for effective regulation of extortionate credit' (National Association of Citizens' Advice Bureaux, 2000) 3.

8 Crowther Committee; as cited in C Ironfield-Smith, K Keasey, B Summers, D Duxbury and R Hudson, 'Consumer debt in the UK: attitudes and implications' (2005) 13(2) *Journal of Financial Regulation and Compliance* 132, 134 (hereinafter 'Ironfield-Smith et al').

9 G Borrie, 'The Credit Society: Its Benefits and Burdens' (1986) *Journal of Business Law* 181, 184–5.

10 C Scott and J Black, *Cranston's Consumers and the Law* (Butterworths, 2000) 231.

11 The Griffiths Commission, 'The Griffiths Commission on Personal Debt – What Price Credit?' (Centre for Social Justice, 2005) 1.

12 Richards et al (n 6).

13 For a more detailed discussion of this legislative framework, see J Macleod, 'Pawnbroking: A Regulatory Issue' (2005) *Journal of Business Law* 155–75.

Acts 1900–1927[14] and the Hire-Purchase Act 1965.[15] The 1980s and 1990s saw the deregulation of these restrictive legislative frameworks and the abolishment of controls on transactions in foreign exchange in 1979, the restrictions on banking lending being lifted, the removal of the reverse asset ratio in 1981 and the abolition of hire purchase controls in 1982.[16] It has been suggested that this deregulation 'transformed borrowing into an acceptable, and necessary, part of many consumers' lives . . . making buying on credit more attractive when compared with saving for consumer goods'.[17] Other important deregulatory measures included the move to allow banks to offer mortgages,[18] the introduction of the Building Societies Act 1986, which liberalised the interest rate fixing agreements,[19] the demutualisation of building societies[20] and an increase in the number of internet mortgage providers.[21] Therefore, these legislative amendments resulted in an increase in the availability of credit.[22] Writing in 2003, the then Department of Trade and Industry (DTI), which has now been replaced by the Department for Business, Innovation and Skills (BIS), concluded that the consumer credit market has fundamentally changed and that the variety of credit commodities available has grown at an unparalleled velocity.[23] Similarly, HM Treasury stated that a majority of households have witnessed a significant increase in ease of access to credit products.[24]

However, the benefits associated with the increased availability of credit has been overshadowed by the 'dark side' to the consumer credit market, fuelled by access to convenient credit and increased competition within the sector. This 'dark side' is illustrated by increasing record levels of consumer debt,[25] increasing evidence of irresponsible lending practices,[26] the imposition of extortionate

14 For a brief discussion, see H Johnson, 'Fair Credit' (1991) 10(6) *International Banking and Financial Law* 94.

15 S Brown, 'The Consumer Credit Act 2006; Real Additional Mortgagor Protection?' (2007) *Conveyancer and Property Lawyer* 316, 317.

16 E Fernandez-Corugedo and J Muellbauer, 'Consumer Credit Conditions in the United Kingdom' (Working Paper No 314, Bank of England, 2006) 4.

17 Ironfield-Smith et al (n 8) 134.

18 During this period mortgage borrowing increased by 300%, largely due to the introduction of 'right to buy' legislation and the Housing Act 1980. See E Kempson, 'Over-Indebtedness in Britain – A Report to the Department of Trade and Industry' (Personal Finance Research Centre, 2002).

19 See J Vaughan, 'The Building Societies Act – A Review of Its Powers' (1986) 7(6) *Company Lawyer* 227.

20 For a more detailed discussion, see R Webb, C Bryce and D Watson, 'The Effect of Building Society Demutualisation on Levels of Efficiency at Large UK Commercial Banks' (2010) 18(4) *Journal of Financial Regulation and Compliance* 333.

21 Fernandez-Corugedo and Muellbauer (n 16) 8–9.

22 E Lomnicka, 'The Reform of Consumer Credit in the UK' (2004) *Journal of Business Law* 129.

23 Department of Trade and Industry, 'Fair, Clear and Competitive – The Consumer Credit Market in the 21st Century' (White Paper, Department of Trade and Industry, 2003).

24 HM Treasury, 'Promoting Financial Inclusion' (HM Treasury, 2004).

25 See The Centre for Social Justice, 'Future Finance: A New Approach To Financial Capability' (The Centre for Social Justice, 2015).

26 See N Ryder, *The Financial Crisis and White Collar Crime: The Perfect Storm?* (Edward Elgar, 2014) 71–9.

interest rates,[27] ineffective legislative protection of consumers and an ineffective regulatory regime.[28] This was a point recognised by Ziegel, who in 1973 stated that 'even under the most favourable circumstances a consumer credit orientated economy is bound to produce a number of casualties. These are the debtors who, for one reason or another, have over-committed themselves and are unable to pay their debts'.[29] The increased availability of convenient credit has resulted in an increasing number of households who are forced to obtain credit from sub-prime providers, who charge higher interest rates than banks or building societies.[30] Sub-prime providers of credit can be divided into three categories: commercial cash loans,[31] non-commercial cash loans[32] and credit tied to the purchase of goods.[33] Sub-prime lenders provide a wide range of financial products that have become synonymous with the financial crisis: 'prime loans', 'alt-A loans' and 'sub-prime loans'. A 'prime loan' is a financial instrument that is used by debtors with a good credit rating.[34] An 'alt-A loan' is used by debtors who generally have a good credit rating that contains some shortcomings.[35] Conversely, a 'sub-prime loan' is aimed at 'high-risk borrowers who typically have poor credit histories';[36] such loans have also been referred to as 'NINJA loans'.[37] It has been suggested that NINJA loans are offered to people who are unable to meet the requirements for prime loans. The sub-prime mortgage sector originated in the United States

27 See generally E Kempson, and C Whyley, 'Extortionate Credit in the UK' (Department of Trade and Industry, 1999).

28 Lomnicka (n 22) 129.

29 J Ziegel, 'Recent Developments in Canadian Consumer Credit Law' (1973) 36(5) *Modern Law Review* 479, 480. See also G Goode, 'A Credit Law for Europe?' (1974) 23(2) *International and Comparative Law Quarterly* 227. For an excellent recent discussion of the issues raised by Professor Roy Goode, see S Brown, 'EU and UK Consumer Credit Regulation: Principles, Conduct, And Consumer Protection: Divergence or Convergence of Approach?' (2015) 26(4) *European Business Law Review* 555.

30 Financial Services Authority, 'In or out? Financial Exclusion: A Literature and Research Review' (Financial Services Authority, 2000) 42.

31 This includes home credit companies, pawnbrokers, sale and buy back, payday loans and unlicensed money lenders. For a graphic illustration of the consequences of utilising home credit companies, see HM Treasury, 'Review of Christmas Savings Schemes' (HM Treasury, 2007).

32 This includes the government-run Social Fund and Budgeting Loan Scheme, credit unions, savings and loan schemes, community-based loan schemes, family and friends, and informal savings and loan schemes.

33 This includes agency mail order companies and rental purchase outlets.

34 According to Mitchell 'lenders steered minorities into taking out subprime loans, though they may have qualified for prime loans that had much lower interest rates and more favourable terms for the borrower'. See T Mitchell, 'Growing Inequality and Racial Economic Gaps' (2013) 56 *Howard Law Journal* 849, 884.

35 Such shortcomings according to Messerschmitt could include an inability to 'verify their income or have high debt-to-income ratios'. See D Messerschmitt, 'Overview of the Subprime Mortgage Market' (2007) 27 *Review of Banking and Financial Law* 3, 3.

36 Ibid 3. For an excellent discussion of sub-prime loans, see O Bar-Gill, 'The Law, Economics and Psychology of Subprime Mortgage Contracts' (2009) 93 *Cornell Law Review* 1073.

37 D Berman, 'The Game: Sketchy Loans Abound: With Capital Plentiful, Debt Buyers Take Subprime-Type Risks', *Wall Street Journal* (27 March 2007) <http://www.wsj.com/articles/SB117495177692049687> accessed 26 October 2015.

in the 1980s, yet it was not until the next decade that they began to make significant inroads into the US mortgage sector. Indeed, it has been suggested by some commentators that by the end of the 1990s only 5 per cent of mortgage loans were considered to be sub-prime.[38] Nonetheless, by 2005 the figure had increased to approximately 20 per cent. Therefore, sub-prime loans grew at an unprecedented level in the United States between the 1980s and the start of the new millennium; by 2006 the amount of money attached to sub-prime mortgages accounted for a quarter of all US mortgages.[39] By 2006 an additional three million sub-prime loans were instigated extending the total value of unsettled debt to $3 trillion. Engel and McCoy concluded that in 2006, mortgages totalling over $600 billion were provided by sub-prime lenders.[40] The growth in the level of sub-prime lending is staggering.[41] The total amount of outstanding loans for the sub-prime mortgage market has increased at an unprecedented rate and has resulted in a 75 per cent increase in the number of repossessions in the United States.

Another illustration of the problems associated with the evolution of the consumer credit market has been the number of people who are at jeopardy from being unable to gain access to affordable credit. For example, it has been estimated that 2.25 million people in the UK are at risk in terms of access to affordable credit.[42] Research conducted by the Financial Services Authority (the former financial watchdog) concluded that 40 per cent of the population have no savings at all.[43] It has also been suggested that people who are unable to access affordable credit are also incapable of accessing the basic services provided by financial services outlets. This has restricted people's access to affordable credit and it has been suggested by some commentators that up to 23 per cent of the population lack access to a current account.[44] However, it has been suggested by the Office of Fair Trading (OFT), which was the consumer credit regulator until the Financial Conduct Authority (FCA) took over in April 2014, that only 12 per cent of the population does not have access to a current account.[45] In April 2014,

38 K Engel, and P McCoy, *The Subprime Virus: Reckless Credit, Regulatory Failure, and Next Steps* (Oxford University Press, 2011).

39 A White, 'The Case for Banning Subprime Mortgages' (2008) 77 *University of Cincinnati Law Review* 617, 618. This is a view supported by T Nguyen, and H Pontell, 'Fraud and inequality in the subprime mortgage crisis' in M Deflem (ed.), *Economic Crisis and Crime* (Emerald, 2011) 12.

40 Engel and McCoy (n 38).

41 A Jacobson, 'The Burden Of Good Intentions: Intermediate-Sized Banks and Thrifts and the Community Reinvestment Act' (2006) *UC Davis Business Law Journal* 6, 16. See also G Udell, 'Wall Street, Main Street, and a Credit Crunch: Thoughts on the Current Financial Crisis' (2009) 52(2) *Business Horizons* 117.

42 P Davis and C Brockie, 'A Mis-signalling Problem? The Troubled Performance Relationship between Credit Unions and Local Government in the UK' (2001) 27(1) *Local Government Studies* 1.

43 Financial Services Authority, 'Levels of Financial Capability in the UK: Results of a Base-Line Survey' (FSA, 2006) 43.

44 E Kempson and C Whyley, 'Access to Current Accounts' (British Bankers Association, 1998).

45 Office of Fair Trading, 'Vulnerable Consumers and Financial Services – The Report of the Director General's Inquiry' (Office of Fair Trading, 1999).

the FCA, citing a report by the Money Advice Service, reported that nine million people are over-indebted with over-indebtedness.[46] Furthermore, in November 2013 the Centre for Social Justice noted that approximately 130,000 people declare themselves insolvent and 1.7 million people have obtained free personal debt advice.[47] If these figures are accurate an increasing number of people are being forced to gain credit from sub-prime providers. In practical terms this means that people are compelled to enter into short-term credit agreements that attract higher levels of interest payments from pawn brokers, catalogues, sale and buyback shops and illegal money lenders.[48]

Due to the diversity and unpredictable nature of the consumer credit market, there has also been a momentous increase in the levels of consumer debt. In 2004, the Department for Work and Pensions reported that the average level of outstanding consumer credit per household had increased from £2,088 in 1995 to £6,464.[49] Similarly, the National Association of Citizens' Advice Bureaux (NACAB) concluded that the number of people facing financial liquidity problems has increased by approximately 50 per cent since 1998.[50] It added that the average level of debt per client was £16,971, almost two thirds higher than in 2001 and that these clients will take an average of 93 years to pay off their debts.[51] In 2009 the BIS stated that 'consumers currently owe around £1.4tn to banks and other financial institutions'.[52] The Money Charity reported in September 2015 that the total level of personal debt in the UK was £1,443 trillion, the total average debt per household was £54,042 and the average debt per adult was £28,535, which amounts to 112 per cent of the average household income.[53] Interestingly, the Office for Budget Responsibility has estimated that by 2021 the total amount of personal debt in the UK in 2021 will be £2,551 trillion.[54] Higher levels of consumer debt have been exacerbated by the most recent financial crisis. The uncertainty in the global financial system has led to a dramatic reduction in the availability of affordable credit.

46 Financial Conduct Authority, 'Consumer Credit and Consumers in Vulnerable Circumstances' (Financial Conduct Authority, 2014) 3.

47 Centre for Social Justice (n 25) 33. See also Friends Provident Foundation, 'Credit and Low-Income Consumers: A Demand-Side Perspective on the Issues for Consumer Protection' (Friends Provident Foundation, 2011).

48 HM Treasury (n 24).

49 Department for Work and Pensions, 'Tackling Over-Indebtedness Action Plan 2004' (Department for Work and Pensions, 2004) 13.

50 As cited in S Bridges and R Disney, 'Use of Credit and Arrears on Debt Among Low-Income Families in the United Kingdom' (2004) 25(1) *Fiscal Studies* 1, 2.

51 National Association of Citizens' Advice Bureaux, 'A Life in Debt – The Profile of CAB Debt Clients in 2008' (National Association of Citizens' Advice Bureaux, 2009) 1.

52 Department for Business, Innovation and Skills, 'Review of the Regulation of Credit and Store Cards – A Consultation: Initial Equality Impact Assessment' (Department for Business, Innovation and Skills, 2009) 7.

53 The Money Charity, 'The Money Statistics September 2015' <http://themoneycharity.org.uk/media/September-2015-Money-Statistics.pdf> accessed 12 October 2015.

54 Office for Budget Responsibility, 'Economic and Financial Outlook: July 2015' (Office for Budget Responsibility, 2015).

However, it is important to note that since the introduction of the first credit card in 1966, the influential recommendations of the Crowther Committee (1971) and the introduction of the Consumer Credit Act (1974), creditors allow debtors to access credit 24 hours a day, 365 days a year. The number of creditors and credit products has grown at an unprecedented level. The evolution of the credit market was hastened by the deregulation of consumer credit legislation in the 1980s and 1990s. This was fuelled by the relaxation of the consumer credit legislative frameworks and resulted in an increase in the availability of 'convenient credit', which is defined as 'credit that is granted by the creditor with little or no reference to the credit worthiness of the debtor'. Access to consumer credit, which 'less than a century ago barely existed', has dramatically altered.[55] This development is summarised by the NACAB:

> In 1979 bank customers wanting to arrange a loan had to ensure that they were able to visit their branch office on a weekday between 9.30 a.m. and 3.30 p.m. Today the proliferation of telephone and Internet banking provides 24-hour access 365 days a year. An ever increasing number of companies have entered the personal finance market offering an ever more bewildering choice of products.[56]

The consumer credit market has undergone a revolution since the 1970s when the government's legislative control over the sector was extremely restrictive.[57] Indeed, prior to the publication of the Crowther Committee and the introduction of the Consumer Credit Act 1974, the consumer credit legislative framework consisted of the restrictive and unsuitable Pawnbrokers Acts 1872–1960, the Moneylenders Acts 1900–1927 and the Hire-Purchase Act 1965. The Griffiths Commission stated that 'there were strict quantitative limits imposed on the banks by the government. Building societies supplied mortgages for house purchases, but again these were rationed on the basis of rigid and conservative debt to income ratios'.[58] The 1980s and 1990s saw the deregulation of the restrictive consumer credit legislation.[59] Such measures included the abolition of controls on transactions in foreign exchange in 1979, the restrictions on banking lending being lifted, the removal of the reverse asset ratio in 1981 and the abolition of hire purchase controls in 1982.[60] Ironfield-Smith et al noted that this deregulation 'transformed borrowing into an acceptable, and necessary, part of many consumers' lives . . . making buying on credit more attractive when compared with saving for consumer goods'.[61] Other important measures included the

55 Richards et al (n 6) 501.
56 National Association of Citizens' Advice Bureaux (n 7) 3.
57 Richards et al (n 6).
58 The Griffiths Commission (n 11) 21.
59 Fernandez-Corugedo and Muellbauer (n 16) 4.
60 National Association of Citizens' Advice Bureaux (n 7) 6.
61 Ironfield-Smith et al (n 8) 134.

move to allow banks to offer mortgages,[62] the Building Societies Act 1986, which liberalised the interest rate fixing agreements, the demutualisation of building societies and an increase in the number of internet mortgage providers in the latter part of the 1990s.[63] Therefore, these legislative amendments have resulted in an increase in the availability of credit.[64] The then Department of Trade and Industry (DTI) shared this view and stated that the consumer credit market has fundamentally changed and that the variety of credit commodities available has grown at an unparalleled velocity.[65] Similarly, HM Treasury stated that a majority of households have witnessed a significant increase in ease of access to credit products.[66]

However, there is a 'dark side' to the consumer credit market, fuelled by access to convenient credit and increased competition within the sector. The 'dark side' of the credit market is illustrated by record levels of consumer debt, increasing evidence of irresponsible lending practices,[67] the imposition of extortionate interest rates,[68] and ineffective legislative protection of consumers.[69] As previously noted above by Ziegel, the rapid expansion of the consumer credit market will have an adverse impact on many debtors who will be unable to repay their debts.[70] Despite an increase in the availability of convenient credit, there are an increasing number of households who are forced to obtain credit from sub-prime providers, who traditionally charge higher interest rates than banks or building societies.[71] Sub-prime providers of credit can be divided into three categories: commercial cash loans, non-commercial cash loans and credit tied to the purchase of goods. In practical terms this means that people are compelled to enter into short-term credit agreements that attract higher levels of interest payments from pawn brokers, catalogues, sale and buyback shops and illegal money lenders.[72]

It has been suggested that 'high-cost credit, in particular payday lending, has recently received unprecedented levels of academic and media interest. In the five years from 2009 to 2014, the market for these products grew significantly – from around £800 million to £2.8–3.5 billion.[73] If the figures are accurate an increasing number of people are being forced to gain credit from sub-prime providers since the crisis of 2008 started to unfold. Research conducted by 'R3', or the Association of British Recovery Professionals, suggested that 3.5 million

62 During this period mortgage borrowing increased by 300%, largely due to the introduction of 'right to buy' legislation and the Housing Act 1980.
63 Fernandez-Corugedo and Muellbauer (n 16) 8–9.
64 Lomnicka (n 22) 129.
65 Department of Trade and Industry (n 23).
66 HM Treasury (n 24).
67 Ibid.
68 Kempson and Whyley (n 27).
69 Lomnicka (n 22) 129.
70 Ziegel (n 29) 480.
71 Financial Services Authority (n 30) 42.
72 HM Treasury (n 24).
73 J Gardner and K Rowlingson, 'High-cost credit and welfare reform' *In Defence of Welfare II* (Social Policy Association, 2015) 32.

people use payday loans. Frances Coulson, R3 President, stated that 'payday loans are not the best way to resolve debt struggles. We know that many who take them out find them to be a negative experience, often escalating financial troubles'.[74] According to the study, this has seen an increase in the number of so-called 'zombie debtors' 'who currently pay only the interest charges on their debt and not the debt itself'.[75] Access to convenient credit resulted in a dramatic 'U-turn' by the UK government towards promoting access to 'affordable credit'. Successive UK governments have attempted to promote convenient credit through, for example, the development of credit unions.[76] These problems have been partly fuelled by the sub-prime mortgage crisis in the United States. It is the global contraction of credit that has caused turmoil in the UK credit market and has resulted in the near collapse and part-nationalisation of several banks.

## Ineffective legislative protection for consumers

Despite the merits afforded by the Consumer Credit Act 1974 (CCA 1974), there is a general consensus among commentators that it is no longer fit for purpose.[77] Reform of the CCA 1974 is an important part of the government's policy towards increasing people's access to affordable credit.[78] The NACAB took the view that 'the dynamic changes in the consumer credit sector have not been matched by changes in the legislation intended to protect consumers from abuse'.[79] Commentators agreed that the CCA 1974 was in desperate need of reform. The DTI took the view that 'the laws governing this market were set out a generation ago . . . the regulatory structure that was put in place . . . is not the same as the regulatory structure required today'.[80] The Griffiths Commission stated that 'since the introduction of the Act, the credit market has been wholly transformed and the current credit market bears little resemblance to that which existed in 1974'.[81] Brown noted that:

> within a few years of the final implementation orders of the Consumer Credit Act being issued, which incidentally was not until the mid-1980s, general dissatisfaction with the working of the Consumer Credit Act, was beginning to surface. Although no reform took place at that time, further suggestion

74 R3, '3.5 million reach for payday loans as "zombie" debtors rise', 12 December 2011 <https://www.r3.org.uk/index.cfm?page=1114&element=14982> accessed 7 April 2016.

75 Ibid.

76 For a more detailed discussion, see N Ryder, 'The Credit Crunch – The Right Time for Credit Unions to Strike?' (2009) 29(1) *Legal Studies* 75.

77 For an excellent analysis of the effectiveness of the CCA 1974, see G Howells, 'The Consumer Credit Litigation Explosion' (2010) 126 *Law Quarterly Review* 617.

78 HM Treasury (n 24).

79 National Association of Citizens' Advice Bureaux (n 7) 1.

80 The DTI stated: 'in 1971, there was only one credit card available; now there are 1,300. 30 years ago, £32 million was owed on credit cards, now it is over £49 billion': Department of Trade and Industry (n 23) 12.

81 The Griffiths Commission (n 11) appendix 2.3.

for change was again mooted a few years later, resulting in the Consumer Credit Review set up by the Government in 2001.[82]

The CCA 1974 was outdated and had not kept pace with the complexity and diversity of the consumer credit market. The Act contained a number of inadequacies – the extortionate credit provisions,[83] the consumer credit licensing regime and the limited enforcement powers of the OFT.[84] Indeed, the DTI took the view that:

> The Act has not provided sufficient protection for consumers where they have been unfairly treated by consumer credit businesses. The rights that the Act accords to consumers and the avenues it provides to them to challenge unfair conduct are restricted. Furthermore, the Act has provided regulators with insufficient powers to tackle improper or unfair conduct by consumer credit businesses.[85]

The reform process began with the publication of a White Paper in 1999, in which the government announced its intention to modernise the CCA 1974 and to ensure that it provided adequate protection for consumers.[86] In October 2000, a Task Force was created with the remit of achieving responsible lending and borrowing.[87] Later that year, the DTI published a consultation paper that sought the opinions of interested parties on the general effectiveness of the CCA 1974.[88] A second White Paper was published in December 2003 with the aim of creating 'a more transparent regime so consumers can make better informed decisions and get a fairer deal'.[89] In conjunction with the White Paper, the DTI published another consultation paper on how the legislative changes were to be implemented.[90] Subsequently, several statutory instruments were introduced

82 Brown (n 15) 318.

83 For an excellent commentary on relevant judicial precedent, see L Bently and G Howells, 'Judicial Treatment of Extortionate Credit Bargains – Part I' (1989) *The Conveyancer and Property Lawyer* 164 and 'Loan Sharks and Extortionate Credit Bargain – Part II' (1989) *The Conveyancer and Property Lawyer* 234.

84 For a more detailed commentary on consumer credit licences, see Office of Fair Trading, 'Consumer Credit Licensing – General Guidance for Licenses and Applications on Fitness and Requirements' (Office of Fair Trading, 2008).

85 Department of Trade and Industry, 'Consumer Credit Bill Full Regulatory Impact Assessment' (Department of Trade and Industry, 2004) 4. Further support for this view is offered by Lomnicka (n 22) 132.

86 Department of Trade and Industry, 'Modern Markets: Confident Consumers' (White Paper, Department of Trade and Industry,1999).

87 Department of Trade and Industry, 'Report by the Task Force on Tackling Overindebtedness' (Department of Trade and Industry, 2001).

88 Department of Trade and Industry, 'Tackling Loan Sharks – And More! – Consultation Document On Modernising The Consumer Credit Act 1974' (Department of Trade and Industry, 2001).

89 Department of Trade and Industry (n 23) 5.

90 Department of Trade and Industry, 'Establishing a Transparent Market' (Department of Trade and Industry, 2003).

to implement some of the proposed amendments to the 1974 Act. However, a majority of the reforms were introduced by the Consumer Credit Act 2006 (CCA 2006), which came into effect on 1 October 2008. The scope of this Act is extensive and applies to the regulation of consumer credit agreements and consumer hire agreements; the provision of information to debtors and hirers after the agreement is made; unfair relationships between debtors and creditors; the licensing of consumer credit and hire businesses and ancillary credit businesses; the powers of the OFT in relation to the licensing of consumer credit and hire businesses and ancillary credit businesses; appeals from decisions of the OFT in relation to the licensing of consumer credit and hire businesses and ancillary credit businesses; and the extension of the jurisdiction of the Financial Ombudsman Service.

However, successive governments are still not satisfied with the measures introduced by the CCA 2006 and believe that that there is the need for further legislative intervention. In May 2008, the government initiated the 'Review of Consumer Law',[91] the aim of which was to achieve a balance between protecting consumers, reducing the unwarranted burdens imposed on businesses and endorsing fair and competitive markets. The Review sought views on four particular areas: the case for reform, options for reform, consumer empowerment and redress, and securing compliance with the law. As a result of this review the BIS took the view that:

> the law is complex, fragmented and inflexible. This can lead to higher levels of consumer detriment as well as unnecessary costs for business and less effectiveness for enforcers. The Government is committed to a fundamental modernisation of the consumer law framework to fit the modern, interconnected and interdependent world. This will ensure consumer rights are fit for purpose in the age of the internet. It will provide consumers, business and enforcers with the clarity and confidence to explain, to exercise and to enforce the protections and responsibilities we all have as consumers.[92]

In July 2009, the government published another White Paper,[93] whose aim was to review the regulations that govern consumer credit and store cards. Writing in 2004 the HM Treasury Select Committee warned that 'store cards charge much higher rates of interest even than credit cards. Although in part this may flow from a pricing model which places all the costs of the operation on the minority who pay interest, there is also evidence to suggest that competition is not working properly'.[94] The White Paper concentrated on four areas of credit and store

91 Department for Business, Innovation and Skills, 'Consumer Law Review: Call For Evidence' (Department for Business, Innovation and Skills, 2008).

92 Department for Business, Innovation and Skills, 'A Better Deal For Consumers – Delivering Real Help Now and Change for the Future, (Department for Business, Innovation and Skills, 2009) 77.

93 Ibid.

94 HM Treasury Select Committee, 'Transparency of Credit Card Charges: First Report of Session 2003–04' (HM Treasury Select Committee, 2004) 78.

cards. This included: 'firstly, the requirement that repayments to a credit or store card are allocated to debts attracting the highest interest rates first; secondly, the level of minimum payments; thirdly, the issue of unsolicited credit limits; and finally, the ability of lenders to raise interest rates on existing debts'.[95] It could be argued that a review of the regulations that apply to credit and store cards is timely given the adverse impact of the 2008 credit crunch and record levels of consumer debt. Indeed, the BIS took the view that:

> Consumers value the flexibility that credit and store cards offer and their use has risen dramatically in the past two decades. However, a significant minority of consumers carry high levels of debt on their credit and store cards with no prospect of paying it off within a reasonable amount of time, if at all. Store cards account for a much smaller proportion of unsecured borrowing than credit cards, but are of particular concern because of the high interest rates they charge. Many consumers are facing financial pressures as a result of the downturn and are now having to deal with unsustainable debts built up on their credit and store cards during the years of easy credit.[96]

The proposals have been largely welcomed by consumer groups. For example, 'Which?' stated that 'for too long, card companies have been allowed to apply the tricks of their trade to the detriment of millions of consumers'. In addition it stated that 'we think it's simply wrong to entice people into spending more than they can afford and then to squeeze as much money out of them as possible'.[97] Similarly, Malcolm Hurlston of the Consumer Credit Counselling Service took the view that 'the government has put its finger on the four main problems that consumers have with credit card debt. We believe that the banks should be able to change their practices on each of these but if they can't, regulation will be necessary'.[98] Furthermore, the BIS published a paper in July 2009 entitled 'A Better Deal for Consumers Delivering Real Help Now and Change for the Future'. According to this publication there are six key principles that underpin the government's consumer strategy. These are protection, responsibility, enforcement, change, proportionality and competition.[99] The Coalition government also published a number of consultation papers in 2010.[100] In a joint consultation paper published by HM Treasury and the BIS, the Coalition government proposed to transfer the regulation of credit from the OFT to the Consumer Protection and Markets Authority. On 1 April 2014, the new FCA

95 Department for Business, Innovation and Skills (n 91) 3.

96 Ibid.

97 *BBC News*, 'Credit card terms "to be curbed"', Tuesday, 27 October 2009 <http://news.bbc.co.uk/1/hi/business/8326485.stm> accessed 11 April 2016.

98 Ibid.

99 Department for Business, Innovation and Skills (n 92) 13.

100 HM Treasury, 'A New Approach To Financial Regulation: Consultation on Reforming the Consumer Credit Regime' (HM Treasury, 2010).

took over the regulation of the consumer credit market.[101] This new authority encompasses much of the conduct-based regulatory responsibility of the Financial Services Authority,[102] coupled with the responsibility for both the prudence and conduct of 23,000 financial services providers.[103]

Therefore, the reform of the 1974 Act and the need to protect consumers and debtors has become a key priority for successive Westminster governments.[104] The NACAB took the view that 'the dynamic changes in the consumer credit sector have not been matched by changes in the legislation intended to protect consumers from abuse'.[105] The DTI stated that 'the laws governing this market were set out a generation ago . . . the regulatory structure that was put in place . . . is not the same as the regulatory structure required today'.[106] Indeed, the Griffiths Commission stated that 'since the introduction of the Act, the credit market has been wholly transformed and the current credit market bears little resemblance to that which existed in 1974'.[107] Furthermore, Brown noted that by the mid-1980s there was 'general dissatisfaction with the working of the Consumer Credit Act'.[108] The Consumer Credit Act 1974 was outdated and had not kept pace with the complexity and diversity of the consumer credit market. The Act contained a number of inadequacies – the extortionate credit provisions, the consumer credit licensing regime and the limited enforcement powers of the OFT.[109] The most ineffective means of consumer protection afforded by the CCA 1974 that applied to high cost credit was the extortionate credit bargain provisions.[110] These provisions permitted a court to intervene with consumer credit agreements.[111] However, this was not the first statutory provision that allowed the courts to perform such a function. The MoneyLenders Act provided that an interest rate above 48 per cent was 'excessive and the credit transaction harsh and unconscionable'.[112] The phrase 'harsh and unconscionable', according to Browne-Wilkinson J, meant that 'the terms of the credit transaction [were] imposed in a morally reprehensible manner'.[113] This is a view also supported by Scott and Black, who opined that

101 A Barber, E Radmore and JJ Manchado, 'Taking the Credit – The Transfer of Consumer Credit Regulation' <http://www.compliancemonitor.com/uk-regulation/regulatory-structure/taking-the-credit--the-transfer-of-consumer-credit-regulation-64192.htm> accessed 8 April 2016.

102 See generally J Perry, R Moulton, G Barwick, R Small, J Green and N Kay, 'The New UK Regulatory Landscape' (2011) 84 *Compliance Office Bulletin* 1, 4.

103 Financial Conduct Authority, 'Business Plan 2014/2015' <http://www.fca.org.uk/static/documents/corporate/business-plan-2014-2015-interactive.pdf > accessed 8 April 2016.

104 HM Treasury (n 24).

105 National Association of Citizens' Advice Bureaux (n 7) 1.

106 The DTI stated 'in 1971, there was only one credit card available; now there are 1,300. 30 years ago, £32 million was owed on credit cards, now it is over £49 billion': Department of Trade and Industry (n 23) 12.

107 The Griffiths Commission (n 11) appendix 2.3.

108 Brown (n 15) 318.

109 Kempson and Whyley (n 27) 36–7.

110 Brown (n 15) 326.

111 Lomnicka (n 22) 137.

112 National Association of Citizens' Advice Bureaux (n 7) 6.

113 *Multiservice Bookbinding Ltd v Marden* [1979] Ch 84, 110.

'rate regulation has a long history deriving from the suspicion with which money lending has always been regarded'.[114] Similarly, Brown took the view that:

> the question of an interest rate ceiling is one that has engaged law reformers for many years. Indeed it was the control of choice under the Usury Laws until their abolition in 1854. When reform of pawnbroking legislation and the establishment of the money-lending legislation were considered, interest rate controls were still seen as appropriate. It was only with the Crowther Committee Report and the passing of the CCA that interest rate controls were finally abandoned.[115]

The extortionate credit bargain provisions of the CCA 1974 were far reaching. They applied to all credit agreements between individuals and creditors and not simply regulated agreements. The Act stipulated that 'if the court finds a credit bargain extortionate it may reopen the credit agreement so as to do justice between the parties'.[116] A 'credit bargain' 'where no transaction other than the credit agreement is to be taken into account in computing the total charge for credit, means the credit agreement',[117] or 'where one or more other transactions are to be so taken into account, means the credit agreement and those other transactions, taken together'.[118] A credit bargain was considered to be extortionate if it required the debtor or a relative of his to make payments which were grossly exorbitant or otherwise grossly contravened ordinary principles of fair dealing.[119] The court was permitted to take into account several factors when determining whether or not the credit bargain was extortionate. This included interest rates prevailing at the time the credit agreement was made,[120] other factors in relation to the debtor,[121] factors in relation to the creditor[122] and whether or not a colourable cash price was quoted for any goods or services included in the credit bargain;[123] and the factors in relation to a linked transaction included the question how far the transaction was reasonably required for the protection of the debtor or creditor, or was in the interest of the debtor.[124] Scott and Black noted that 'the wide discretion given to the courts in considering bargains for their extortionate character, and the fact that so much can depend upon individual circumstances of a credit transaction, meant that little control of credit charges has resulted from the enactment of this provision'.[125]

114 Scott and Black (n 10) 254.
115 Brown (n 15) 326.
116 CCA 1974, s 137(1).
117 Ibid, s 137(2)(i).
118 Ibid, s 137(2)(ii).
119 Ibid, s 138(1)(a) and (b).
120 Ibid, s 138(2)(a).
121 Ibid, s 138(2)(b).
122 Ibid, s 138(4).
123 Ibid, s 138(4).
124 Ibid, s 138(5).
125 Scott and Black (n 10) 256.

A credit bargain was considered extortionate if it involved making payments that were grossly exorbitant or which disregarded the principles of fair dealing.[126] The second part of this definition – a credit bargain was extortionate if it otherwise grossly contravened ordinary principles of fair dealing[127] – was, according to Howells and Bently, 'more nebulous than the first'.[128] Howells and Bently illustrated the inconsistent approach adopted by the judiciary towards the interpretation of the world 'grossly' and cited several cases to support this contention.[129] When a court was considering whether or not a credit agreement was extortionate, it would take into account several factors in relation to the debtor, for example the personal conditions and status of the debtor such as their age, experience, business capacity and their state of health and whether or not the debtor was under any financial pressure.[130] It is difficult to determine how much weight was actually afforded to the personal circumstances of the debtor.

The CCA 1974 provided the courts with a list of factors that they could take into account when determining whether a credit agreement was to be reopened.[131] This included such factors as the interest rates prevailing at the time the agreement was made;[132] the debtor's age, experience, business capacity and state of health; the degree to which, at the time of making the credit bargain, the debtor was under financial pressure; and the nature of that pressure.[133] Furthermore, in relation to the creditor, a court would consider such factors as the degree of risk accepted by him, having regard to the value of any security provided;[134] his relationship to the debtor;[135] and whether or not a colourable cash price was quoted for any goods or services included in the credit bargain.[136] If a court determined that a credit agreement was extortionate, it had a broad range of powers under the Act 'for the purpose of relieving the debtor or surety from payment of any sum in excess of that fairly due and reasonable'.[137]

In relation to interest rates, Howells and Bently took the view that:

> the Act directs the court to have regard to interest rates prevailing at the time the bargain was made. The courts have recognised that the section covers many types of credit bargains and that therefore there is no one market rate for all bargains, so they have compared the rate charged in the case in hand with the prevailing rate for 'these sort of loans'.[138]

126 Ibid, s 138(1)(a) and (b).
127 Ibid, s 138(1)(b).
128 Bently and Howells (n 83) 166.
129 Ibid 165.
130 CCA 1974, s 138(2) and (3).
131 Ibid, s 138(2)(a).
132 Ibid, s 138(3)(a).
133 Ibid, s 138(3)(b).
134 Ibid, s 138(4)(a).
135 Ibid, s 138(4)(b).
136 Ibid, s 138(4)(c).
137 Ibid, s 139(2).
138 Bently and Howells (n 84) 169.

It is fair to state that, when considering the interest rates charged in consumer credit agreements, the courts have correctly investigated the type of institution lending to the debtor. Howells and Bently, citing *Davis v Direct Loans*,[139] highlighted the approach adopted by the court, which divided the then credit market into such providers of credit as banks, building societies, finance houses and secondary finance associations. Similarly, in *Leamington Spa Building Society v Jindal*,[140] the court rejected that two mortgages with interest rates of 17.75 and 18.75 per cent were extortionate because they were similar to the rates offered by other building societies and within the interest rate band recommended by the Building Societies Association. However, on some occasions it is difficult for the court to obtain a direct like-for-like comparison between various credit agreements.[141] The imposition of varying levels of interest rates on consumer credit agreements was extremely contentious and it is the part of the extortionate credit provisions that received a great deal of judicial discussion. For example, in *Nash and Staunton v Paragon Finance plc*,[142] Nash, the mortgagor, appealed against the decision of the first instance court to strike out a defence and counterclaim to a possession action initiated by Paragon Finance plc, the mortgagee, after Nash had fallen into mortgage arrears. Counsel for Nash postulated that the mortgage agreement was an extortionate credit bargain following the decision by Paragon Finance not to reduce the interest rates in line with those issued by the Bank of England.[143] In this case the difference between the interest rates charged by Paragon Finance and the Halifax had increased from 2 per cent to somewhere between 4 and 5 per cent, which Paragon Finance asserted was necessary as its own source of funds had become more expensive due to an increase in the number of mortgagees who defaulted on payments. Therefore, Paragon Finance had no other choice but to pass on the increase costs to its customers. It is important to note that the mortgage agreement contained a variable interest clause, which resulted in Nash attempting to argue that this clause was an implied term that required Paragon Finance to vary its interest rates accordingly. The Court of Appeal dismissed the claim by Nash and stated that the mortgage agreement was not an extortionate credit bargain and that Paragon Finance was permitted to pursue the possession action. The decision in *London North Securities v Meadows*[144] will almost certainly be remembered for the court's comments concerning the extortionate credit bargain provisions under the CCA 1974. However, his consideration of those provisions was purely obiter. The primary issue in *Meadows* raised important questions about the meaning of the terms 'credit' and 'total charge

139 [1986] 1 WLR 823.

140 1985 WL 1167649.

141 See, for example, *Patel v Patel* [1983] CLCLR 11.

142 [2001] EWCA Civ 1466.

143 Nash argued in this case that the mortgage agreement should have been reopened by virtue of the CCA 1974, s 139(1).

144 Unreported, 28 October 2004 (Liverpool County Court); summarised at [2005] 1 P & CR DG16.

for credit' under the Consumer Credit Act 1974. Indeed, on appeal, the Court of Appeal[145] preferred, somewhat controversially, to focus solely on the latter issue.[146] It appears that a credit agreement is not extortionate if the debtor had been advised of the cost of credit and that the level of interest charged by the lender was justified due to the level of risk undertaken by the lender and that it was comparable with other lending institutions.[147]

While undertaking its review of the provisions of the CCA 1974, the then DTI considered whether or not to impose a ceiling on interest rates covered by The Act.[148] In the 2003 White Paper, the DTI took the view that 'it has been suggested by some consumer groups that one mechanism for controlling the cost of credit is to limit the rate of interest charged. The overwhelming advantage claimed for this mechanism is its simplicity. Several other EU Member States and some of the States in the United States of America have ceilings'.[149] The government decided against introducing a cap on interest rates for several reasons. For example, the introduction of such a cap would lead to many practical difficulties in introducing a capping regime that would apply to a very broad range of credit providers and credit agreements. In particular, the DTI felt that a high APR would not automatically label the consumer credit agreement as extortionate. Furthermore, it considered that creditors would be able to abuse the interest rate cap by simply extending the length of the loan. The DTI felt that unscrupulous lenders would find other ways to increase the cost of credit for consumers such as 'encouraging rates to gravitate towards that ceiling'. Finally, it added that 'a rate ceiling may also result in some lenders withdrawing from the market. This, in turn, may lead to groups of consumers being denied ready access to alternative forms of credit, forcing them to resort to illegal moneylenders'.[150] Lomnicka took the view that:

> the desirability of generally controlling interest rates and, more specifically, of imposing interest rate 'caps' or ceilings was considered but provisionally dismissed on the usual grounds that market forces are the best regulator of interest rates. Previous experience suggests that interest rates gravitate upwards towards any cap and that caps render credit unavailable (from legitimate sources) to certain high-risk borrowers.[151]

145 [2005] EWCA Civ 956, [2005] All ER (D) 351 (Lord Phillips of Worth Matravers MR, Waller and Lloyd LJJ).

146 For a more detailed commentary on this case, see J Devenney and N Ryder, 'The Cartography of the Concept of "Total Charge for Credit" under the Consumer Credit Act 1974' (2006) *The Conveyancer and Property Lawyer* 475.

147 *Davis v Directloans* [1986] 1 WLR 823. The court followed the test advocated by Browne-Wilkinson J in *Multiservices Bookbinding Ltd v Marden* [1979] Ch 84.

148 Department of Trade and Industry, 'A Consultation Document on Making the Extortionate Credit Provisions Within the CCA More Effective' (Department of Trade and Industry, 2003).

149 Department of Trade and Industry (n 23) 66.

150 Department of Trade and Industry (n 23) 63.

151 Lomnicka (n 22) 139.

Despite calls from consumer groups to impose a cap on the interest rate charges, the HM Treasury Select Committee stated that:

> The high interest rates charged by some credit and store cards are excessive, as the banks have conceded, and are a considerable cause for concern. There is an impression that they result in part from a lack of transparency in pricing which obstructs effective competition. Excessive rates would not exist in a genuinely transparent and competitive market. Consumers cannot shop around if they lack the mechanisms to compare products. It is not for Government, or this Committee, to state what rates are acceptable, but *it* is for Government to ensure that competitive forces can work.[152]

In July 2009, the OFT announced a review of high costs lending which 'focused on the high cost area of the sector, where APRs are high, and where consumers may have an urgent need of credit, be more vulnerable and face a smaller number of products to choose from'.[153] The OFT noted that it would concentrate upon four specific areas: understanding consumer behaviour; understanding lender dynamics; considering relevant practices in other countries; and quantifying any consumer detriment found in relation to high cost credit and the development of appropriate remedies where necessary.[154] In response to the publication of this review the 2009 White Paper stated:

> There is considerable political, media and stakeholder concern about the role of high cost credit particularly against a backdrop of rising credit exclusion. People on low incomes or with poor credit records can struggle to obtain access to cheaper credit from high street banks and building societies. Instead, they may use home credit (also known as doorstep lending), unauthorised overdrafts or sub-prime personal loans, all of which are typically more expensive than mainstream credit, reflecting the flexibility of the product, the cost of collecting the debts and the higher risk of default The Government welcomes the OFT's announcement that its review of the consumer credit sector will focus on high cost credit and whether competition in these markets is effective in current conditions.[155]

This review document forms an important wider policy initiative by the OFT, its 'Financial Services Strategy'.[156] The OFT was asked by Alistair Darling MP, the Chancellor of the Exchequer in 2008, to publish a Financial Services Plan.[157] In its

152 HM Treasury Select Committee (n 94) 55.
153 Office of Fair Trading, 'High Cost Consumer Credit – Scope and Reasons for a Review' (Office of Fair Trading, 2009) 3–5.
154 Ibid 1.
155 Department for Business, Innovation and Skills (n 92) 37.
156 Office of Fair Trading, 'Financial Services Strategy – A Consultation Document' (Office of Fair Trading, 2009).
157 HM Treasury, '2008 Pre-Budget Report' (HM Treasury, 2008) 62.

2008 pre-budget report HM Treasury stated that 'the OFT will set out a specific financial services plan, detailing how it will build on its strong track record of tackling abusive behaviour and consumer detriment'.[158] The OFT took the view that it would concentrate more upon its financial services focus, which is based on two issues: first, to promote 'fairness and responsibility in the relationship between the credit industry (including banks and debt businesses) and their customers, to deal with the immediate issues facing consumers'; and secondly, 'to play a strong role as an advocate of choice and competition in the UK and internationally, to ensure that as public decisions are made to deal with the current crisis, they do not harm competition over the long term and thus reduce the future growth of the UK economy'.[159] The extortionate credit bargains test of the CCA 1974 was severely criticised by many commentators. For example, Kempson and Whyley concluded that there 'appear to be three main problems with the existing legislation: very few cases are brought to court because the onus is on the borrower to initiate proceedings; the wording of the Act is too imprecise and judicial decisions have tended to be based on a restrictive interpretation of its provisions; the penalties set down in the Act are inadequate'.[160] The effectiveness of these provisions was restricted because the relevant terms were extremely difficult to define. Kempson and Whyley, quoting a district judge who was interviewed as part of a research study for the Department of Trade and Industry (DTI), stated:

> firstly we don't have the knowledge. Secondly, we aren't well versed in the Consumer Credit Act as it's just a small part of our work . . . We are not equipped to deal with interest rates, we don't have the information at our fingertips. Generally speaking we tend not to take a proactive role, through lack of knowledge. That's the honest answer.[161]

The effectiveness of these provisions were criticised by a number of commentators. For example, Johnson stated that 'the problem of the extortionate credit agreement is one that has, like the poor, been always with us and appears to be no nearer solution today than it has ever been'.[162] Patient took the view that 'the extortionate credit bargain provisions have proved ineffective as a means of consumer protection with only a few cases reaching court and even fewer proving successful'.[163] This point is supported by the DTI, which noted that 'there are

158 Ibid.

159 Office of Fair Trading (n 154) 10.

160 Kempson and Whyley (n 27) 29.

161 Ibid 32.

162 Johnson (n 14) 94. Johnson cited an OFT report which stated 'the extortionate credit bargain provisions of the Act have not effectively dealt with the problems they have addressed. There have been very few cases in the courts indeed and in most of these cases which have reached the courts, a restrictive interpretation of the provisions has been adopted': Office of Fair Trading, 'Unjust Credit Transactions: A Report by the Director General of Fair Trading on the Provisions of ss 137–140 of the Consumer Credit Act 1974' (Office of Fair Trading, 1991) para 1.7

163 J Patient, 'The Consumer Credit Act 2006' (2006) 21(6) *Journal of International Banking Law and Regulation* 309, 311–12.

only about 30 published court judgments that we are aware of where a court has considered the issue, although we are aware that the issue has been raised in proceedings more frequently'.[164] In particular, the DTI identified three major criticisms. First, the provisions were too narrow and they focused on the cost of credit rather than taking a holistic approach towards the terms of the agreement.[165] Secondly, the measure of the term 'extortionate' was too high to effectively prevent creditors adopting practices that were unjust and manipulative.[166] Thirdly, a large number of potential applicants were prevented from seeking redress against the creditor due to such issues as the cost of litigation.[167] Furthermore, the judiciary tended to concentrate upon examining the terms of the credit agreement at the time it was entered into. This meant that the courts did not take into account any later conduct that could make the overall agreement unfair.[168] The NACAB has highlighted numerous examples where consumers have not been adequately protected by these provisions. For example, a client entered into a hire purchase agreement for a car which stated that the APR was 53.6 per cent. The price of the car was £1,400. The client was forced to repay £3,045.[169] Similarly, the NACAB reported that a client who had taken out a loan of £5,800 over a 15-year period, where the APR was 36.3 per cent, was expected to repay £27,550 when all of the repayments had been made.[170] In addition, the extortionate credit provisions of the CCA 1974 had not provided any level of protection for low income consumers.[171] For example, the NACAB reported that a single parent entered into a credit agreement for £800, which was to be repaid at a rate of £18 per week over an 80-week period. The interest charge was £640, resulting in an APR of 132.5 per cent.[172] Furthermore, people entered into agreements where the APR was 1,355 and 1,834 per cent.[173] Therefore, it is somewhat unsurprising that the NACAB concluded that 'there is no doubt that extortionate credit is a persistent and undesirable feature of the UK consumer credit sector and significant consumer detriment will continue unless effective measures are put in place to solve the problem'.[174]

164 Department of Trade and Industry, 'Full Regulatory Impact Assessment – Consumer Credit Bill' (Department of Trade and Industry, 2004) 29.

165 Ibid 3.

166 Department of Trade and Industry (n 164) 29.

167 Ibid 30.

168 See, for example, the decisions in *Paragon Finance plc v Nash and Staunton* [2001] EWCA Civ 1466, [2002] 1 WLR 685 and *Broadwick Financial and Services Ltd v Spencer and another* [2002] EWCA Civ 35, [2002] 1 All ER 446.

169 National Association of Citizens' Advice Bureaux (n 51) 11.

170 Ibid.

171 The most commonly used threshold of low income is a household income that is 60% or less of the average UK household income. For a more detailed commentary of low income in the United Kingdom, see T MacInnes, P Kenway and A Parekh, *Monitoring Poverty and Social Exclusion* (Joseph Rowntree Foundation, 2009).

172 National Association of Citizens' Advice Bureaux (n 51) 11.

173 Ibid 13.

174 Ibid 21.

It is important to note that the CCA 2006 repealed CCA 1974, sections 137 to 140, and replaced the 'extortionate credit' bargain test with a new test, the 'unfair relationship' test, under CCA 1974, sections 140A to 140C. The new test covers the main credit agreement and also any related agreements. Section 140C(4) states what can be regarded as a related agreement to the main credit agreement. In principle, the new 'unfair relationship' test should be able to protect consumers against an extortionate interest rate. Section 140A(1)(a) provides the court with the power to intervene if 'any terms of the agreement or any related agreement' are unfair to the debtor, and this should include the terms related to interest rates charged by creditors. Unfortunately, the application of this new test by the court in a number of cases concerning high cost short term credit agreements showed that this test does not offer better protection to low income consumers than that of the extortionate credit bargain test. The court has not regarded the vulnerability of some of those borrowers as an important factor to be considered in deciding the fairness of the agreement once it was established that the charged price was, at the time, the market price.[175]

## Irresponsible lending

Creditors and financial institutions must accept some of the blame for the increase in consumer debt due to their lending practices. This has been referred to as irresponsible or predatory lending.[176] It has also been called 'socially harmful lending', which can include such practices as targeting low-income households, targeting people who are facing financial problems and soliciting credit on the doorstep.[177] The OFT stated that irresponsible lending is a business practice that it would consider deceitful, oppressive, unfair and improper for the purposes of revoking a consumer credit licence. It has been suggested that the deregulation of consumer credit laws in the 1970s and 1980s has contributed towards an increase in irresponsible lending practices by creditors.[178] Creditors have been accused of irresponsible lending practices and have been subject to much criticism; in response Inderst stated that 'in the UK various reports and taskforces on consumer lending practices have brought up the issue of irresponsible lending'.[179]

175 See AK Aldohni, 'Loan Sharks v. Short-Term Lenders: How do the Law and Regulators Draw the Line?' (2013) 40(3) *Journal of Law and Society* 436, for a detailed discussion on the 'unfair relationship' test and its application to these cases: *Khodari v Al Tamimi* [2009] EWCA Civ 1109 (Official Transcript); *Barons Finance Ltd v Lara Basirat Abeni Olubisi* [2011] EWCA Civ 1461; *Robert Shaw v Nine Regions Limited* [2009] EWHC 3514 (QB); *Nine Regions (t/a Logbook Loans) v Sadeer* (14 November 2008) Bromley County Court, Case No 8QT25415 (All England Official Transcript).

176 For a more detailed discussion of predatory lending in the US, see A Pennington-Cross and G Ho, 'Predatory Lending Laws and the Cost Of Credit' (2008) 36(2) *Real Estate Economics* 175 and M Spector, 'Taming the Beast: Payday Loans, Regulatory Efforts, and Unintended Consequences' (2008) 57(4) *Depaul Law Review* 961.

177 Kempson and Whyley (n 27) 8.

178 Ibid.

179 R Inderst, 'Irresponsible Lending with a Better Informed Lender' (2008) 118(532) *The Economic Journal* 1499, 1499–500.

What practices constitute irresponsible lending? Examples include increasing the credit card and overdraft limits without the customer's consent; not requesting proof of income when determining the level of credit to be offered; and providing loans and credit cards to the unemployed and people who are dependent on state benefits. Other examples of irresponsible lending practices are the speed and simplicity of credit applications; the prominence given to very high credit limits; the importance given to very low interest rates for cards; incentives to use a particular brand of credit card; unwanted mail shots for credit card cheques; important information in small print; and the indiscriminate targeting of direct mail shots.[180] In relation to such activities the HM Treasury Select Committee took the view that 'issuers should never raise credit limits without carrying out appropriate internal and external credit checks. Lenders also need to recognise that in many cases, for over indebted consumers, increases in credit limits are wholly inappropriate'.[181] Therefore, it is imperative that the UK has in place an appropriate and effective regulatory system for irresponsible lending.

As a result of these concerns a self-regulation system has been proposed by the banks which includes a voluntary Responsible Lending Index that seeks to encourage best practice in credit lending.[182] Furthermore, Part 13 of the Banking Code provided that 'before we [the bank] lend you any money or increase your overdraft, we will assess whether we feel you will be able to repay it'.[183] It is interesting to note that this part of the Banking Code did not apply to high cost short term credit or even sub-prime commercial cash loans. In fact, the Banking Code was voluntary and not legally binding. However, the extent to which the voluntary measures and codes of practice have contributed towards a reduction in the use of irresponsible lending is extremely debatable and their overall effectiveness can be questioned. Subsequently, a second consultation paper was published outlining the position regarding the irresponsible lending test under the CCA 2006.[184] In July 2009, the OFT published its draft guidance on irresponsible lending with the aim of:

> Producing clear guidance on the test for irresponsible lending for the purposes of s25(2B) of the Consumer Credit Act 1974. The subsequent guidance will outline the types of deceitful or oppressive or otherwise unfair or improper business practices which, if employed by a consumer credit business, would call into consideration its fitness to hold a consumer credit licence.[185]

180 HM Treasury Select Committee (n 94) 43.

181 Ibid 38.

182 See generally Ironfield-Smith et al (n 8) 141.

183 For a brief comment, see P Cartwright, 'Retail Depositors, Conduct of Business and Sanctioning' (2009) 17(3) *Journal of Financial Regulation and Compliance* 302.

184 Office of Fair Trading, 'Irresponsible Lending – OFT Guidance for Creditors' (Office of Fair Trading, 2011).

185 Ibid.

The draft guidance provided that creditors should employ the use of appropriate business practices and procedure; there should be transparency in dealings between creditors and borrowers; there should be proportionality in dealings between creditors and borrowers; and creditors should not treat borrowers unfairly. Section 25(B) provides that irresponsible lending is a business practice that the OFT would consider deceitful, oppressive, unfair and improper for the purposes of revoking a consumer credit licence. It is also important to note that the 2010 Consumer Credit Directive amended the Act so that creditors are now required to undertake a creditworthiness check on the debtor.[186] However, this was subsequently repealed in 2013 by the Financial Services and Markets Act 2000 (Regulated Activities) Order (Amendment (No 2) Order 2013.[187] Writing in 2006, Patient took the view that 'some of the most significant changes to be introduced by the [Consumer Credit] Act [2006] relate to the powers of the OFT'.[188] She stated that the OFT should 'be able to impose a financial penalty on anyone who fails to comply with a requirement imposed on them. The fines may be up to £50,000'.[189] Additionally, the OFT has the ability to suspend, vary and revoke a licence, it can refuse applications, impose requirements on existing and new licences and grant licences on different terms. The ability to impose requirements on a licence is a new enforcement power for the OFT.[190] Under section 33A the OFT is permitted to impose requirements on a licence where it is dissatisfied with 'any matter in connection with a business being carried on, or which has been carried on, by a licensee or by an associate or a former associate of a licensee', or 'a proposal to carry on a business which has been made by a licensee or by an associate or a former associate of a licensee'[191] and 'any conduct not covered by paragraph (a) or (b) of a licensee or of an associate or a former associate of a licensee'.[192] The requirement could compel or stop the licensee from doing something which the OFT is displeased about.[193] In addition, the OFT has the ability to impose a financial sanction of up to £50,000 if the requirements imposed are not fully complied with.[194] There are four principles that the OFT will consider before imposing a fine: proportionality; changing behaviour; no financial benefit obtained from non-compliance and consistency; or limited financial benefit obtained from non-compliance and consistency.[195] The OFT published a statement on its policy towards the imposition of civil penalties for

186 Directive 2008/48/EC of the European Parliament and of the Council on credit agreements for consumers (OJ L133/66), implemented by the Consumer Credit (EU Directive) Regulations 2010 (SI 2010/1010).

187 SI 2013/1881.

188 Patient (n 163) 314.

189 Ibid.

190 CCA 1974, s 33A.

191 Ibid, s 33A(1)(b).

192 Ibid, s 33A(1)(c).

193 Ibid, s 33A(2)(a) and (b).

194 CCA 2006, s 39A(3).

195 Office of Fair Trading, 'Consumer Credit Licensing Statement of Policy on Civil Penalties' (Office of Fair Trading, 2008) 1.

breaches of the credit licensing regime under the CCA 2006.[196] The OFT is permitted to impose a financial penalty when a licensee fails to observe a requirement that has been imposed on a standard licence or as a reasonable person in relation to a group licence.[197] In determining whether or not to impose a financial penalty the OFT will consider a non-definitive list of factors. This includes, for example, whether or not the non-compliance is simply a one-off breach or a series of habitual breaches. Has the licensee taken the necessary measures to ensure that the non-compliance has stopped and has the licensee complied with the OFT? Was the firm's senior management aware of the non-compliance? Furthermore, prior to imposing a fine the OFT is required to inform the recipient of the financial penalty that is to be imposed.[198] Macleod took the view that 'the OFT may give a person notice that he is minded to impose such a penalty, what may be termed a "yellow card", so that the alleged defaulter may make representations to try to dissuade it'.[199] In addition, the notice must: state the anticipated amount of the penalty;[200] justify the reasons for imposing a penalty;[201] state the proposed period for the payment of the penalty;[202] and invite the defaulter to make representations in accordance with section 34 of the 1974 Act.[203] Additionally, the OFT can inflict a financial sanction if a licensee fails to provide it with information as specified.[204] This is also referred to as a 'penalty notice' or 'red card', which outlines the reasons for the imposition of a financial penalty and the methods and time period within which the payments must be made.[205]

In light of these ineffective measures the FSA implemented a number of measures aimed at tackling irresponsible lending. For example, it introduced a mortgage affordability test for lenders which: provides that lenders are responsible for assessing and determining the ability of consumers to meet their monthly repayments; bans so-called 'toxic combination' loans (which are worth more than 90 per cent of the value of a house for people with poor credit histories); bans charges for borrowers who are behind on payments but who are at least able maintain an arrangement to repay these debts; and broadens the scope of FSA regulation to all mortgage advisers and arrangers.[206] Perhaps more importantly, the financial regulator has an extensive array of enforcement powers under the Financial Services and Markets Act 2000 (FSMA 2000). The most commonly used enforcement power in relation to irresponsible lending has been

196 Ibid.
197 CCA 1974, ss 33A and 33B.
198 Ibid, s 39A(1).
199 J Macleod, *Consumer Sales Law* (Routledge, 2007) 253.
200 CCA 1974, s 39A(2)(a).
201 Ibid, s 39A(2)(b).
202 Ibid, s 39A(2)(c).
203 Ibid, s 39A(2)(d).
204 Ibid, s 36A.
205 Ibid, s 39C(6).
206 See, generally, Financial Services Authority, 'Mortgage Market Review: Responsible Lending' (Financial Services Authority, 2010).

its ability to impose unlimited financial penalties.[207] In November 2010, the FSA imposed its first financial penalty for irresponsible lending. Bridging Loans Ltd, a mortgage lender, was fined £42,000, and its director Joseph Cummings was fined £70,000 for 'serious failures relating to lending practices and for failing to treat customers fairly in arrears'.[208] The FSA imposed a financial penalty because it considered the actions of the company and its directors to be extremely severe due to consistent failings and conduct over a five-year period. Furthermore, both Bridging Loans Ltd and Joseph Cummings treated their customers unfairly and did not attempt to investigate these allegations. As a result of the conduct of the company and Mr Cummings, several customers, who were already suffering from financial hardship, were in danger of entering into inappropriate regulated mortgage contracts. It is arguable that if the firm's customers had entered into these contracts, they would have suffered even greater financial difficulties. In particular, the FSA noted that the conduct of Bridging Loans Ltd and its directors was 'serious because your failings impacted on customers who were financing or re-financing their homes; the most significant transaction that many customers make'.[209] Additionally, the FSA banned Mr Cummings and took other action against several other directors of the company. The importance of this groundbreaking financial penalty by the FSA cannot be underestimated. It is the first reported instance of a firm being fined by a regulatory body for irresponsible lending practices.[210] The FSA must be commended for tackling the problems associated with irresponsible lending, an issue that has received little regulatory attention. However, it is important to note that financial penalties have not been imposed in instances of high cost short term credit. It will be interesting to see whether the FCA will use these powers now that it regulates the consumer credit market.

The OFT's Irresponsible Lending Guidance has heavily influenced the provisions of the Consumer Credit Source Book.[211] The creditworthiness test provides that 'before making a regulated credit agreement the firm must undertake an assessment of the creditworthiness of the customer'.[212] The Consumer Credit Handbook from the Financial Conduct Authority, CONC, also provides any firm undertaking an assessment of the creditworthiness of a customer must consider 'the potential for the commitments under the regulated credit agreement to adversely impact the customer's financial situation . . . [and] the ability of the customer to make repayments as they fall due over the life of the regulated credit

207 Financial Services and Markets Act 2000, s 206(1).

208 Financial Services Authority, 'Final Notice: Bridging Loans Ltd', 20 October 2010 <http://www.fsa.gov.uk/pubs/final/bridging_loans.pdf> accessed 26 October 2015.

209 Ibid.

210 Financial Services Authority, 'FSA Fines Mortgage Lender and its Director for Irresponsible Lending and Unfair Treatments of Customers in Arrears', 4 November 2010 <http://www.fsa.gov.uk/pages/Library/Communication/PR/2010/159.shtml> accessed 26 October 2015.

211 See Financial Conduct Authority, *Consumer Credit Sourcebook, Chapter 5 Responsible Lending* (Financial Conduct Authority, 2015) (hereinafter 'Consumer Credit Sourcebook').

212 Ibid 5.2.1R(1).

agreement'.[213] Additionally, and even as importantly as the introduction of the creditworthiness test, the CONC also introduces the notion of sustainability. Therefore, lenders are required to take into consideration the ability of the customer to make the repayments without 'undue difficulty'.[214] In determining the creditworthiness of the customer, firms are required to consider the customer's 'record of previous dealings; evidence of income; evidence of expenditure; a credit score; a credit reference agency report; and information provided by the customer'.[215]

## A new regulator

The regulation of the consumer credit market was ineffectively pursued by the OFT, which was hampered by a weak credit licensing scheme and enforcement powers. The transfer of the regulation of the consumer credit market from the OFT to the FCA took place on 1 April 2014, since when there has been a period of transition that includes amending the Consumer Credit Act 1974 and the incorporation of the relevant FCA rules.[216] The decision to transfer regulation was preceded by an extensive period of consultation where the FSA and HM Treasury published important documents that outline the aims and objectives of the new regime. The FSA consultation paper contained proposals on: providing an interim permission for OFT licence holders to continue to carry on regulated consumer credit activities; its authorisation process; the supervision of credit advertising being subject to the FSMA 2000 financial promotions regime; prudential requirements for debt management firms; a number of the CCA provisions being kept as part of the new FCA credit regime; the supervision of and reporting by firms; and how the regime would be funded.[217] The HM Treasury Consultation Paper was published in March 2013 and outlined the plans to introduce a 'high-level regulatory model and approach for regulation of the consumer credit market under the FCA, and also describes the secondary legislation the government proposes to make to underpin the transfer'.[218] The aim of the proposals was to ensure that a highly competitive and economically important consumer credit market should be supported and reinforced by a strong regulatory regime. In particular, HM Treasury hoped that the regime would be able to achieve four objectives. First, the regulatory regime should be able to maintain

213 Ibid 5.2.1 R.

214 Ibid 5.3.1G(6).

215 Ibid 5.2.4(G).

216 For a more detailed discussion of this, see J Patient, E Greaves, P Finch, R Savary, C Loughrey and S Timbrell, 'Consumer Credit' (2015) 127 *Compliance Bulletin* 1 (hereinafter 'Patient et al').

217 Financial Services Authority, 'CP13/7 Consumer Credit Regulation – Our Proposed Regime' (Financial Services Authority, 2013).

218 HM Treasury, 'Consultation Outcome: A new approach to financial regulation: transferring consumer credit regulation to the Financial Conduct Authority' (16 January 2014) <https://www.gov.uk/government/consultations/a-new-approach-to-financial-regulation-transferring-consumer-credit-regulation-to-the-financial-conduct-authority> accessed 23 October 2015.

pace with an inventive and rapidly expanding market. Second, that it provides the FCA with the power and financial means to protect the users of the credit market. Third, that it imposes proportionate and practical burdens on businesses. Fourth, that it produces a healthy working consumer market that continues to support the UK economy.[219] As a result of this consultation process, the consumer credit market is now regulated by the FCA. Patient et al stated that:

> In order to preserve certain consumer protections contained within the CCA, a hybrid statutory structure has been adopted. This was necessitated by a government commitment to ensure that the transfer of the regime did not lead to a reduction in consumer protection. Broadly speaking the authorisation and supervision regimes have been fully integrated into the FSMA with relevant sections of the Handbook applying to all regulated firms. The conduct of business regime is split with large sections of the CCA and various underlying statutory instruments retained, but supplemented by the Consumer Credit Sourcebook which is part of the FCA's Handbook.[220]

Therefore, any new participants to this market will be required to comply with the FCA's authorisation regime[221] and be approved by the regulator.[222] Importantly, authorised firms will be subjected to the wrath of the FCA's extensive array of enforcement powers under the FSMA 2000. For example, one of the most frequently used powers by the FCA has been its ability to impose unlimited financial penalties. Such penalties have already been imposed on firms that have breached the FCA's Principles for Business and for not acting in the best interest of customers. The ability of the FCA to fine the regulated sector has been clearly illustrated by the manipulation of both the LIBOR and FOREX sectors by banks. This compares favourably with the weak powers of the OFT to impose financial sanctions (limited to a maximum of £50,000) on licensed creditors who breach the related provisions of the CCA 1974. Additionally, the FCA is able to impose prohibition orders where 'it appears to it that an individual is not a fit and proper person to perform functions in relation to a regulated activity'.[223] In 2008/2009, the FSA imposed prohibition orders on 58 individuals.[224] The number of prohibition orders slightly decreased in 2009/2010 to 56,[225] but increased to 71 in

219 HM Treasury, 'A New Approach to Financial Regulation: Transferring Consumer Credit Regulation to the Financial Conduct Authority' (HM Treasury, 2013) 5.

220 Patient et al (n 216).

221 See Financial Conduct Authority, 'Authorisation: Consumer Credit' (22 September 2015) <https://www.the-fca.org.uk/authorisation-consumer-credit> accessed 23 October 2015.

222 Ibid. For a brief discussion, see E Lomnicka, 'The Future of Consumer Credit Regulation: A Chance to Rationalise Sanctions for Breaches of Financial Services Regulatory Regimes?' (2013) 34(1) *Company Lawyer* 13.

223 FSMS 2000, s 56(1).

224 Financial Services Authority, 'Enforcement annual performance account 2008/2009' (Financial Services Authority, 2009) 7.

225 Financial Services Authority, 'Enforcement annual performance account 2009/2010' (Financial Services Authority, 2010) 4.

2010/2011.[226] However, the numbers dropped to 47 in 2011,[227] 45 in 2012[228] and 26 in 2013.[229] Additionally, the FCA is able to pursue reparation for consumers who have suffered maltreatment by a licensed creditor.[230] The highest profile action that has been undertaken by the FCA related to Wonga being ordered to recompense consumers £2.6 million.[231] In October 2015, Dollar Financial UK entered into an agreement with the FCA and agreed to provide £15.4 million to redress 147,000 customers who had been subjected to unfair practices.[232] The FCA conducted a review of Dollar Financial UK's lending decisions in July 2014 with the aim of determining whether the firm's customers had been treated fairly. The review concluded that 'many customers were lent more than they could afford to repay' and the FCA stated that it 'expects all credit providers to carry out proper checks to ensure that borrowers don't take on more than they can afford to pay back'.[233] This is not the first time Dollar Financial UK has been sanctioned by the FCA. For example, in July 2014, the firm agreed to refund approximately £700,000 to its customers who had received loans that had exceeded the firm's own lending criteria.[234] Additionally, one of the most important amendments to the regulation of the consumer credit sector has been the imposition of the credit cost cap as a preventative measure by the FCA. However, it is interesting to note that in 2013 the FCA indicated that the imposition of an interest rate cap could not be beneficial for all consumers as some could be 'worse off by caps on APR'.[235] The imposition and effectiveness of the interest rate cap has also been questioned by some commentators, including Collins who noted

226 Financial Services Authority, 'Enforcement annual performance account 2010/2011' (Financial Services Authority, 2011) 8.

227 Financial Services Authority, 'Enforcement annual performance account 2011/2012' (Financial Services Authority, 2012) 8.

228 Financial Services Authority, 'Enforcement annual performance account 2012/2013' (Financial Services Authority, 2013) 5.

229 Financial Conduct Authority, 'Enforcement annual performance account 2013/2014' (Financial Conduct Authority, 2014) 3.

230 FSMA 2000, s 404. See Financial Services Authority, 'Kensington Mortgage Company – Final Notice' <http://www.fsa.gov.uk/pubs/final/kensington.pdf> accessed 23 October 2015. For a more detailed discussion of this instance, see T Smith, 'Regulatory Investigations Group FSA Enforcement Action: Themes and Trends' (2010) 76 *Compliance Officer Bulletin* 1, 20–21.

231 Financial Conduct Authority, 'Wonga to Pay Redress for Unfair Debt Collection Practices' (15 June 2014) <http://www.fca.org.uk/news/wonga-redress-unfair-debt-collection-practices> accessed 26 October 2015.

232 Financial Conduct Authority, 'Payday Lender Dollar to Provide £15.4 Million Redress to over 147,000 Customers' (26 October 2015) <http://www.fca.org.uk/news/payday-lender-dollar-to-provide-154-million-redress> accessed 26 October 2015.

233 Ibid.

234 Ibid.

235 S Dale, 'FCA Says It May Stay Its Hand on Payday Rate Caps' <http://www.mortgagestrategy.co.uk/news-and-features/latest-news/fca-says-it-may-stay-its-hand-on-payday-rate-caps/1069405.article> accessed 25 March 2016. See Financial Conduct Authority, 'Proposals for a Price Cap on High-Cost Short-Term Credit' (Consultation Paper 14/10, June 2014) para 5.15. The consultation paper suggests that around 11% of current payday loans consumers would no longer be able to access these loans.

that this measure would not limit the debtor's use of payday lenders who would continue to make significant profits.[236]

## Conclusion

This chapter began by identifying the problems that have been caused by access to convenient credit and it has argued that these have been exacerbated by the irresponsible lending practices of creditors and the inappropriate level of protection provided by the CCA 1974.

The lack of access to affordable credit for individuals can lead to higher credit charges, limited access to financial products and services and lack of security, and it can prevent employment.

It is also important to note that the government's policy towards the provision of credit in the UK has reverted to that prior to the recommendations of the Crowther Committee on Consumer Credit and the introduction of the CCA 1974. After three decades of what can be best described as a 'laissez faire' approach towards the regulation of the consumer credit market, the government has decided, no doubt influenced by the impact of the 2008 financial crisis and increasing levels of consumer debt, to improve the regulation of the consumer credit market. The extension of the remit of the FCA to include the regulation of the consumer credit market must be welcomed. Not only will creditors be subject to a higher standard of regulation than that provided by the OFT, but the FCA will be able to utilise its more extensive enforcement powers to protect vulnerable consumers who use short term credit.

236 D Collins, 'Payday Loans: Why One Shouldn't Ask For More' (2013) 28(2) *Journal of International Banking Law and Regulation* 55, 56.

# 5 Contingent convertible capital: a perfect tool for more resilient banks

*Gabriel Adeoluwa Onagoruwa*

## Introduction

In the aftermath of the global financial crisis of 2007 to 2009 (the 'GFC'), the need to reform the extant framework for the regulatory capital held by banks became a prioritised policy objective for bank regulators as the ineffectiveness of the extant framework as a buffer for banking risks became evident. The failings of the extant framework necessitated various forms of emergency intervention actions by governments and applicable regulatory agencies in various jurisdictions.

Although the failings of the extant capital regulatory framework brought about a consensus in the policy arena on the need for reforms, there were divergent views on the nature of the reforms that were to be adopted. Leading the initiatives as it did when it adopted the 1988 Capital Accord, which recommended methodologies for calculating capital requirements to be held by banks for loss absorbency,[1] the Basel Committee for Banking Supervision (the 'Basel Committee'), adopted Basel III: Global Regulatory Framework for More Resilient Banks and Banking Systems ('Basel III')[2] as a build-up on the quality and quantity of capital requirements in previous accords.

In the European Union, the recommendations in Basel III have been implemented through the Capital Requirements Regulation (Regulation 575/2013) ('CRR'),[3] which is directly applicable in the UK, and the CRD IV Directive (Directive 2013/36/EU).[4] The phased implementation of Basel III effectively

1 Prior to the 1988 Accord, banks in each of the jurisdictions represented on the Basel Committee had different regulatory capital requirements and the definition of what constituted capital varied significantly. S Gleeson, *International Regulation of Banking – Basel II: Capital and Risk Requirements* (Oxford University Press, 2010) 34.

2 Basel Committee on Banking Supervision (BCBS), 'Global Systemically Important Banks: Assessment Methodology and the Loss Absorbency Requirement' (Bank for International Settlement, 2011); Basel Committee, 'Basel III: Global Regulatory Framework for More Resilient Banks and Banking Systems' (Bank for International Settlement, 2011).

3 Regulation (EU) No 575/2013 of the European Parliament and of the Council of 26 June 2013 on prudential requirements for credit institutions and investment firms and amending Regulation (EU) No 648/2012 Text with EEA relevance (OJ 2013 L176/1).

4 Directive 2013/36/EU of the European Parliament and of the Council of 26 June 2013 on access to the activity of credit institutions and the prudential supervision of credit institutions and

doubles the equity capital requirements for banks and tripled the minimum equity requirements for globally significant financial institutions[5] but a number of commentators and academics have expressed concerns regarding the inadequacy of the Basel III capital requirements.[6]

In order to meet up with the requirements of Basel III and reinforce resilience, a number of banks have issued convertible debt instruments that also double as loss absorbents. Regulators are also mulling over the development of an effective framework to enable the loss absorbent convertible debt instruments, described variously as contingent capital certificates,[7] reverse convertible debt,[8] enhanced capital notes, mandatory capital notes[9] and convertible contingent capital,[10] to function as supervisory tools.

Considering that the main aim of this edited collection is to highlight the implicit effects of the GFC, this chapter identifies the use of contingent convertible capital ('Coco') by banks, as a means of complying with the new banking capital regulatory requirements, as one of the new trends that emerged in the wake of the GFC. First, the chapter addresses the nature and function of regulatory bank capital. Then it examines the nature of Cocos as ideal complements for equity by considering the arguments in favour of and against the adoption of Cocos as part of the framework for regulatory capital requirements.

## The importance and nature of capital

The Basel Committee, in its Core Principles for Effective Bank Supervision, which is generally regarded as the *locus classicus* on bank regulation, stipulates that 'supervisors must set prudent and appropriate minimum capital adequacy requirements for banks that reflect the risks that the banks undertake, and they must also define the components of capital, bearing in mind the ability to absorb losses.[11]

Capital requirements are intended to serve as the first line of defence against

investment firms, amending Directive 2002/87/EC and repealing Directives 2006/48/EC and 2006/49/EC (OJ 2013 L176/388).

5 BCBS, 'Basel III: A Global Regulatory Framework for More Resilient Banks and Banking Systems' (Bank for International Settlement, 2011).

6 For this, see Institute of International Finance, 'Interim Report on the Cumulative Impact on the Global Economy of the Proposed Changes in Banking Regulatory framework' (June 2010) <http://www.ebf-fbe.eu/uploads/10-Interim%20NCI_June2010_Web.pdf> accessed 6 October 2015.

7 MJ Flannery, 'Stabilising Large Financial Institutions with Contingent Capital Certificates' (6 October 2009) 3 <http://ssrn.com/abstract=1485689> accessed 6 October 2015.

8 N Doherty and S Harrington, 'Investment Incentives, Bankruptcies and Reverse Convertible Debt' (Wharton School Working Paper, March 2005).

9 O Fernandez, 'Contingent Convertible Instruments and the Brave New World of Regulatory Capital', *Practical Law Company*, 6 April 2010.

10 RJ Herring and CW Calomiris, 'Why and How to Design a Contingent Convertible Debt Instrument' (11 April 2011) 6 <http://papers.ssrn.com/sol3/papers.cfm?abstract_id=1815406> accessed 6 October 2015.

11 BCBS, Core Principles for Effective Banking Supervision (1997) principle 6.

the loss of depositors' funds and the possibility of a contagion resulting from risk exposures by ensuring that banks remain sound and able to perform pivotal intermediation and lending functions. Banks are generally exposed to a number of risks which may be classified differently by commentators and analysts. These include the risk of the failure of its borrowers to repay the loans extended, which is generally known as credit risk; the fluctuation of asset prices particularly in the form of a decline in prices, which presents what is known as market risk (examples of this include interest rate risk and foreign exchange risk); and operational risks, which arise as result of 'inadequate or failed internal processes, people and systems or from external events'.[12] Other forms of risks include liquidity risk, which arises from the inability to purchase or otherwise obtain the necessary funds, either by increasing liabilities or converting assets to meet obligations as they become due without incurring unacceptable losses; and legal risk, which could arise from non-compliance with laws, rules and regulations. Regulators therefore seek to safeguard financial stability by ensuring that banks hold sufficient level of capital as cushioning against unforeseen losses from exposure to risks and engender confidence among market participants.[13] Although some academics contend that there is no validated proof of the effect of capital regulation on risks, most regulators and academics seem to agree with the proposition that 'well-conceived capital requirements will generally discourage undue risk taking'.[14]

The most fundamental issue in capital regulation has been and remains the question of the level and nature of capital that a bank should hold in order to effectively weather the storms of banking risks and prevent losses to depositors and the taxpayer. While the regulation of capital as a matter of regulatory concern is traceable to countries like the United States, France, Switzerland and the UK, the mode, pattern and approach to capital regulation varied significantly between these countries, and the deteriorating capital levels of some international banks was the key event that earned the issue of capital adequacy its prominent significance in the global regulatory space.[15] It prompted the introduction of the 1998 Capital Accord (the 'Accord') by the Basel Committee for Banking Supervision (the 'Basel Committee') with the methodologies for the calculation of capital requirements for loss absorbency in order to strengthen the stability of the international banking system and create a level playing field to combat competitive inequality that could result from differences in national capital regulatory

12 BCBS, Implementation of Basel II: Practical Considerations (2004).

13 Gleeson (n 1) 22.

14 In D Kim and AM Santomero, 'Risk in Banking and Capital Regulation' (1988) 43 *Journal of Finance* 1219, the authors devise models which suggest that capital regulation could in some circumstances increase risk taking rather than reduce it. See also E Scott, *Capital Adequacy Beyond Basel* (Oxford University Press, 2005). For authorities on the positive effect of capital regulation, see J Santos, 'Bank Capital Regulation in Contemporary Banking Theory: A Review of Literature' (2001) 10 *Financial Markets, Institutions and Instruments* 2, 41–84.

15 See DK Tarullo, *Banking on Basel: The Future of International Financial Regulation* (Peterson Institute, 2008) 29–44.

requirements.[16] The next section of this chapter examines this Accord and subsequent initiatives that have been developed by the Basel Committee to set the minimum capital requirements for internationally active banks.

## The Basel Accord of 1988 (Basel I)

Basel I was essentially focused on the calculation of capital requirements to safeguard against credit risk. The accord was characterised by three essential features: the allocation of assets among risk categories; conversion factors on how off-balance sheet items like lines of credit, letter of credit, underwriting facilities and contingent obligation were to be assessed for risk-weighting purposes; and the prescription of a two-tiered definition for capital.

Under the Basel I framework, the assets of a bank were to be grouped into five different credit risk categories with corresponding risks weights of 0 per cent, 10 per cent, 20 per cent, 50 per cent and a 100 per cent on the basis of the generic attribute of the borrower/counter party to reflect the varying risk characteristics of the asset.[17] The Accord dealt with off-balance sheet items by converting them to their credit risk equivalent. This is done by multiplying the notional principal amount of the off-balance sheet asset by a credit conversion factor.[18] The part of the Basel I dealing with the definition of capital was the most contested part during its negotiations and this led to the emergence of the dual approach to the definition of capital in the form of Tier 1 and Tier 2 capital. The Tier 1 capital, which is also known as the core capital, was defined to consist of disclosed reserves from post-tax retained earnings and other capital paid for by the sale of bank equity such as ordinary shares, common stock and non-cumulative per-

16 Prior to the 1988 Accord, banks in each of the jurisdiction represented on the BCBS had different regulatory capital requirements and the definition of what constituted capital varied significantly; Gleeson (n 1) 34.

17 The first class of assets, like cash, claims on central governments and central banks denominated in national currency and funded in the relevant national currency, claims on OECD countries, central governments and central banks and claims collateralised by cash of OECD central government securities or guaranteed by OECD central governments, are assigned a zero capital risk weight, which effectively means that these assets are completely riskless; the second class of assets, which includes claims on domestic public sector entities, the debt guaranteed by such entities and claims collaterised by securities of public sector entities other than the central government, could be allotted risk weight varying from 0 to 100% subject to national regulatory discretion. The third class consists of loans that are fully secured by mortgage on residential property that is or will be occupied by the borrower or that is rented, which is allotted the 50% credit risk weight; and the final class of assets, which consists of claims on the private sector, claims on banks incorporated outside the OECD with residual maturity of over one year, claims on central governments outside the OECD (unless denominated and funded in national currency), claims on commercial companies owned by the public sector, premises, plants and equipments, real estate and other investments, capital instruments issued by other banks and all other assets, were allotted the credit risk weight of 100%.

18 For example, standby letters of credit serving as financial guarantees for loans carry a 100% credit risk conversion, while revolving underwriting facilities require 50%.

petual preferred stock.[19] Tier 2 capital consists of elements such as undisclosed reserves, revaluation reserves, general loan-loss reserves, subordinated term debt with a minimum maturity term of five years, and hybrid debt/equity instruments such as perpetual cumulative preference shares, perpetual debt instruments and other mandatorily convertible debt instruments.[20]

There was no specific ratio regarding the volume of equity capital to disclosed reserve from retained earnings under the Tier 1 capital but there was no limit to the total amount of Tier 1 capital a bank could hold under Basel I. The Accord, however, required internationally active banks to hold at least equal amounts of Tier 1 and Tier 2 capital and, as a minimum requirement, the Tier 1 capital of the bank should be at least 4 per cent of the bank's risk weighted capital, while the total capital in relation to its risk weighted assets should be a minimum of 8 per cent.[21]

The Basel 1 Accord was generally successful in terms of implementation. All the states represented on the Basel Committee (except Japan, which was then faced with the banking crisis of the late 1980s) were in compliance with its recommendations by 1992. By 1999, virtually all countries in the world claimed to be in compliance with its recommendations.[22] The Accord was criticised, however, on the grounds of perceived omissions in terms of its concentration of credit risks at the expense of other forms of risks, crude calibration of risks that made it insufficiently risk sensitive and arbitrage opportunities resulting from imprecision in the rules that led to a divergence in the implementation of the recommendations in various jurisdictions. It also failed to include risk mitigating efforts with only a minimal relief for collateral.[23]

## Basel II

As an offshoot of the criticisms of Basel I and the banking crisis of the 1990s, the Basel Committee came up with the report titled *A Revised Framework on International Convergence of Capital Measurement and Capital Standards*, which was informally known as Basel II.[24] In aiming to correct the faults of Basel I, it

19 Tier 1 capital, however, excluded cumulative preferred stock. See BCBS, 'International Convergence of Capital Measurement and Capital Standards' (Bank for International Settlements, 1988) 3.

20 Ibid 5–6. The Accord further stipulates that although the instruments that would qualify as hybrid instruments under this category may carry an obligation to pay interest that cannot be reduced or waived, they must be unsecured, subordinated, and fully paid-up; not redeemable at the initiative of the holder or without the prior consent of the supervisory authority; available to participate in losses without the bank being obliged to cease trading; and permit the service of obligations to be deferred where the profitability of the bank would not support them. See BCBS (n 19) 15.

21 BCBS (n 19) 13.

22 BCBS, 'Report on International Development in Banking Supervision' (Bank for International Settlements, 1992).

23 Tarullo (n 15) 77–83; R Cranston, *Principles of Banking Law* (2nd edn, Oxford University Press, 2002) 90–91.

24 BCBS, 'International Convergence of Capital Measurement and Capital Standards: A Revised Framework' (Bank for International Settlements, 2004).

adopted a more risk-sensitive approach that sought to capture a more extensive range of risks to which banks are exposed. It incorporated earlier amendments that had been made to the framework to reflect capital requirements for market risks and introduced the novel idea of capital requirements for operational risks.[25] It introduced special rules on areas that were not covered under the previous Accord, like securitisation and allowance for adjustments to take account of credit risk mitigation techniques in banks. It also enabled eligible banks to adopt their own internal risk assessment models for the determination of regulatory capital requirements. In the words of the Committee, 'the objective of the committee's work to revise the 1988 accord has been to develop a framework that would further strengthen the soundness and stability of the international banking system while maintaining sufficient consistency that capital adequacy regulation will not be a significant source of competitive inequality among internationally active banks'.[26]

The Basel II framework is composed of three broad interlocking pillars of minimum capital requirements, supervisory review and market review. The first pillar of the framework, known as 'Minimum Capital Requirements', deals extensively with the issue of the capital requirements for the various risks faced by banks. This pillar seeks to allocate minimum capital requirement for credit, market and operational risks. In dealing with credit risks, the Accord provides for two alternative methods for the rating of credit risks, in the form of the Standardised Approach and the Internal Ratings Based (IRB) Approach. The IRB is further divided into the Foundation IRB and Advanced IRB approaches ('IRB approaches'). The Standardised Approach introduces a 150 per cent risk category to the 0, 20, 50 and 100 per cent in operation under the Basel I risk weight categories. It made provision for the assessment of risk ratings by external credit assessment institutions, retained the credit conversion factor approach for off-balance sheet exposures and granted supervisory discretion for the reduction of capital requirements for collaterised debts. The IRB approaches encourage banks to adopt their own internal risk rating systems in order to engender a self-surveillance practice and potentially reduce the cost of regulation. These approaches are therefore incentivised by requiring banks to 'scale up' their risk weight reserves by 6 per cent if they use the Standardised Approach instead of the IRB approaches. Under the Foundation IRB, a bank with the approval of the regulators uses in-house ratings for its risk exposures but the regulators supply the 'essential variables' for the internal model.[27] However, under the Advanced IRB approach, the bank itself supplies all the variables for its risk calculation models.

To calculate the capital requirements needed to guard against operational risks resulting from failure in internal processes and external events, pillar I of Basel

25 The 2004 Accord essentially incorporated most of the changes proposed to the 1988 Accord.

26 BCBS (n 24) para C.

27 These variables include the loss given default (the probability of loss on each type of asset), exposure at default (the exposure of a bank to the risk asset at the time of default) and maturity (the risk at maturity on each type of asset).

II recommends three exclusive methods: first, the Basic Indicator Approach, which requires a capital charge of 15 per cent of the bank's average annual gross income for the preceding three years; second, the Standardised Approach, which divides business of eligible banks along eight business lines and requires a capital charge of between 12 and 18 per cent of the bank's average annual gross income in the preceding three years for each line of business; and finally, the Advanced Measurement Approach, which requires a capital charge that is equal to risk measure generated by the bank's internal operational risk measurement systems.[28] Pillar I also specifies the methodology for the quantification of the capital requirements to be held as safeguards against market risk.[29]

As was the case under Basel I, the total capital ratio for credit, market and operational risks under Basel II must be no less than 8 per cent of the bank's risk weighted assets. The definitions of the constituents of Tier 1 and Tier 2 capital remained largely the same under Basel II.[30] Basel II, however, introduced a third tier of capital, Tier 3, which is composed of subordinated debt instruments with a two-year maturity.[31] Subject to national regulatory approval, Tier 3 capital could be used to satisfy some of the capital requirements for market risks.[32]

Pillars II and III of the Basel II framework are focused on supervisory review and market discipline. The supervisory review relates to risk management, transparency and accountability, which are aimed at ensuring that the managers of banks 'develop and use better risk management techniques in monitoring and managing risk',[33] where supervisors would be expected to effectively assess the internal processes of banks in the areas of internal limits, provisioning, reserves and internal controls, and take prompt corrective action when appropriate. Pillar II, therefore, generally seeks to ensure that the bank's financial position is in tune with its risk profile and seeks to enable prompt supervisory intervention where necessary. Market discipline serves as a complement to pillars I and II by focusing on disclosure requirements, which balances out the ample discretion allowed under pillars I and II. This permits the use of internal process in the models for capital requirements calculations by requiring relevant information to be placed in the domain of market participants in order to enable them to play a more active role in demanding compliance with regulatory requirements under the framework.

Following the GFC, it was generally noted that the capital regulatory

28 Tarullo (n 15) 125.

29 BCBS, 'Amendments to the Capital Accord to Incorporate Market Risks' (Bank for International Settlements, 1996).

30 BCBS, 'International Convergence of Capital Measurement and Capital Standards: A Revised Framework' (Bank for International Settlements, 2006).

31 Thus, to be eligible, the subordinated debt must be unsecured, fully paid, have a maturity of at least two years as opposed to five years under Tier 2, not be repayable before the agreed repayment date and subject to a lock-in clause which stipulates that neither interest nor principal will be paid if such payment would lead to a depletion of capital below the minimum capital requirement.

32 See BCBS (n 30) 16–17.

33 Ibid.

requirements as construed prior to the crisis failed woefully as loss absorbents given that they were incapable of preventing bank failures or ensuring orderly resolution of banks.[34] As a result of this, a number of amendments to the Basel II framework were suggested and these included: first, the call for the scope of coverage of capital requirements to be extended to other financial institutions and financial activities that could trigger systemic crisis; second, capital requirements to be uniformly defined in all jurisdictions; third, capital requirements to be sufficiently dynamic and market sensitive as opposed to being static during boom periods and market downturns in order to reduce the procyclicality that makes banks willing to lend during boom periods but unwilling to do so during downturns; and, fourth, capital requirements to be more loss absorbent by increasing common equity requirements in the definition of capital, and more importantly introducing some form of contingent capital that will be able to absorb losses during market downturns and thereby operate as countercyclical mechanisms.[35]

## Basel II.5

After the GFC, amendments were made to the Basel framework in order to require banks to hold additional capital for market risks under rules that require banks to break down their risk portfolios and hold capital against: value at risk (VAR), i.e. how much could be lost on a normal trading day; stressed VAR, which indicates how much could be lost in extreme conditions; default risk and migration of unsecuritised credit products; and the risk on securitised loans.[36] This initiative was followed by the Basel III framework.

## Basel III

Following the amendments made under Basel II.5, the Basel Committee adopted further reforms under Basel III that are aimed at 'raising the required quality and quantity of capital in the banking system, improving risk coverage, introducing a leverage ratio to serve as a back stop to the risk-based regime, introducing capital conservation and countercyclical buffers as well as a global standard for liquidity risk' in order to 'improve the banking sector's ability to absorb shocks arising from financial and economic stress' and reduce 'the risk of spillover from the

34 Committee on Capital Markets Regulation, 'The Global Financial Crisis, A Plan for Regulatory Reform' (Committee on Capital Markets Regulation, May 2009).

35 Variants of these recommendations can be found in the following reports: The de Larosière Group, 'Report of the High-Level Group on Financial Supervision in the EU' (Brussels, 2009); Congress Oversight Panel, 'Special Report on Regulatory Reform' (US Congress, 2009) <http://www.sec.gov/comments/4-579/4579-24.pdf> accessed 7 March 2012; Financial Services Authority (FSA), 'The Turner Review: A Regulatory Response to the Global Banking Crisis' (Financial Services Authority, 2009); Financial Stability Forum, 'Report of Financial Stability Forum on Enhancing Market and Institutional Resilience' (Financial Stability Board, 2008).

36 BCBS, 'Revision to Basel II Market Risk Framework' (Bank for International Settlements, 31 December 2010).

financial sector to the real economy'.[37] The reforms were approved by the Group of Governors and Heads of Supervision (GHOS) on 12 September 2010 and endorsed at the Seoul G20 Leaders Summit in 12 November 2010.[38]

Under the reforms, which have been phased in since 2013 and are intended to be completely operational by 1 January 2019, banks will be required to hold three different categories of regulatory capital in the form of minimum capital requirements, capital conservation buffers and countercyclical buffers. In addition, systemically important banks would be required to hold an additional surcharge.[39] The reforms would be applicable at the consolidated level but national supervisory authorities would also have the option to apply the regime on a solo basis where it is considered necessary to conserve capital in certain parts of the banking group.[40]

### *Minimum capital requirements*

With particular reference to loss absorbency, the new framework essentially builds on the previous framework. It retains the requirement for minimum total capital ratio to be no less than 8 per cent of risk weighted assets of the bank but it extensively varies the constituent and definition of capital. While retaining the tiered definition for capital, it emphasises the need for Tier 1 capital to be dominated by loss-absorbing instruments such as common shares and retained earnings. It clarifies and sets very stringent rules for qualification as Tier 1 capital. It makes provision for the inclusion of provisions or loan-loss reserves in the calculation of Tier 2 capital subject to a limit of 1.25 per cent of the risk weighted assets of the bank under the standardised approach. It phases out the so-called Tier 3 capital instruments which were intended to be capable of being used to satisfy a part of the capital requirement for market risk under the Basel II framework. Under the framework, banks are required to hold a minimum Common Equity Tier 1 capital (CET1) of 4.5 per cent after stipulated deductions as opposed to the situation under the Basel I and II frameworks, which merely stated that Tier 1 capital elements were to be composed of fully paid shares or cash reserves from retained earnings without specifying the proportion in which they were to be held.[41] It increases the minimum total Tier 1 capital from 4 per cent under the Basel II framework to a minimum of 6 per cent of the bank's risk weighted

37 BCBS, 'Global Systemically Important Banks: Assessment Methodology and the Loss Absorbency Requirement' (Bank for International Settlements, 2011); BCBS, 'Basel III: A Global Regulatory Framework for More Resilient Banks and Banking Systems' (Bank for International Settlements, 2011).

38 Cited in H Hannoun, 'The Basel III Capital Framework: A Decisive Breakthrough' (BOJ-BIS High Level Seminar on Financial Regulatory Reform: Implications for Asia and the Pacific, Hong Kong, 22 November 2010).

39 BCBS, 'Global Systemically Important Banks: Assessment Methodology and Additional Loss Absorbency Requirement Rules Text' (Bank for International Settlements, 2011).

40 BCBS, 'Basel III' (n 37) 12, 56.

41 Some of the deductions include investments in own shares, reciprocal cross-holdings in the capital of banking, financial and insurance entities, investments in the capital of banking, and financial and

assets. Although it is contemplated that the rest of the Tier 1 capital requirements under the Basel III framework could be satisfied by either CET1 capital or Additional Tier 1 capital, a review of the qualifying attributes of the instruments to be classified as Additional Tier 1 capital reveals that the regulation is basically asking for additional CET1 capital or instruments that are essentially similar to it in attributes and loss absorbency function. The framework further stipulates that the difference between Tier 1 capital and the total minimum capital requirements could be met with either Tier 2 capital, which would be largely populated by the debt instruments that are subordinated to the depositors and general creditors of the bank, or any form of the Tier 1 capital.

As set out in more detail in subsequent sections of this chapter, the fact that an investor in Coco could face a write down or conversion even when equity holders continue to receive dividends means that the loss absorbency capacity of these instruments makes them ideal supplements and buffers to the regulatory capital requirements under the Basel III framework when they meet the other parameters set out for Tier 1, Additional Tier 1 or Tier 2 capital.

### *Conservation buffer*

In addition to the minimum capital requirements, banks will be required to hold a capital conservation buffer of 2.5 per cent in the form of Common Equity Tier 1 capital to withstand future periods of stress, which brings the total Common Equity Tier 1 requirement of the Basel III framework to 7 per cent. The capital conservation buffer is intended to make banks build up capital buffers well above the minimum capital requirement during boom time from which they can draw during periods of market downturns or when they are individually facing stressed periods. These conservation buffers would also double as an extra layer of defence for minimum capital requirements.

Under the capital conservation buffer framework, which is recommended to be applied on a consolidated basis and scheduled to be phased in between 1 January 2016 and 1 January 2019, when the regulatory capital of the relevant bank falls within the stipulated regulatory range it would be required to hold and retain a certain level of its earnings to reflect the plunge in capital levels.[42] The deeper the bank falls into the range specified for this purpose, the higher the level of the bank's earnings to be retained for the purpose of rebuilding the reserve. The capital conservation framework is structured to ensure that banks are inhibited from engaging in generous distributions of earnings to shareholders and other stakeholders in difficult times and that the bank is able to access much needed capital.[43]

insurance entities that are outside the scope of regulatory consolidation. See BCBS, 'Basel III' (n 37) 21–7 for a full discussion.

42 The framework also recommends that national authorities could also require the buffer to be held by banks on a solo basis. See BCBS, 'Basel III' (n 37) 56.

43 BCBS, 'Basel Committee on Banking Supervision Reforms – Basel III' (Bank for International Settlements, 2011).

### *Countercyclical buffer*

The third capital requirement to be imposed on banks under the Basel III framework is the countercyclical buffer that is required to be built up during periods of 'excess aggregate credit growth', which has been associated with the build-up of system-wide risk for the banking sector. In effect, depending on the economic climate, national regulatory authorities are given the discretion to set countercyclical capital levels under the framework, which would mandate that banks hold additional Common Equity Tier 1 or other fully loss absorbing capital within the range of 0 to 2.5 per cent as the level of countercyclical buffer. This effectively increases the CET1 ratio under Basel III framework to 9.5 per cent. National regulatory authorities are also required to pre-announce increases in countercyclical buffer levels by up to 12 months, while decreases in countercyclical levels could take effect immediately.

It is projected that this countercyclical buffer would help conserve capital during periods of economic growth that may then be used up by the banks during periods of economic stress. It is proposed that these buffers would be activated by applicable authorities when they judge that aggregate credit growth is excessive. A bank with purely domestic credit exposures will be subject to the full amount of the buffer determined by the national authorities while internationally active banks would be required to calculate a buffer add-on for each jurisdiction in which they have credit exposures, using the applicable buffers in effect in each host jurisdiction.[44] It is intended that the countercyclical buffers would serve as extensions to the conservation buffer.[45] A failure to satisfy regulatory requirements for countercyclical buffers would therefore result in the extension of the restrictions on distributions by the relevant bank. Just like the capital conservation buffer, the countercyclical buffer would also be phased in through the period of 1 January 2016 and 1 January 2019.

### *G-SIFI surcharge*

In spite of these additional capital requirements, in the immediate aftermath of the development of the Basel III framework, doubts were expressed about the adequacy of these proposals for big, complex, interconnected and systemic cross-border banks. The Financial Stability Board and the Independent Commission on Banking in the UK expressed the view that systemically important financial institutions should be required to hold additional equity as loss absorbency mechanisms in excess of the minimum agreed under the Basel III Standards to reflect the greater risks and cross-border negative externalities associated with

44 BCBS, 'Countercyclical Capital Buffer Proposal' (Bank for International Settlements, 2010); DX Chen and I Christensen, 'The Countercyclical Bank Capital Buffer: Insights for Canada' in Bank of Canada (ed.), *Financial System Review* (Bank of Canada, 2010).

45 M Drehmann, C Borio, L Gambacorta, G Jimenez and C Trucharte, 'Countercyclical Capital Buffers: Exploring Options' (Bank for International Settlements, Working Papers No 317, 2010) 1, 26.

these institutions.[46] Following its considerations of the concerns in relation to cross-border systemic financial institutions and in furtherance of the call by the Financial Stability Board (FSB), the Basel Committee developed an assessment methodology for the identification of globally systemically important financial institutions (G-SIFI), which are currently listed to consist of 29 banks globally. And it decided on an additional G-SIFI surcharge for SIFIs in the form of Common Equity Tier I capital ranging from 1 to 3.5 per cent, depending on the bank's systemic importance.[47]

## Bank capital beyond Basel III

Throughout the process of the consultations for the Basel III framework and following the release of its revised update in June 2011 and the publication of the paper on the regulatory framework for more resilient banks,[48] views regarding the inadequacy of the Basel capital requirements have been expressed by academics and other commentators. Although some dissenting opinions on the need to increase capital requirements up to or beyond the Basel III standards have been expressed,[49] the overwhelming opinions support the Basel III thresholds and a number of others advocate for increases beyond the current thresholds.

In this regard, the Independent Commission on Banking specifically suggested that the minimum leverage ratio of equity to total assets should be increased to a minimum of 10 per cent, with an additional surcharge element of 3 per cent for large UK retail banks; while the combination of large retail and UK banking groups should generally have a loss-absorbing capacity of at least 17 to 20 per cent.[50] The Basel Committee in its study on the cost and benefits of higher capital ratios using conservative estimates, suggests optimal capital ratios in the region of 13 to 14 per cent.[51] Taking this study a step further, Miles, Yang and Marcheggiano, realising the omission of the BCBS study to take account of the effect of the increase in capital requirements on the cost of equity and debt,

46 GHOS, 'Group of Governors and Heads of Supervision announces higher global minimum capital standards' (2010); Financial Stability Board (FSB), 'Reducing the Moral Hazard Posed by Systemically Important Financial Institutions, FSB Recommendations and Time Lines' (Financial Stability Board, 20 October 2010); Independent Commission on Banking, 'Final Report – Recommendations' (Independent Commission on Banking, September 2011).

47 See FSB (n 46) para 48. The indicator based approach of the Committee makes use of five selected multiple indicators of interconnectedness, size, substitutability, complexity and substitutability to define which institutions should be classified as G-SIFIs. See BCBS, 'Basel III' (n 37).

48 BCBS, 'Basel III' (n 37).

49 For this, see Institute of International Finance, 'Interim Report on the Cumulative Impact on the Global Economy of the Proposed Changes in Banking Regulatory framework' (Institute of International Finance, June 2010) <http://www.ebf-fbe.eu/uploads/10-Interim%20NCI_June2010_Web.pdf> accessed 28 May 2012; V Pandit, 'We Must Rethink Basel, or Growth Will Suffer', *Financial Times* (10 November 2010).

50 Independent Commission on Banking (n 46) 13.

51 BCBS, 'An Assessment of the Long-term Economic Impact of Stronger Capital and Liquidity Requirements' (Bank for International Settlements, August 2010) 28–31.

reworked the model using data from UK bank assets and stocks from different parts of the world. This led them to suggest an optimal loss absorbing capacity of capital to risk weighted assets between the ranges of 16 and 20 per cent as being sufficient to counter the risk of failure in a crisis, which is higher than the level of the minimum targets agreed under the Basel III capital framework.[52] Similarly, while acknowledging that Basel III is a 'good starting point' Andrew Haldane of the Bank of England notes that the capital requirements under the framework are insufficient to stave off another round of financial crisis and could therefore not be regarded as the 'right finishing line'.[53] Explaining the rationale for his stance, he notes that the average risk weight of a global bank is 40 per cent, and points out that this means that 10 per cent capital ratio of risk weighted assets means that banks would still be allowed a leverage of 25 times of equity, and an unexpected loss of 4 per cent would be enough to render the bank insolvent, while a loss of a lesser percentage would be enough to render the bank illiquid.[54]

While the policy direction in the international policy arena has been supportive of the need for increased regulatory capital levels for banks, there has been a sharp divide with regards to the form and nature of bank capital. Counteracting the popular belief that high equity levels on a bank's balance sheet would mean an increase in funding cost and a decrease on the return on equity in comparison to having banking operations funded by debt,[55] Admati, De Marzo, Hellwig and Pfleiderer[56] have led a school of thought that argues that equity in fact leads to better capitalised banks that require less external finance and are capable of more retained earnings to fund growth and reduce the potential for default risk and losses to depositors.[57] They contend that the tax advantage of debt to equity amounts to a social misnomer which privatises banking profits while socialising its cost.[58] They further argue that the case for the introduction of convertible debt instruments like contingent capital and bail-in instruments is yet to be effectively made due to the complicated nature of the design, valuation and mode of implementation of these instruments by regulators.[59]

In subsequent sections of this chapter, it is argued that the high level of equity capital maintained by banks during the GFC cast substantial doubt on the need to further increase capital requirements beyond the Basel Committee

52 D Miles, J Yang and G Marcheggiano, 'Optimal Bank Capital' (External MPC Unit Discussion Paper No 31, Bank of England, April 2011) 34–9.

53 A Haldane, 'Control Rights (and Wrongs)' (Wincott Annual Memorial Lecture, London, 24 October 2011) 14.

54 Ibid.

55 F Allen, E Carletti and RS Marquez, 'Credit Market Competition and Capital Regulation' (2011) 24(4) *Review of Financial Studies* 983.

56 AR Admati, PM De Marzo, MF Hellwig and P Pfleiderer, 'Fallacies, Irrelevant Facts, and Myths in the Discussion of Capital Regulation: Why Bank Equity is Not Expensive' (23 March 2011) <http://ssrn.com/abstract=1669704> accessed 6 October 2015 ('Admati et al').

57 Ibid 4.

58 Ibid.

59 Ibid.

requirements. It is argued that the capital requirements for banks under Basel III should incorporate convertible debt instruments that will satisfy the requirements of Tier 1, Additional Tier I capital and Tier 2 capital and in turn serve as prudential market discipline tools and loss absorption instruments. In making this case, the subsequent sections of this chapter examine the nature and operational framework for and concerns regarding the viability of Cocos.

### *The case for contingent convertible capital*

From the information obtainable from Bloomberg Dealogic, the total amount of Cocos issued by banks between January 2009 and September 2015 stands at about $450 billion and financial institutions registered in the UK account for about 14.3 per cent of this value.[60] This is a significant figure that highlights the emergence of Cocos as a consequence of the GFC.

Two major variants of convertible debt instruments that function as loss absorbents and complements for equity have been identified by Mark Flannery,[61] John Coffee Jr,[62] Richard Herring and Charles Calomiris,[63] George Pennachi,[64] the Squam Lake Working Group,[65] the Association for Financial Markets in Europe (AFME),[66] and Canada's principal bank regulator.[67] The first, which is described in this chapter as contingent convertible capital, generally refers to contractual subordinated debt instruments that are capable of being converted into equity or of being written down in order to absorb the losses of a bank following the occurrence of a triggering event in order to recapitalise the bank and keep it functioning as a going concern well before it gets to the point of becoming unviable. This therefore qualifies as a going-concern capital. Investors in these instruments would accept the prospect of conversion under agreed conditions,

60 Examples of recent issuers include Lloyds Bank, Barclays Bank and Royal Bank of Scotland.

61 MJ Flannery, 'No Pain, No Gain: Effecting Market Discipline via Reverse Convertible Debentures' in HS Scott (ed.), *Capital Adequacy Beyond Basel: Banking, Securities and Insurance* (Oxford University Press, 2005); Flannery (n 7).

62 JC Coffee, Jr, 'Systemic Risk after Dodd-Frank: Contingent Capital and the Need for Regulatory Strategies Beyond Oversight' (2011) 111(4) *Colombia Law Review* 795.

63 Herring and Calomiris (n 10).

64 G Pennachi, 'A Structural Model of Contingent Bank Capital' (University of Illinois College of Business Working Paper, 2010).

65 Squam Lake Working Group on Financial Regulation, 'An Expedited Resolution Mechanism for Distressed Financial Firms: Regulatory Hybrid Securities' (Working Paper, Council on Foreign Relations – Centre for Geoeconomics Studies, April 2009); the Squam Lake Working Group includes a collection of prominent financial economists from major institutions and universities.

66 M Austen, 'Too Big to be Bailed Out: There is a Way to Rescue Banking Giants and the Economy Without Making the Taxpayer Cough Up', *The Guardian* (17 August 2010).

67 Canada's Office of the Superintendent of Financial Institutions (OFSI) has announced a policy of requiring all subordinated debt issued by financial institutions under its jurisdiction to contain a conversion provision under which the debt will convert into equity under specified circumstances of financial distress. See B Keefe, 'Canada Pushes Embedded Contingent Capital', *Mondaq* (25 August 2010).

and would require compensation for bearing this risk.[68] However, in order to avoid a dilution of their interest, shareholders would usually be motivated to raise more equity to avoid conversion and this will help keep banks well capitalised at all times.

The other major variant is described here as bail-in instruments. These refer to forms of regulatory or statutory debt instruments that absorb losses at the point of non-viability. Just like the going-concern contingent capital instruments, these instruments are capable of being converted into equity or being written down in order to recapitalise a bank. However, they differ from going-concern contingent capital in that while contingent capital conversion or write down is triggered by the occurrence of a contractually stipulated event while the bank is still viable, bail-in instruments conversion or write down is triggered at the point when the banks becomes unviable and would usually be triggered at the discretion of applicable national or consolidated regulatory or resolution authorities. The resulting buffer from the write down or conversion of the debt instrument would have the effect of reducing the liability of the bank, improving the chances for the bank to continue with the provision of essential functions or simply facilitating the bank's orderly wind down and reducing the likelihood of the cost of resolution being borne by the taxpayer. Just as is the case with the contingent capital, the possibility of the converted instrument diluting the interest of existing shareholders also operates as an incentive for shareholders to do all that is within their powers to obviate the dilution and raise additional capital to keep the bank adequately capitalised.[69] It is however doubtful that shareholders would be sufficiently motivated to raise additional capital at this point in the life of a failing bank. This variant of convertible debt instrument therefore qualifies as gone-concern capital.

In view of the special nature and functions of banks, the going-concern variant of Coco as described above is preferred as it presents a mechanism for risk governance in banking by providing a credible signal for default risk through the conversion or write-down mechanism. Therefore, it averts the uncertainty that occasions distress periods by necessitating a bank to scale down its liabilities and embark on timely recapitalisation well in advance of troubled times and during a period when it could still afford to choose its own preferred method of recapitalisation. The potential substantial dilution of shareholders' interest upon the exercise of the conversion mechanism presents a substantial incentive for voluntary pre-emptive issuance of equity capital in order to avoid conversion and subsequent dilution. Although bail-in instruments could complement the loss absorption function of equity capital at the time of distress, the going-concern variant of the convertible debt instrument performs a different but uniquely complementary function to equity capital in view of the earlier conversion or

68 C D'Souza, T Gravelle, W Engert and L Orsi, 'Contingent Capital and Bail-In Debt: Tools for Bank Resolution' in Bank of Canada (ed.), *Financial System Review* (2010) 51 <http://www.bankofcanada.ca/wp-content/uploads/2010/12/fsr_1210.pdf> accessed 6 October 2015.

69 Independent Commission on Banking, 'Final Report – Recommendations' (Independent Commission on Banking, September 2011).

write-down feature for recapitalisation of troubled banks. This makes bank insolvency extremely unlikely and prevents the potential follow-on failure of other institutions that may have resulted from such failures if attention were paid to the point when a bank becomes unviable. It also privatises the costs of banking that could have been socialised (i.e. borne by taxpayers) in the event of a bailout because it effectively transfers the cost of bank recapitalisation to the debt instrument holders, who would have negotiated compensation for the risk being taken, and it ensures better market discipline as a result of periodic extensive disclosure requirements. It is argued here that the nature of Coco impels its incorporation as a complement to equity capital requirements for banks and this argument will be buttressed throughout the discussion in the following three subsections.

### *Equity as a lagging indicator of losses*

The last GFC has clearly indicated that government and regulatory authorities are generally reluctant to permit a large financial institution to fail.[70] This disposition could mean that the taxpayer could still be exposed to the burden of bank bailouts even though equity capital requirements suggested under the Basel III requirements or beyond are adopted. Also, the International Monetary Fund (IMF) notes that most banks that required bailouts in the GFC reported higher than average capital levels in the build-up to the crisis.[71] Simply increasing capital levels or the equity capital levels does not therefore guarantee that much will change. Herring and Calomiris note the practice of banks engaging in regulatory arbitrage and manipulating the accounting treatment of equity in order to conceal losses through complex transactions that are hard for regulators to uncover and they recommend the use of contingent capital as an incentive-based regulatory tool that could be used to force banks to replace lost capital.[72] While not implying that the Coco provides an alternative to effective supervision, it is argued here that it provides an additional mechanism for regulatory compliance by compelling prompt recapitalisation; and because the regulator is not omniscient, additional tools compelling compliance with regulatory thresholds can only do more 'regulatory good' for the banking industry.

### *Difficulty and cost of replenishing equity*

The ability of banks to manipulate accounting treatment of losses and equity enables them to hide risk exposures. But when losses are eventually recognised, the fall in the level of confidence during periods of market downturn following the recognition of losses or during a market downturn would affect the success

70 While the case of Lehman Brothers presents an exception in this regard, the effect of the decision to allow it to fail had reverberating effects that compelled the authorities in the US to further strengthen and fortify responses to the crisis, which included large bail-out programmes.

71 International Monetary Fund, 'Detecting Systemic Risk' in *Global Financial Stability Report* (International Monetary Fund, April 2008) ch 3.

72 Herring and Calomiris (n 10) 6–7.

and cost of an attempt at equity issuance. The well-acknowledged asymmetric nature of information on a bank's net worth, which will be aggravated during a crisis, would also make the issue of equity during this period particularly costly.[73] In the words of Walter Bagehot, 'Every banker knows that if he has to prove he is worthy of credit, however good may be his arguments, in fact his credit is gone'.[74] Embarking on a successful equity issuance programme during a period of market downturn would therefore be a difficult if not impossible task.

Another challenge of issuing equity is described by economists as the debt overhang problem. This refers to the disincentive of management who would themselves hold shares in the banks to issue additional shares after a bank may have suffered losses because such an issue of shares could result in a significant dilution of the interest of current shareholders and the transfer of value to the existing bondholders in the bank, who instead of experiencing a reduction in the value of their interest would be protected from losing any value as the equity issuance would guarantee the funds for their repayment. The management and shareholders may therefore prefer to satisfy regulatory capital requirements in the interim by selling assets and reducing lending activities; while banks that are in compliance with regulatory capital requirements may simply rely on potential government bailouts, which could lead to the transfer of banking cost to the taxpayer.[75] Although Admati et al argue that this debt overhang problem could be alleviated by restricting equity payouts and mandating new equity under regulatory framework,[76] this argument ignores the difficulty and costs related to share issuance during a market downturn.[77]

In comparison to equity, the fact that Cocos are to be issued and converted well in advance of crisis situations means that pricing, costs and confidence levels in the market will be better. These instruments are, therefore, unlikely to suffer the challenges that could be faced by the issuance of equity during a period of market downturn for the purpose of recapitalisation. The fact that Cocos would not lead to a dilution in shareholder interest at the time of their issuance also means that it bypasses the debt overhang problem with which equity is saddled. Therefore Cocos provide a veritable complement to equity in the regulation of bank capital even though they may subsequently be converted to shares.

### *Disclosure, market transparency and discipline*

A major advantage of Cocos as advocated in this chapter relates to the fact they would encourage market transparency and enable market operators to assess the specific status of banks, as potential investors/creditors are likely to require more and better disclosure from the banks before making investments in the

73 P Bolton and X Freixas, 'Corporate Finance and the Monetary Transmission Mechanism' (2006) 19(3) *The Review of Financial Studies* 829.

74 W Bagehot, *Lombard Street: A Description of the Money Market* (HS King, 1873) 68.

75 Herring and Calomiris (n 10) 7.

76 Admati et al (n 56) 4.

77 Coffee (n 62) 834.

instruments on offer.[78] Once investors buy into these instruments, they are likely to constitute a lobby group in the governance of the bank that would constantly clamour for prudence. Unlike regulators who may find it difficult to prove that a bank is taking excessive risks when trying to impose sanctions, the holders of the Coco instruments would place the burden of proving the level of risk undertaken on the bank management. This would in turn have the advantage of bolstering market discipline and confidence.[79]

Mandating banks to issue these subordinated convertible debt instruments on a periodic basis would impose a continuous and periodic disclosure obligation on the banks and amount to an effective market discipline tool. Further, considering that investors are likely to shy away from the instruments issued by unstable or unviable banks, the lack of appetite of investors for these debt instruments could constitute a warning signal for official supervisors with regard to the issuing bank.

It must be noted that the potency of the market discipline effect of debt instruments has been questioned by Admati et al and Morgan and Stiroh, as they argue that the last GFC makes it difficult to accept the argument that debt has a disciplinary role on managerial processes.[80] However, it must be pointed out that their argument in this regard is focused on the ability of creditors to prevent managers from taking excessive risks and not on the benefit of more periodical disclosure required by the disclosure conditions to which banks are subjected in order to issue these instruments.

## The design of contingent convertible capital instruments (Cocos)

The FSB and the Basel Committee have pointed out that developing a framework for contingent convertible capital instruments would require laying down clear rules for its operation.[81] Thus, in order to be effective, issues relating to the trigger for conversion or write down, the details of the process for the conversion or write down, the consequences of the conversion or write down on shareholders and the investors' interests and market for the issuance of the instruments must be considered well in advance, and some of these issues are addressed below.

78 Goldman Sachs Global Markets Institute, 'Contingent Capital: Possibilities, Problems and Opportunities' (Goldman Sachs Global Markets Institute, March 2011) 5 <http://www.goldmansachs.com/our-thinking/public-policy/regulatory-reform/contingent-capital-feb.html> accessed 6 October 2015.

79 D Evanoff and L Wall, 'Subordinated Debt and Bank Capital Reform' (Working Paper No 2000-24, Federal Reserve Bank of Chicago, November 2000).

80 Admati et al (n 56) 4.

81 BCBS, 'Global Systemically Important Banks: Assessment Methodology and the Loss Absorbency Requirements' (Bank for International Settlements, July 2011) 17–20; Financial Stability Board, 'Reducing the Moral Hazard Posed by Systemically Important Financial Institutions: FSB Recommendations and the Time Lines' (Financial Stability Board, 20 October 2010) 3.

### *The trigger and time inconsistency challenge*

In order for these instruments to be effective, the trigger event for the conversion or write down of the contingent capital would have to be carefully specified and implemented. Some trigger mechanisms suggested in existing literature include the systemic crisis triggers,[82] bank specific and market indicator triggers that are activated by indices such as bank book value,[83] bank capital ratio[84] or market valuation of the stock of the relevant bank.[85] A combination of systemic triggers and bank-specific triggers[86] or more than one bank-specific trigger that would help avoid market manipulation or unwarranted conversions or write downs resulting from unusual short-term market conditions have also been suggested.[87] The major challenge in deciding the appropriate mechanism is attributable to the time inconsistency challenge. This refers to the challenge that what appears like the best policy option when announced may in reality turn out not to be as good as contemplated. Further, a reversal of the policy on realisation of this shortcoming could in fact lead to worse outcomes, which compels adherence to the original policy option even though it may not effectively achieve the policy objective.[88]

In this regard, as long as the conversion or write down of the debt instrument to equity would be subject to the discretion of the bank management or the regulatory authorities, it is unlikely to be effective. This is because it is impossible to guarantee that the management of the bank or regulators will pull the trigger for conversion/write down on the basis of the terms that were agreed when the banks were viable and the market was normal. This challenge of time inconsistency can be addressed by ensuring that the triggers for Cocos are automatic and are not dependent on indicators that can be manipulated by the management of the relevant banks or dependent on the discretion of regulators. A review of recent issues of Cocos reveals that capital adequacy ratios have been adopted as the preferred trigger mechanism. However, due to the fact that an indicator like bank capital ratio is dependent on financial reporting, which can be subject to accounting manipulations, this measure may be questionable. Therefore, in some respects, and as early intervention mechanisms in bank regulation are already based on bank capital ratios, the adoption of a separate trigger indicator like

82 Squam Lake Working Group on Financial Regulation (n 65) 4.

83 O Hart and L Zingales, 'How to Make a Bank Raise Equity', *Financial Times* (7 February 2010).

84 T Huertas, 'Too Big to Fail, Too Complex to Contemplate: What to Do about Systemically Important Firms' (Financial Markets Group Conference, London, 15 September 2009) <http://www.fsa.gov.uk/library/communication/speeches/2009/0915_th.shtml> accessed 12 March 2014.

85 Flannery (n 7) 3.

86 R Rajan, 'More Capital Will Not Stop the Next Crisis', *Financial Times* (1 October 2009).

87 RL McDonald, 'Contingent Capital with Dual Price Trigger' (2013) 9(2) *Journal of Financial Stability* 230.

88 For a discussion of time inconsistency in financial policy making after the crisis, see JM Nason and CI Plosser, 'Time-Consistency and Credible Monetary Policy after the Crisis' (2012) Q2 *Business Review* 19.

share prices for the Cocos would provide an additional supervisory monitoring mechanism.

Stock price triggers may be criticised on the grounds that they may be manipulated and only offer a rough estimate of an institution's financial health.[89] Also, it is suggested that declining equity values can only be regarded as reliable measures if they are sufficiently persistent. To address these shortcomings of stock prices, a write-back provision could be incorporated into the conversion or write-down feature of the Coco instrument. This feature would ensure that investors are protected and compensated for abnormal and temporal movements in share prices that are not related to deterioration in a bank's financial health by enabling them get back some, if not all, of their investment if the bank bounces back to a healthy financial status within a defined period.[90] Adopting this approach would ensure that the recapitalisation takes place in the first instance automatically to protect the bank and avoid the time inconsistency challenge, but a provision is made for abnormal blips.

### *Pricing and other conversion considerations*

A key issue for the success of the conversion or write down of the Coco instruments relates to pricing. As investors could have their interest completely wiped out, a justification exists for investors in Cocos to charge the bank a high coupon or interest.

Where Cocos are to be converted into common stock following the occurrence of the triggering event, it would be essential to determine the formula for ascertaining the value and volume of shares to be ascribed to the converting debt instruments. Flannery suggests that the conversion price of the debt instrument to equity should be the market price at the point of conversion.[91] Herring and Calomiris and the Squam Lake Group, however, note that the adoption of such an approach could prompt investors in the debt instruments to manipulate the share price of the bank in order to force a conversion, dilute the interest of existing shareholders and thereafter proceed to sell the shares at a premium.[92] While the potential for this can be curbed by lock-in provisions that prohibit the sale of banks shares within a particular period after purchase, such a lock-in approach carries the danger of the transmission of risks from the bank to the investors. An effective alternative approach to pricing would be to use a fixed share premium conversion approach, which will be based on allocating a percentage stake in the equity of the bank to investors irrespective of monetary value at the point of conversion. This must, however, be priced in a way that would ensure that Cocos are still able to incentivise voluntary recapitalisation to avoid the trigger. Such a predefined premium will reduce the incentive for investor market manipulation.

89 Herring and Calomiris (n 10) 24–5.

90 Goldman Sachs Global Markets Institute (n 78).

91 Flannery (n 7) 4.

92 Squam Lake Working Group on Financial Regulation (n 65) 4; Herring and Calomiris (n 10) 42–3.

***Market for contingent convertible capital instruments and the need to protect retail investors***

Cocos have been described as risky and highly complex instruments that combine the worst features of debt and equity.[93] Unlike equity that has the potential to enjoy the upside of a prosperous business, Cocos do not increase in value as investors would only be entitled to agreed coupons and would not share in the profits of the business. Unlike secured debt that may enjoy some form of security, Cocos are largely unsecured and investors take the risk of losing out completely on their investments in the event that the conversion or write-down feature is triggered. The projected growth in the issuance of Cocos and the increasing focus on yields in an environment of low interest rates on cash savings make these instruments attractive to all investors.

In order to protect the ordinary retail customers or clients who may be unable to adequately assess the risks relating to these debt instruments in view of the information asymmetries that are characteristic of the financial markets, the Financial Conduct Authority (FCA), exercising its powers under sections 137D and 138M of the Financial Services and Markets Act 2000 (FSMA 2000) (as amended by the Financial Services Act 2012) and acting in line with the European Securities and Markets Authority's (ESMA's) published concerns about the risks with Cocos investments,[94] introduced temporary explicit product intervention rules, which came into effect on 1 October 2014.[95] This was followed by the permanent rules from the FCA (the 'Final Rules') restricting the sale of Cocos to retail investors in the European Economic Area from October 2015 on the basis that requisite investment analysis for Cocos can only be done with the skills and resources available to institutional investors.[96] However, the FCA has clarified that intermediation activities that give effect to transactions in Cocos do not fall within the scope of the restriction in the Final Rules.

## Conclusion

The complexity of Cocos are hardly in doubt but investors have been drawn by the relatively high interest rates on offer, while the banks offering the instruments are delighted by the flexibility that the instruments offer in shoring up the capital base to meet regulatory capital requirements. Although regulators are keen

93 The Owl, 'Avoid Contingent Convertible Bonds: All The Qualities Of A Bond, Except Security' (2015) <http://seekingalpha.com/article/2496585-avoid-contingent-convertible-bonds-all-the-qualities-of-a-bond-except-security> accessed 6 October 2015.

94 European Securities and Market Authorities, 'Potential Risks Associated with Investing in Contingent Convertible Instruments' (European Securities and Market Authorities, 31 July 2014).

95 See Financial Conduct Authority, 'Temporary Product Intervention Rules: Restrictions in relation to the Retail Distribution of Contingent Convertible Instruments' (Financial Conduct Authority, August 2014).

96 See Financial Conduct Authority, 'Restrictions on the Retail Distribution of Regulatory Capital Instruments: Feedback to CP14/23 and Final Rules' (Financial Conduct Authority, June 2015).

to protect the interest of retail investors, the reversal in the hierarchy of losses offered by conversion or write-down triggers in Cocos make them attractive to regulators who are also keen to protect the taxpayer from the burden of bank failures and preserve the utilitarian function performed by banking institutions as financial intermediaries.

Having said that, it is important to note that despite their popularity there has been a decline in trading in Cocos at the time of submitting this chapter. This was attributed to a number of factors, among which were the underperformance of a number of European banks, such as Deutsche Bank, which happened to be major issuers of Cocos, and the question of whether they will be able to pay the interest due on their Cocos.[97] Additionally, there was some regulatory confusion over the rules with regard to Cocos where the European Banking Authority issued a paper stating that coupon payments from existing Cocos may be deferred (i.e. regulators force banks not to pay interest to investors in Cocos) due to concerns regarding banks' capital levels (i.e. concerns in relation to the way in which their capitals were measured).[98]

Therefore, the future prospects of this financial innovation will depend on the ability of the issuers and the regulator to address these concerns and reassure their investors.

97 T Hale and D McCrum, 'Why Coco Bonds are Worrying Investors', *Financial Times* (9 February 2016); and see also 'Deutsche Bank's Unappetising Cocos, Discomforting Brew', *The Economist* (13 February 2016).

98 T Hale, M Arnold and L Noonan, 'Bank Coco Market Faces Uphill Struggle', *Financial Times* (23 February 2016).

# 6 Exploring the myth of ethical finance in the UK financial market post the 2008 financial crisis: the prospects and challenges

*Abdul Karim Aldohni*

## Introduction: The state of the UK financial market in the run-up to the 2008 financial crash

There is no doubt that the 2008 global financial crisis uncovered some major defects in the legal and regulatory structure of the global financial sector. More importantly the global financial crash of 2008 exposed a questionable business culture that undermined almost all the functions of this vital sector and led to catastrophic economic and social consequences. This culture created a work environment in which the market players' reckless behaviour became widely acceptable or even the norm. In this regard, some major financial institutions became involved in highly speculative financial products with a complicated structure, which made it even more difficult for these institutions to understand all the risks that they were exposed to. Further, other financial institutions started to make less prudent lending decisions relying on excessive credit, only made available through leveraging, in order to make short-term gains.[1] The UK's fifth-largest mortgage provider, Northern Rock, structured a product called 'Together' mortgage, which allowed borrowers, who were not necessarily very creditworthy, to borrow up to 125 per cent of the value of the property they wished to purchase.[2] The credit that Northern Rock relied on to finance these operations was mostly obtained through short-term interbank borrowing (i.e. it was not based on retail funding). It is important to note that Northern Rock was also involved to a certain extent in the complicated business of securitisation.[3] This reckless business strategy weakened the bank's resilience and significantly increased its exposure to

1 JC Coffer, Jr, 'What Went Wrong? An Initial Inquiry into the Causes of the 2008 Financial Crisis' (2009) 9(1) *Journal of Corporate Law Studies* 2.

2 'Together' mortgages combined a secured loan of 95% of the value of the property and an unsecured loan up to 30% of the value of the property, or £30,000, whichever was the lowest. National Audit Office, 'HM Treasury: The Nationalisation of Northern Rock' (20 March 2009) 32 <https://www.nao.org.uk/wp-content/uploads/2009/03/0809298.pdf > accessed 10 January 2016. See also R Winnett, 'Northern Rock Lent £1.8billion in Risky Mortgages after Government Bail-Out', *The Telegraph* (20 March 2009).

3 HS Shin, 'Reflections on Modern Bank Runs: A Case Study of Northern Rock' (August 2008) 3–9, 12–16 <https://www.princeton.edu/~hsshin/www/nr > accessed 15 January 2016.

credit and liquidity risks, which consequently led to its failure and then nationalisation in February 2008.[4]

The questionable business culture of the financial sector in the run-up to the 2008 financial crisis fostered some serious manipulative/exploitative and – in some cases – fraudulent practices that undermined public trust in the sector. The mis-selling of financial products has been one of the key systemic problems that the UK financial market has repeatedly suffered. The period that preceded the 2008 financial crash witnessed a major episode of mis-selling of personal protection insurance (PPI)[5] and interest rate hedging products (IRHPs or interest rate swaps).

The post 2008 investigation into the selling of these products found that individual and business consumers were subjected to undue pressure to buy these insurance products. Consumers were made to believe by the selling institutions that they had no other option but to buy these products as part of their credit agreements,[6] while in reality these insurance products were separate products. On many occasions it was found that business consumers were mis-sold inappropriate, complicated structures of IRHPs, which were difficult to understand and the business need for these products was questionable. It was also found that the selling of PPI was primarily driven by the institutions' need to generate cash to subsidise the relatively cheap credit made available to borrowers.[7]

Further, more serious forms of exploitative and manipulative practices were also uncovered in the wake of the 2008 financial crisis, the most serious of which was the LIBOR scandal. This scandal exposed the worst side of a business culture that allowed systemic fraudulent practices to corrupt the financial sector and erode any trust left in its main players.

Considering the vital role that interbank lending plays in facilitating the financial market's operations it is essential for market players to set a rate for their internal borrowing. Therefore, the LIBOR (London Inter-Bank Offered Rate) is used as an estimate of the cost that banks incur in their wholesale short-term unsecured borrowing. The calculation of this rate is based on averaging the submissions made by the largest and most creditworthy banks operating in London after discarding the top and bottom four submissions.[8]

In this regard, it is important to note that the LIBOR is uniquely different from other financial benchmarks or interest rates considering its wide global use and its significant influence over different aspects of the financial markets. A wide

4 BBC, 'Northern Rock to Be Nationalised'(17 February 2008) <http://news.bbc.co.uk/1/hi/business/7249575.stm>.

5 E Ferran, 'Regulatory Lessons from the Payment Protection Insurance Mis-selling Scandal in the UK' (2011) 13(2) *European Business Organization Law Review* 249.

6 Parliamentary Commission on Banking Standards, 'Changing Banking for Good – Volume II: Chapters 1 to 11 and Annexes, together with formal minutes' (June 2013) 90–91.

7 Parliamentary Commission on Banking Standards, 'Changing Banking for Good – Volume II: Chapters 1 to 11 and Annexes, together with formal minutes' (June 2013) 91, 95.

8 D Hou and DR Skeie, 'LIBOR: Origins, Economics, Crisis, Scandal, and Reform' (Staff Report No 667, Federal Reserve Bank of New York, March 2014) 1–2.

range of financial instruments around the globe use the LIBOR as a reference rate to set interest rates.[9] It is estimated by the US Commodity Futures Trading Commission that in 2012 around $350 trillion worth of derivatives and $10 trillion worth of loans were based on LIBOR.[10] The fact that the borrowing rate for 10 currencies and 15 maturities is set according to the LIBOR shows its significant influence.[11] The LIBOR measures performance relatively with regard to investment return and funding cost and indicates the overall financial health of the market.[12]

The above important features of the LIBOR would not have existed if it were not for the fact that the financial markets and their participants have trust in the honest nature of its calculation. The significance of the LIBOR is based on the honesty and trustworthiness of the institutions involved in setting this rate. This is because the submissions made by the banks involved in setting the LIBOR are actually an estimate of the borrowing cost. It can be suggested, therefore, that on the one hand this shows the need to maintain the market's trust in the honesty of the process that produces the LIBOR in order for this benchmark to function well, and, on the other hand, this makes the LIBOR very susceptible to abuse and manipulation.

Unfortunately, the findings of the investigations into the LIBOR scandal demonstrated that systemic fraudulent behaviour was the dominant feature, and this eroded the key foundation upon which the LIBOR was found, namely trust. In manipulating the banks' submissions and eventually rigging the LIBOR final fixing, traders in some of these trusted banks, such as Barclays and Royal Bank of Scotland (RBS), saw a great opportunity to secure financial gains. It was found that, in order to signal false financial strength of their financial institutions at the height of the 2008 financial crisis, these traders submitted discounted estimates of the true cost of their borrowing.[13] Further, with regards to LIBOR-based financial contracts, the traders manipulated their submissions in order to fix the LIBOR at a figure that increased their profits, or reduced losses.[14] For example, while conspiring with other banks' traders, Barclays' traders used this technique to increase profits or reduce losses on their derivative exposures.[15]

The above overview of the UK financial market in the run-up to the 2008 financial crash shows that something has gone badly wrong with the ethos of the financial sector. On the one hand, greed and selfishness were widely tolerated, if not accepted, as part of the business drive. On the other hand, it seems to have allowed a dangerous process of malpractice normalisation where the different forms of wrongdoing that went on in the market, such as reckless and exploitative practices, were not the actions of a rogue player or two. Instead, they represented

9 Ibid 2.
10 J Nocera , 'Libor's Dirty Laundry', *The New York Times* (6 July 2012).
11 'The LIBOR Scandal: The Rotten Heart of Finance', *The Economist* (7 July 2012).
12 Hou and Skeie (n 8) 2–3.
13 Ibid 6.
14 Ibid.
15 'The LIBOR Scandal' (n 11).

a new way of executing business, which participants – one way or another – found themselves drawn into and accepted them as the new business norm. An apparent representation of this point can be seen in the argument made by Barclays in the wake of the LIBOR scandal. Barclays maintained that it tried to submit honest estimates but the action of its counterparts had prevented it from doing that. It was alleged that almost all banks on the panel were deliberately submitting manipulated estimates, which had created a market trend that every participant had to follow otherwise they risked looking financially weaker than their distinctly weak counterparts.[16] There are other relevant examples that can be pointed out to support this argument. For instance, the mass mis-selling of PPI and IRHP was not primarily associated with only one or two major credit providers but was endemic, involving almost all credit providers in this exploitative practice. The tale of Northern Rock's failure can also be used to further advance this argument as it has been suggested that the risky mortgage lending policy that dominated the business strategy of Northern Rock was part of a wider market practice.[17] In other words, Northern Rock was following what other competitors were doing in terms of making credit for mortgages easily available to all borrowers without giving much consideration to their creditworthiness. Therefore, Northern Rock was not an outlier among other big banks in the UK in terms of using non-retail funding for its highly leveraged operations.[18] It is worth noting that the directors of Northern Rock enjoyed their bonuses in the same year (2008) the bank was nationalised and made a 1.4 billion loss.[19] This signifies a selfish attitude towards the business in general and their shareholders in particular.

Accordingly, it can be suggested that the new ethos of the financial sector, which underlined the business practices in the run-up to the 2008 financial crash, accommodates some unhealthy traits. The first is the prioritisation of self-interest that is driven by greed and the relentless pursuit of personal gains, by the institutions or their members, without any consideration for the social context of their actions. In this regard, it can be argued that this new financial business ethos is highly influenced by Objectivist ethics that consider the prioritisation of self-interest as a moral concept. In *The Virtue of Selfishness* Ayn Rand, the founder of the Objectivism philosophy, defended 'selfishness'. Rand argued that 'every living human is an end in himself, not the means to the ends or the welfare of others – and . . . man must live for his own sake'.[20] This makes self-interest a moral concept as it helps an individual achieve the sole and ultimate purpose of

16 Ibid.

17 AK Aldohni, 'The Bank that Rocked: Does the problem lie in the global business model of conventional banking?' in J Gray and O Akseli (eds), *Financial Regulation in Crisis?: The Role of Law and the Failure of Northern Rock* (Edward Elgar, 2011) 93–4.

18 HS Shin, 'Reflections on Modern Bank Runs: A Case Study of Northern Rock' (August 2008) 7–8 <https://www.princeton.edu/~hsshin/www/nr > accessed 15 January 2016.

19 J Kirkup, 'Northern Rock Executives to Get Bonuses after £1.4 billion Loss', *The Telegraph* (23 February 2009).

20 A Rand, *The Virtue of Selfishness: A New Concept of Egoism* (with additional articles by Nathaniel Branden, Penguin, 1964) 23.

his existence, namely his happiness, and it cannot be morally questionable unless it was contaminated by fraud or brutal force.[21] This was described by Rand as rational selfishness where an individual pursues the ultimate goal of any man's life that is his happiness while avoiding 'irrational whims'.[22]

Accepting that the relentless pursuit of personal interest is a virtue led executives in some of the banks that were bailed out by taxpayers' money in the UK to pay themselves handsomely while the share price of their institutions was falling significantly in the market.[23] Such conduct shows no concern even with the self-interest of the institution represented by its shareholders, let alone any concern with wider social interest. Quite the reverse; it is a clear manifestation of the type of self-interest pursuit advocated by Objectivists, such as Ayn Rand, where the person is the end and his personal happiness is the ultimate goal irrespective of the effects on others.

It must be noted that the type of self-interest drive that was uncovered by the 2008 crisis even pushed Rand's acceptable moral boundaries. The LIBOR scandal showed that traders' pursuit of their personal gains was largely tainted by fraudulent submissions of prices. In this regard, Rand made it clear that the use of fraud in the selfish pursuit of personal happiness would make it morally questionable.

The second unhealthy trait is the lack of mechanisms that hold individuals accountable for fulfilling the long-term commitments of their institutions and for the long-term consequences of their actions. As transpired post 2008, the executives of most of the failing financial institutions were handsomely rewarded through the remuneration system for their (deceptive) short-term success. However, there was hardly any retribution for the long-term damages caused by their short-sighted strategies.[24]

It is important to note that the significant danger posed by this new business ethos, and its unhealthy features, lies in its ability to gradually erode some of the fundamental ethical foundations of financial business, such as honesty, trust and responsibility, to the point where they are no longer enshrined in business culture. This leads to the million-dollar question: what can be done about the erosion of the ethical foundations of the financial sector in the UK market?

This chapter aims to address this question through examining the process in which the corrupt ethos of the financial business can be contained and the ethical foundations of the financial business can be re-enshrined.

21 Ibid 20. See also DW Snyder Belousek, 'Greenspan's Folly: The Demise of the Cult of Self-Interest', *America Magazine* (30 March 2009).

22 Rand (n 20) 25.

23 It is reported that staff in the Royal Bank of Scotland (RBS) were paid £588 million in bonuses despite suffering an £8.24 billion loss in 2013 when the share price fell 6.7%. Also in 2014 RBS staff were handed out £421 million in bonuses despite suffering £3.5 billion loss and RBS shares slipped 4.4%. See S Farrell, 'RBS Pays Out £588m In Bonuses Despite Suffering £8.24bn Loss', *The Guardian* (27 February 2014); J Treanor, 'RBS Paid Out £421m in Bonuses in 2014 Despite £3.5bn Loss', *The Guardian* (26 February 2015).

24 Parliamentary Commission on Banking Standards, 'Changing Banking for Good – Volume I: Summary, Conclusion and Recommendations' (June 2013) 9.

In pursuing this objective this chapter argues that the ethical finance sector in the UK may well be the solution or part of the solution to the ethical concerns; however, such presumption should be addressed with caution considering that some of the ethical financial institutions in the UK market were not immune to the influence of the new corrupt business ethos. The second part of this chapter investigates the meaning of ethical finance and its relevance to the challenges posed by the new business ethos of the financial sector. It also surveys the ethical finance sector in the UK market. The third part provides a critical assessment of the potential contribution of the ethical finance sector in the UK to the solution to the financial business corrupt ethos problem. The chapter concludes by highlighting the challenges and prospects of the ethical finance sector in the UK.

## Surveying the ethical finance sector in the UK financial market

Before examining the layout of the ethical finance sector in the UK, and its relevance to the challenge posed by the corrupt new financial business ethos, it is important to understand what ethical finance means. In this regard, it has been suggested that finance is only a tool to serve an end; therefore, what differentiates ethical finance from other forms of finance is the way in which this tool is used and the end that it is achieving. Ethical finance aims to use this tool in a 'collective and supportive' manner in order to spread the benefits of the gains obtained by its operations.[25] As for the ends it serves, ethical finance institutions make it clear that their investment decisions are based on non-economic as much as economic considerations.[26] This means that their allocation of finance aims primarily to promote the social and environmental context in which they operate and that monetary gains are not their ultimate objective.

It is clear that what ethical finance stands for captures some of the key ethical foundations of the financial business, such as responsibility and trust, which the financial sector no longer has. Therefore, it comes as no surprise that ethical finance is considered as the solution or part of the solution to what the Archbishop of Canterbury, Justin Welby, describes as the 'cultural contamination' in the financial business in the UK. The Archbishop stressed the need to reintroduce ethical values into the vision of the financial industry as part of the solution to the problem.[27]

These views have also been echoed by the Governor of the Bank of England, Mark Carney, who has spoken on a number of occasions about the lack of public confidence in the financial sector and the clear sense of mistrust among its

25 I Palmisano, 'Thematic Guide 1: Introduction to Ethical Finance and Responsible Investments' (Promoting Responsible Investment and Commerce in Europe – the PRICE project, 2014) 4 <http://ideasfactorybg.org/ifactory/wp-content/uploads/2015/02/IntroFinanceIng.pdf?iframe=true&width=100%&height=100%> accessed 10 June 2016.

26 A Baranes, 'Towards Sustainable and Ethical Finance' (2009) 52(3) *Development* 417.

27 J Welby, 'The Future of Banking Standards and Ethics' (New City Agenda, House of Lords, Westminster, 17 June 2014) 3, 7 <http://www.archbishopofcanterbury.org/articles.php/5353/archbishops-lecture-on-the-future-of-banking-standards> accessed 15 January 2016.

participants due to the systemic nature of the misconduct that took place in the financial market in the run-up to the 2008 financial crisis.[28] For Mr Carney the reinvigoration of the ethical dimension of financial business is also an essential part of reinstalling confidence in it.[29] In this regard, the Bank of England has already taken some formal steps to achieve this objective, such as the establishment of the Banking Standards Review Council (BSRC),[30] whose main mandate is to 'work with banks and encourage a process of continuous improvement, and regularly assess and disclose the performance of each bank under the three broad headings of culture, competence and development of the workforce, and outcomes for customers'.[31]

### *The key ethical finance players in the UK financial market*

The landscape of the ethical financial sector in the UK is very diverse as there are different types of ethical financial institutions that operate in the UK financial market. One of the very early pioneering institutions in this respect is the Co-operative Bank.

The genesis of the Co-operative Bank can be found in the establishment of the Rochdale Equitable Pioneers Society as a retail society by 28 working men in 1844. Later, other retail societies followed the Rochdale Equitable Pioneers Society footstep and eventually they formed the foundation of the Co-operative movement.[32] The Co-operative Wholesale Society (CWS) was created in 1863, as a result of the amalgamation of these retail societies, in which the Co-operative Bank was initially established as the CWS Loan and Deposit Department,[33] providing banking services to the other CWS departments and retail members. The actual birth of the Co-operative Bank as we know it today came in 1971 when the CWS Loan and Deposit Department was registered as a separate, wholly owned subsidiary of the CWS and started to offer its banking services to the public.[34]

The emergence of the Co-operative Bank out of the Co-operative movement

28 M Carney, 'Building Real Markets for the Good of the People' (Lord Mayor's Banquet for Bankers and Merchants of the City of London at the Mansion House, 10 June 2015) 4 <http://www.bankofengland.co.uk/publications/Documents/speeches/2015/speech821.pdf> accessed 15 January 2016.

29 M Carney, 'Inclusive Capitalism: Creating a Sense of the Systemic' (Conference on Inclusive Capitalism, London, 27 May 2014) 8 <http://www.bankofengland.co.uk/publications/Documents/speeches/2014/speech731.pdf> accessed 15 January 2016.

30 The BSRC was launched in 2014 and is funded by the UK's largest seven lenders. See ibid 9. See also S Goff, 'Sir Richard Lambert launches UK Banking Standards Council', *Financial Times* (19 May 2014); Emma Dunkley, 'Treasury Official to Lead UK Banking Standards Council', *Financial Times* (13 January 2015).

31 Carney (n 29) 9–10.

32 B Harvey, 'Ethical Banking: The Case of the Co-operative Bank' (1995) (14) 12 *Journal of Business Ethics* 1006.

33 The Co-operative Group, 'Our History' <http://www.co-operative.coop/corporate/aboutus/ourhistory/> accessed 18 January 2016.

34 Ibid. See also Harvey (n 32).

in the UK has had a significant impact on its business strategy. Since the bank started offering its banking services to the wider public, it has always made its investment decisions with the wider societal interest in mind; hence, the bank has never been driven only by profits generation. A clear manifestation of the Co-operative Bank's wider societal commitments can be seen in its decision not to invest in certain lucrative industries, such as tobacco and cigarette manufacturing, and arms manufacturing and its export trade, due to their long-term adverse effect on societies. Also, as a manifestation of its human rights commitment, the bank refuses to deal with oppressive regimes or governments.[35]

Further, in implementing its socially responsible business agenda the Co-operative Bank has taken proactive steps to promote social and economic development in Britain, which entails supporting charities, credit unions and community finance initiatives. For instance, around 60 per cent of the credit union sector relies on the Co-operative Bank for its banking facilities.[36] The bank also supports initiatives that help finance small businesses and social enterprises that focus on the promotion of local economies and the creation of employment opportunities within the local communities.[37]

The bank's ethical policies are enshrined in its constitution as stated in its articles of association. It should be noted that the ethical finance movement, in general, has evolved over the years and its ethical agenda has consequently expanded to include a wider range of socially concerning issues beyond issues such as gambling and tobacco.[38] For instance, the Co-operative ethical policy now has a clear environmental focus. Also, the ethical agenda of other financial institutions now includes cultural objectives in addition to their environmental commitments.

The Co-operative Bank is not the only fully fledged ethical bank operating in the UK market; there are a number of others, among which is Triodos Bank. This Bristol-based bank is a Dutch ethical bank that opened its UK first branch in 1995. The ethical focus of Triodos is sustainability; as such, the bank's business strategy is based on promoting the quality of life for the members of the communities in which the bank operates through investing in those communities. Triodos has a number of ways to execute this business strategy. First, it provides finance to 'microfinance banks in developing countries, innovative fair trade enterprises and social housing providers'.[39] Second, it expands the sustainability focus of its business agenda to include investments in culture and environment. This covers a range of cultural activities and welfare initiatives (schools, medical centres) and sustainable environmental enterprises (renewable energy and organic farming).[40]

35 Harvey (n 32).

36 The Co-operative Bank, 'Our Ethical Policy'<https://www.co-operativebank.co.uk/assets/pdf/bank/aboutus/ethicalpolicy/ethical-policy.pdf > accessed 18 January 2016.

37 Ibid.

38 H Chelawat and IV Trivedi, 'Ethical Finance: Trends and Emerging Issues for Research' (2013) (2)2 *International Journal of Business Ethics and Developing Economies* 34.

39 Triodos Bank <https://www.triodos.co.uk/en/about-triodos/> accessed 20 January 2016.

40 Triodos Bank, 'Lending Strategy' <https://www.triodos.co.uk/en/about-triodos/what-we-do/lending-strategy/> accessed 20 January 2016.

Given the sustainability focus of its business agenda Triodos has no option but to align its finance activities with the real economy. This not only prevents profit generation from becoming the ultimate aim of its business but also influences its business model. Accordingly, Triodos relies on a diverse investment portfolio made of tangible commodities (energy, food and real estates).[41] More importantly, it is prevented from using the lending model of other conventional banks that is based on originate-to-distribute.[42] Instead, Triodos maintains a direct relationship with its investments.[43] These important factors, which are connected to its sustainability agenda, protected Triodos from exposure to the market volatility in 2007/08 that affected complicated securities, such as mortgage-backed securities in the sub-prime mortgage crisis. They also ensured that the bank's growth was not slowed down by the 2008 financial crisis.[44]

It must be noted that the treatment of profit as a means to an end rather than an end in itself lies at the heart of the Triodos sustainable banking strategy. This is not to say that profitability is not an important factor in any investment the bank makes; however, its significance from Triodos' point of view stems only from its use to maximise social, environmental and cultural sustainability.[45] Therefore, the bank designed its lending criteria on the basis of a 'self-consciously positive approach'. This means that primarily it assesses an investment's contribution to a more sustainable society and only then measures its negative impact in this respect.[46] In other words, in the decision-making process, meeting financial and commercial objectives is considered by Triodos as important as the objectives of creating social, cultural and environmental added value in order to achieve real and meaningful benefits to the wider community.[47]

There is also another type of ethically oriented financial institution that provides banking services in the UK market without being a bank, namely mutual organisations such as building societies and credit unions.

The ideas and values of credit unions have their origins in the corporate movement, with Robert Owen being one of the main pioneers in the UK in this respect.[48] However, compared to the United States, Canada and Ireland, credit unions in the UK needed some time before they took off.[49] Given their roots in the co-operative movement, credit unions are owned and controlled by their

41 Triodos Bank, 'Our Sustainable Banking Expert' <https://www.triodos.co.uk/en/about-triodos/what-we-do/our-expertise/sustainable-banking/our-susb-expert/> accessed 20 January 2016.

42 Making loans with the intention of converting them into securities (i.e. originating them by issuing debt instruments) and selling them to other financial institutions.

43 Triodos Bank (n 41).

44 Ibid.

45 Ibid.

46 Triodos Bank, 'Lending Criteria' <https://www.triodos.co.uk/downloads/our-approach-to-lending.pdf> accessed 20 January 2016.

47 Ibid.

48 Association of British Credit Unions Limited (ABCUL), 'The History of Credit Unions' <http://www.abcul.org/credit-unions/history-world-facts> accessed 11 June 2016.

49 Ibid.

members and are not-for-profit financial institutions. The simple premise of their co-operative model is based on the idea that individuals can save together and lend to each other at a favourable rate of interest. However, there is the requirement that those individuals should have a 'common bond' that is geographical, associational or occupational. It has been suggested that the requirement of the common bond has an important role in strengthening the community element of these institutions.[50] The ethical dimension of these institutions can be seen not only in their co-operative model, which prevents them from prioritising profit maximisation, but also in the type of community that they serve. Credit unions are well known for their role in making finance available to those who are less financially able and who would otherwise resort to high cost short term credit (discussed in Chapter 4).[51]

Therefore, it can be seen that the financial welfare of their members is the key foundation of credit unions, whose objectives include using the members' savings for their mutual benefits, promoting thrift and educating and training their members to make better use of their money.[52]

With regards to building societies, given their mutual structure most of these institutions do not answer to shareholders because they are owned by their members/customers (savers and borrowers). Accordingly, their business decisions tend to prioritise the interests of their members, which eventually brings prosperity to the local community in which the members are based and creates a special bond between the institution and the local community.[53] Therefore, it is not surprising that some of these institutions, for instance the Coventry, Cumberland and Ecology Building Societies, were recently featured in the *Ethical Consumer* magazine guide to ethical banking, occupying top positions.[54] The ethical agenda

50 Timothy Edmonds, 'Credit Unions' (House of Commons, Briefing Paper No 01034, January 2015) 4.

51 For more details with regard to the role of credit unions in the financial inclusion agenda, see D Fuller, 'Credit Union Development: Financial Inclusion and Exclusion' (1998) 29(2) *Geoforum* 145; D Fuller and AEG Jonas, 'Institutionalising Future Geographies of Financial Inclusion: National Legitimacy Versus Local Autonomy in the British Credit Union Movement' (2002) 34(1) *Antipode* 85; and AM Ward and DG Mckillop, 'An Investigation into the Link between UK Credit Union Characteristics, Location and their Success' (2005) 76(3) *Annals of Public and Cooperative Economics* 461.

52 HM Treasury, 'Call for Evidence: British Credit Unions at 50' (December 2014) <https://www.gov.uk/government/consultations/british-credit-unions-at-50-call-for-evidence/call-for-evidence-british-credit-unions-at-50> accessed 3 August 2016.

53 For example, see Coventry Building Society ('The Coventry') 'Genuinely Different' <http://www.coventrybuildingsociety.co.uk/your-society/genuinely-different.aspx#tabs-1> accessed 20 January 2016. The Coventry immerses its staff in the local communities by encouraging them to volunteer and work with community-based groups. See 'Community' <http://www.coventrybuildingsociety.co.uk/your-society/community.aspx> accessed 20 January 2016. See also Ecology Building Society, 'What We Believe' <http://www.ecology.co.uk/eco-difference/beliefs/> accessed 20 January 2016.

54 'Shopping guide to Banking Current Accounts, from Ethical Consumer', *Ethical Consumer* <http://www.ethicalconsumer.org/buyersguides/money/bankingcurrentaccounts.aspx> accessed 20 January 2016. And see also 'Shopping Guide to Savings Accounts, from Ethical

of these institutions may vary from one to another. Some have environmental focus, such as Ecology Building Society, where finance is used to provide mortgages to promote green building practices in order to create a greener society;[55] while the ethical agendas of others, such as the Coventry and Cumberland Building Societies, have a clear social orientation – hence, their investment decisions prioritise maximising the benefits of their local communities and their members. Regardless of the focus of their ethical agenda these building societies share two common features: first, they are not driven by profits generation; and, second, they only use their savers' money for their investments (i.e. no wholesale money market is accessed to finance their operations).

## Ethical finance and the 2008 financial crisis: the case of the UK financial market

As demonstrated earlier in this chapter, the widespread misconduct in the financial markets that largely contributed to the 2008 financial crisis was partly the result of a corrupt new business ethos, which fostered some unhealthy traits including self-interest and lack of accountability. Given that addressing the cultural contamination in the UK financial sector is an essential part of the response to the 2008 financial crisis, it is important to review the role that ethical finance may play in this respect. This requires examining whether the unhealthy traits of the financial business ethos have also corrupted the ethical finance sector in the UK, which would certainly undermine its contribution to solving the cultural contamination problem.

### *Ethical finance in the UK financial market: what went right?*

Earlier in this chapter it was established that ethical financial institutions have distinguished themselves from their counterparts through their structure or their business agenda, or even both.

It can be argued, therefore, that ethical financial institutions are better equipped to ensure that the selfish pursuit of financial gains by those running the business is not institutionally accommodated. This is a major problem that seems to have corrupted the majority of the participants in the UK financial market and contributed largely to the financial crisis of 2008.

Whether due to the mutual/cooperative business structure of some of these institutions, which means that there are no shareholders to prioritise, or because of their central social or environmental substratum, the self-interest ideology does not drive the business of ethical institutions. The type of ideology that the Objectivist ethics long defended proved to be a failure that brought disastrous

Consumer', *Ethical Consumer* <http://www.ethicalconsumer.org/buyersguides/money/banksavingsaccounts.aspx >accessed 20 January 2016.

55 Ecology Building Society, 'What We Believe' <http://www.ecology.co.uk/eco-difference/beliefs/> accessed 20 January 2016.

outcomes. One of Ayn Rand's inner circle members since the 1950s, Alan Greenspan, former Chairman of the Federal Reserve of the United States, stated before a congressional committee in 2008 that: 'Those of us who have looked to the self-interest of lending institutions to protect shareholders' equity, myself included, are in a state of shocked disbelief. . . . The whole intellectual edifice . . . collapsed last summer'.[56] He further admitted that he: 'made a mistake in presuming that the self-interests of organisations, specifically banks and others, were such that they were best capable of protecting their own shareholders and their equity in the firms'.[57] Although these statements were made with regard to the US financial markets, they also extend to other global financial markets including the UK where the same self-interest ideology was allowed to drive business, and as a result a wide range of malpractices took place.

Having said that, there is no doubt that ethical finance institutions are interested in making profits, but this does not make profits their only end. The structure of these institutions and/or their ethical agenda prevents their individuals from becoming driven by a selfish pursuit of financial gains at any cost. Instead, they aim to make profits while achieving their wider social, environmental and cultural objectives. Accordingly, profits become the means to their end. Therefore, they do not sell or invest in financial products that do not serve their customers, the local community in which they operate or their social and environmental commitments. For instance, the mutuality of the business model of some of the building societies has kept them close to the local communities in which they operate. Considering that they only have members (customer savers and borrowers) they have no option but to remain connected to the roots of those members by serving their communities instead of being driven by self-interest. Another added benefit of their mutual structure is that they are bound to be prudent with their lending decisions given that they only lend their savers' money. This prevents them from using the complicated financial products available on the wholesale money markets, and as a result it reduces the level of leveraging that drives short-term financial gains, which only benefit those running the business.

Further, the financial mediation of ethical financial institutions has two important features in this context. First, through mediating between savers and borrowers they create conditions that are communal to all individuals and help them realise their potential, while at the same time balancing this with their commitments to social and environmental sustainability. Second, their financial intermediation is based on linking finance with real productive economic activities, which serves as a means to achieve the personal good of the individuals involved while simultaneously advancing the wider social and environmental agenda of these institutions. For example, the sustainability agenda adopted by

56 A statement made before the House Committee on Oversight and Government Reform; cited in DW Snyder Belousek, 'Greenspan's Folly: The Demise of the Cult of Self-Interest', *America Magazine* (30 March 2009).

57 Cited by Andrew Clark and Jill Treanor, 'Greenspan – I was Wrong about the Economy. Sort of', *The Guardian* (24 October 2008).

Triodos Bank prevented it from getting involved in activities that are not connected to the real economy, including a range of speculative financial products that only profit traders without maximising social, environmental and cultural sustainability.

### *Ethical finance in the UK financial market: what went wrong?*

The 2008 financial crisis demonstrated how the lack of any form of accountability increases the self-interest drive of individuals and that unless those individuals are held accountable for any costs associated with their selfish pursuit of personal gains this unhealthy trait will continue to corrupt the UK financial market. Take, for example, the use of complicated/speculative financial products. These products handsomely rewarded bankers in the short run. However, in the long term they proved to be a complete failure resulting in high level of toxic debt and institutional deficit. Yet, those who widely traded these products and rendered their financial institutions nearly bankrupt remained unaccountable for their actions.

Having earlier considered how ethical financial institutions have certain mechanisms to contain the selfish pursuit of financial gains, it is essential to examine their success in implementing these processes and to measure the accountability of individuals with regard to the commitments of their institutions.

In this regard, it is evident at the outset that ethical finance has not been successful in dealing with the problem of unaccountability. The near collapse of the Co-operative Bank in 2013 was a major blow to the reputation of the ethical finance sector in the UK. There is no doubt that this scandal was not systemic in nature and only related to one institution, yet its significance stems from the origins of the problem and its effect on the ethical brand championed by the Co-operative Bank for many years.

It is important to note that the ethically questionable personal behaviour (drugs possession) of the Co-operative's former chairman, Paul Flowers, was not the reason for the Co-operative Bank's troubles in 2013. The Co-operative Bank was investigated by the Prudential Regulatory Authority (PRA) and the Financial Conduct Authority (FCA) with regard to prudential issues and governance concerns.[58] Eventually, instead of receiving a substantial fine for serious risk management and transparency failings, the regulator decided to publicly censure the bank. One of the most troubling findings of the PRA, for the purpose of the discussion here, was the fact that 'Co-op Bank had a culture which encouraged prioritising the short-term financial position of the firm at the cost of taking prudent and sustainable actions for the longer-term'.[59] Additionally, the FCA

58 HM Treasury, 'Chancellor Confirms Independent Inquiry into Events at Co-Op Bank' (22 November 2013) <https://www.gov.uk/government/news/chancellor-confirms-independent-inquiry-into-events-at-co-op-bank> accessed 20 January 2016.

59 Bank of England, 'PRA censures Co-operative Bank for Serious Risk Management and Transparency Failings' (11 August 2015) <http://www.bankofengland.co.uk/publications/Pages/news/2015/066.aspx> accessed 20 January 2016.

found that the Co-operative Bank published misleading information regarding its capitalisation for the period 21 March 2013 to 17 June 2013.[60]

The findings of the investigations show that the Co-operative Bank was prioritising short-term financial gains, which is the exact same practice that led to the 2008 financial crash. In other words, the bank was not executing its business in line with its claimed ethical agenda, which required the bank to pursue long-term sustainable goals. The bank in this sense was no different from other banks that never claimed to have an ethical agenda beyond the self-interest of the institution or its individuals. However, with regard to the Co-operative Bank the issue of executives' compensation never came across as the drive behind this pursuit of short-term gains. Despite the importance of this difference it cannot be used as an excuse for jeopardising the bank's long-established ethical brand. Further, the integrity of the institution in general and its ethical claim more specifically was also badly damaged by its publication of misleading information in breach of the Listing Rules.

It can be argued, therefore, that these breaches boil down to a major flaw in the accountability mechanisms in the Co-operative Bank. Sir Christopher Kelly found in 'the report of the independent review into the events leading to the Co-operative Bank's capital shortfall' that the Co-operative Bank suffered from 'confused or diffused accountabilities in a number of important areas'.[61]

It is important to note that it is not suggested here that because the Co-operative Bank has had a major accountability flaw then all ethical financial institutions suffer or will suffer from the problem of unaccountability similar to all other mainstream banks. Instead, the main argument to be made here is that installing the mechanisms required to deal with the problem of the selfish pursuit of financial gains does not automatically and on its own improve the accountability culture within ethical finance institutions. Therefore, it is vital for ethical finance institutions to be equally concerned with ensuring the ability of their governance systems to hold those in charge accountable for undermining the institution's ethical commitments.

In this regard, in order to reassure its customers about its ethical brand the Co-operative Bank has taken a number of steps to respond to this challenge. First, the bank 'codified values and ethical policies in the Bank's constitution by writing reference to them into [its] Articles of Association'. Second, the bank 'established a new, independently chaired Values and Ethics Committee as a subcommittee of the bank's Board to ensure accountability for values and ethics'.[62] There is no doubt that these steps show that the Co-operative Bank is committed

60 Financial Conduct Authority, 'The Financial Conduct Authority censures the Co-operative Bank for Listing Rules Breaches and Failing to Be Open with the Regulator' (11 August 2015) <http://www.fca.org.uk/news/fca-censures-the-co-operative-bank-for-listing-rules-breaches> accessed 20 January 2016.

61 Sir C Kelly, 'Failings in Management and Governance: Report of the Independent Review into the Events Leading to the Co-Operative Bank's Capital Shortfall' (30 April 2014) 9.

62 The Co-operative Bank, 'Our Ethical Policy' <https://www.co-operativebank.co.uk/assets/pdf/bank/aboutus/ethicalpolicy/ethical-policy.pdf> accessed 20 January 2016.

to remain on its ethical path; however, their effectiveness in addressing the unaccountability problem remains to be tested.

## Conclusion: ethical finance in the UK, challenges and prospects

The post-mortem of the 2008 financial crisis in the UK showed that a key factor in the failures of 2008 was the disconnection between finance and the real world. In other words, financial institutions became less interested in real productive economic activities given that they were primarily investing in ever more complicated financial products existing only on trading platforms in wholesale money markets.[63] This was predominantly driven by two key elements that corrupted the financial sector and led to its downfall: first, the self-interested pursuit of financial gains, with financial products only being offered short term and to a very exclusive elite; second, the lack of any accountability for fulfilling the commitments of their institutions and for the long-term effect of their actions.

The level of cultural contamination in the financial sector that was uncovered by the 2008 financial crisis has brought focus to its underlying corrupt ethos and the need to re-enshrine some key ethical foundations such as prudence, responsibility and trust. This is where ethical finance comes into play, especially since its underlying foundation stands at odds with the mainstream – no longer desirable – ideology, which suggests that this sector has the potential to grow and play an important role in addressing the cultural contamination problem.

In this regard, when it came to dealing with the selfish pursuit of personal gains ethical finance institutions operating in the UK did not disappoint. Ethical finance participants in the UK market have made creating social, environmental and cultural value their ultimate objective. Accordingly, profit has become a by-product and a means to achieve better ends. It can be suggested, therefore, that having such an ethical agenda plays a crucial role in containing the selfish pursuit of financial gains, which contaminated the business ethos and largely contributed to the 2008 financial crisis.

As for the challenges that face the ethical finance industry in the UK, as argued earlier in this chapter the problem of unaccountability represents the most significant challenge that the industry should address head-on in order to avoid losing its very unique selling point, that is its ethical brand. As demonstrated in the crisis of the Co-operative Bank, adopting an ethical agenda that addresses the self-interest ideology problem is not enough on its own to ensure its effective application. Ethical finance institutions should ensure that their governance systems are capable of holding those in charge accountable for fulfilling the institution's ethical commitments. This is an area where the Co-operative Bank has failed significantly, and as a response, it has decided to establish a Values and Ethics Committee as a subcommittee of the bank's Board to ensure accountability. It is a welcome step but its effectiveness is still to be tested. In any case, the forms in

63 B Davis, 'Can Ethical Finance Break Through to the Mainstream?' (2015) August–September *The European Financial Review* 31.

which this could be achieved are a subject that requires significant research and goes beyond the remit and the capacity of this chapter.

With regard to the prospects of the ethical finance sector in the UK there are a few key points that can be made. It can be argued that the UK ethical finance sector has a real opportunity to join the mainstream and stop being a niche sector; this is primarily because the gap between these two forms of finance is supposed to shrink.

On the one hand, there is a political will to positively change mainstream finance in the UK and make the sector more caring and so bring ethical standards more into mainstream. Among a number of initiatives to help effect this change the Banking Standards Review Council was established to look into the banks' behaviour, their culture and effects on customers. This means that banks will have to improve their culture and customers' outcomes. This can be achieved if self-interest and short-term financial gains are no longer the sole drive of the banking business.

Further, the government has taken a special interest in empowering credit unions as 'the only other realistic option' to serve low income consumers.[64] However, the current organisational and business structure was found to be an obstacle and would need to be modernised in order for credit unions to stand as a sustainable, credible and effective source of finance to individuals on low income. Therefore, the government took a number of steps in this respect. First, the Department of Work and Pension (DWP) in May 2012 launched the 'DWP Credit Union Expansion Project', the feasibility study of which examined 'the sustainability of credit unions' and 'what more can be done to expand them to serve many more people on lower incomes'.[65] In April 2013 the government awarded the Association of British Credit Unions Ltd (ABCUL) the contract (worth £38 million) to deliver DWP's Credit Union Expansion Project in order to modernise and grow credit unions.[66] The project was planned to end in April 2016; however, a request has been made for a further extension which is, at the time of writing this chapter, under government consideration.[67] Given that the modernisation project is not yet complete it is difficult to assess its effectiveness. Nonetheless, it is fair to suggest that by investing in credit unions the government has taken an important step to promote financial institutions, which have the wider interest of society in mind. Credit unions are 'strongly embedded in their local communities and are committed to assisting those on low incomes' and 'often appeal to low income consumers as bodies which are local, accessible and convenient and which are community based'.[68] Second, as of 1 April 2014

64 DWP Credit Union Expansion Project, Project Steering Committee, Feasibility Study Report (May 2012) 4 <http://webarchive.nationalarchives.gov.uk/20130102224139/http:/www.dwp.gov.uk/docs/credit-union-feasibility-study-report.pdf > accessed 10 June 2016.

65 DWP announcement in the House of Commons; cited in T Edmonds, House of Commons Library, 'Credit Unions' Briefing Paper' (No 01034, 5 January 2015) 30.

66 DWP, 'Credit union £38 million expansion deal signed' (16 April 2016).

67 UK Parliament, 'Credit Union: Written Question–11604' (19 October 2015).

68 Sajid Javid, the then Economic Secretary to the Treasury; cited in Edmonds (n 65) 32.

the government introduced a statutory change to section 11(5) of the Credit Union Act 1979 that allowed credit unions to charge interest up to 3 per cent per month (i.e. 42.6 per cent APR).[69] This 1 per cent increase was specifically brought to ensure that credit unions do not make a loss when they lend short-term small loans (up to £1,000) which improves their ability to provide this type of credit.[70]

On the other hand, investors in the UK and around the globe learned that short-term quick gains come at an expensive cost in the long run. Therefore, the business of ethical finance institutions could hugely benefit from the sobering experience of 2008 and its unfolding events. Those who are looking for a sustainable outcome that is 'a combination of financial and ethical return'[71] can rightly find ethical finance as a real alternative for their investments. Additionally, the UK market is very well equipped to empower this sector. The Ethical Investment Research Services (EIRIS) has long been established in the UK, since 1983, to provide the most needed research and information on the available responsible investments.[72]

To sum up, the ethical finance sector in the UK seems to have a real opportunity not only to help deal with the cultural contamination problem but also to grow its share of the market if only the sector can effectively address the problem of unaccountability, which is a very challenging task.

69 The Financial Services and Markets Act 2000 (Regulated Activities) (Amendment) (No 2) Order 2013 (SI 2013/1881) (art 6); and see also HM Treasury, 'Raising the maximum interest rate cap: response to consultation' (June 2013) 12.

70 HM Treasury, 'Credit union maximum interest rate cap' (December 2012) 9 <https://www.gov.uk/government/uploads/system/uploads/attachment_data/file/221917/credit_union_maximum_interest_rate_cap181212.pdf >.

71 Davis (n 63).

72 Robert M Burlando, 'Ethical Finance: Its Achievements in Great Britain and Italy' (2001) 56(4) *World Futures* 376; and see also EIRIS <http://www.eiris.org/> accessed 26 April 2016.

# 7 SMEs and access to finance: a vulnerability perspective

*Orkun Akseli*

## Introduction

The global financial crisis has highlighted the vulnerability of small businesses[1] in economic downturns, particularly in relation to access to finance. It has become clear that, at such times, the law of credit and security does not enable small businesses to find effective solutions.[2] This is problematic in light of the role of small businesses in economic growth and social renewal at times of economic crisis. The limited availability and the cost of credit make small businesses vulnerable to market uncertainties caused by financial crisis.[3] Finance to small businesses is generally refused on the grounds that they are new to the market, insufficiently profitable or cannot provide acceptable collateral. Small businesses present certain distinctive problems for lenders in terms of lending. These challenges include low capitalisation, small size, varied profitability and growth in the market, problems of information asymmetry and monitoring (difficulties with differentiating the financial position of business from the owner's financial standing), low credit rating, relatively weak bargaining power, dependency on external finance and credit (which becomes acute at times of recession and financial crisis), and inability to access financial markets.[4] Research conducted post 2008 financial crisis has revealed that banks' criterion for lending is based on the size of the firm, which indicates that micro-businesses (0–9 employees) have been most vulnerable to access to finance. Furthermore, it was also pointed out that the demand

1 There is no agreed definition of small and medium-sized enterprises (SMEs). The term has been further diversified as small firms, medium-sized firms and micro firms. See p 120 below. Therefore, as an umbrella terminology 'small businesses' and 'SMEs' will be used interchangeably in this chapter in order to differentiate them from large firms.

2 See e.g. 'Secured Transactions Law: The Case for Reform' <http://securedtransactionsproject.wordpress.com/case-for-reform/> accessed 20 September 2015. For example in England the secured transactions law regime is restrictive in the sense that unincorporated businesses and SMEs feel that they need to incorporate as companies in order to create a charge and access to secured credit.

3 For the effects of market liberalisation on development and SMEs, see e.g. JA Ocampo and JE Stiglitz (eds), *Capital Market Liberalization and Development* (Oxford University Press, 2008).

4 See OECD Centre for Entrepreneurship, SMEs and Local Development, *The SME Financing Gap Theory and Evidence volume 1*, 17–19 (OECD Publishing, 2006).

for and supply of credit during the recession period fell and credit rationing affected 119,000 small businesses where credit was denied.[5] However, there is a justifiable widespread view that facilitating small businesses' access to finance may support economic growth[6] and contribute to social mobility and renewal. The failure of small businesses may not only have individual consequences (e.g. personal bankruptcies of employees and members of businesses) but also universal repercussions (e.g. failure of economies and decline in economic growth).

The majority of world trade relies on credit supplied by banks and financial institutions to small businesses. Small businesses account for about 90 per cent of businesses worldwide with 50 per cent of employment around the world[7] and 58 per cent in the UK by employing 13.5 million people.[8] However, they experience particular difficulties in raising finance.[9] Unlike large businesses, they are usually only able to borrow on a secured basis.[10] Yet, they play an important role in securing economic growth and social renewal. From an Ordoliberal perspective, at times of financial crisis the state must assume its pragmatic duties to ensure that markets achieve their maximum capacity to fulfil their theoretical foundations. This argument suggests that as a political task the state needs to establish and sustain measures for the entrepreneurial cohesion of society. Therefore, the responsibility of the state is to establish a financial and legal framework that understands the barriers to access to finance, and either addresses those barriers or enables small businesses to negotiate them.

Since the 2008 financial crash several national and international policy documents and empirical publications on the effect of financial crisis on small businesses and the pathways to access to finance have been published.[11] However,

5 M Cowling, W Liu and A Ledger, 'Small Business Financing in the UK before and during the current financial crisis' (2012) 30 *International Small Business Journal* 778, 794–5.

6 See generally e.g. 'SME Access to External Finance' (BIS Economics Paper No 16, Department for Business Innovation and Skills, January 2012); T. Beck, A. Demirguc-Kunt and R. Levine, 'SMEs, Growth and Poverty' Working Paper No 11224, National Bureau of Economic Research, March 2005); T Beck, A Demirguc-Kunt, L Laeven and R Levine, 'Finance, Firm Size and Growth' (Working Paper No 10983, National Bureau of Economic Research, December 2004).

7 IFC Issue Brief, 'IFC and Small and Medium Sized Enterprises' (2012) <http://www.ifc.org/wps/wcm/connect/277d1680486a831abec2fff995bd23db/AM11IFC+IssueBrief_SME.pdf?MOD=AJPERES> accessed 20 September 2015. In the OECD area small businesses account for 99% of all enterprises and employ half of the work force. See OECD Centre for Entrepreneurship, SMEs and Local Development, *The Impact of the Global Crisis on SME and Entrepreneurship Financing and Policy Responses* (OECD Publishing, 2009) 6.

8 Federation of Small Businesses, 'Number Crunching the Credit Crunch' <http://www.fsb.org.uk/frontpage/assets/credit%20crunch%20figures.pdf> accessed 26 February 2014).

9 EU Survey, 'SMEs' Access to Finance' (2013) <http://ec.europa.eu/enterprise/policies/finance/data/index_en.htm#h2-1> accessed 27 September 2015. For results of surveys taken in 2009, 2011 and August to October 2013, see particularly Memo, 'Joint Commission/ECB Report: Access to Finance and Finding Customers the most pressing problems for SMEs' (Brussels, 14 November 2013).

10 The Law Commission, 'Company Security Interests A Consultative Report' (Consultation Paper No176) (2004) xiv.

11 For example Department for Business Innovation and Skills, 'Small Business Survey 2012: SME Employers' (April 2013); Department for Business, Innovation and Skills, 'SME Access to Finance

legal doctrinal analysis of small businesses' access to finance from the lens of vulnerability has been sparse.[12] It can be argued that there is a legal theoretical gap that does not allow the conceptualisation of small businesses' vulnerability to financial crisis and market changes and their role in social renewal. Although conceptualising small businesses' vulnerability to market volatilities and financial crisis would have a significant positive impact on our understanding as to their role in economic growth, the existing legal literature seems to have largely ignored this important aspect of the subject.

In this regard, this chapter particularly focuses on one of the main implicit effects of the 2008 crisis on the UK financial market, that is the shortage of funding for SMEs. The chapter highlights the importance of SMEs in the process of economic recovery in the UK and examines their vulnerable positon at this current stage. It investigates the limited access to finance problem from a legal and regulatory perspective and provides an in-depth critical legal analysis of how this problem can be addressed. The legal context of access to finance provides an optimal lens through which to explore questions of vulnerability and resilience of small businesses, the role and responsibilities of the state in responding to the risks to which vulnerable businesses are exposed in the aftermath of the financial crisis and the implications of being vulnerable to market volatilities in terms of social renewal.

The chapter begins by defining the 'small business'. Then, it continues by examining vulnerability and access to finance. In this context, first, vulnerability of small businesses will be discussed. Its philosophical foundations, the significance of small businesses and access to finance and their challenges in this process will be examined. The discussion in this part asks what makes small businesses vulnerable in access to finance, why and how they are vulnerable and the law's role in making them more resilient. It is argued that the essential starting point must shift from a desire to fund them only at times of crisis to an analysis of why they are vulnerable and why they need to be financed. This will require conceptualisation of vulnerability in the light of access to finance. In doing so,

Schemes – Measures to support SME Growth' (April 2013); OECD Centre for Entrepreneurship, SMEs and Local Development (n 7); A Cosh and A Hughes, *British Enterprise: Thriving or Surviving?* (ESRC Centre for Business Research, 2007); Department for Business Innovation and Skills, 'Results from the 2009 finance survey of SMEs' (2010) <http://webarchive.nationalarchives.gov.uk/20121212135622/http://www.bis.gov.uk/assets/biscore/enterprise/docs/10-636-2009-finance-survey-smes-results> accessed 20 September 2015; Business Finance Taskforce, 'Supporting UK Businesses: The report of the UK Business Finance Taskforce' (British Bankers Association, 2010) <https://www.betterbusinessfinance.co.uk/images/pdfs/Business_Finance_Taskforce_report.pdf> accessed 20 September 2015.

12 See e.g. J Freedman, 'Small Businesses and the Corporate Form: Burden or Privilege?' (1994) 57(4) *Modern Law Review* 555; M Hesselink, 'SMEs in European Contract Law' in K Boele-Woelki and W Grosheide (eds), *The Future of European Contract Law: Essays in Honour of Ewoud Hondius* (Kluwer, 2007) 349; RJ Mokal, 'Priority as Pathalogy: The Pari Passu myth' (2001) 60(3) *Cambridge Law Journal* 581, 587 et seq.; J Armour, 'The Law and Economics Debate About Secured Lending: Lessons for European Lawmaking' in H Eidenmüller and E-M Kieninger (eds), *The Future of Secured Credit in Europe: European Company and Financial Law Review* (De Gruyter Recht, 2008) 3.

the chapter will explain why small businesses need to be protected, their weak bargaining positions, issues of information asymmetry and monitoring and, more philosophically, their role in social renewal and improvement of social well-being. While the analysis will focus on the vulnerability of small businesses, it is axiomatic that lenders also have vulnerabilities in their dealings with small businesses and these will be flagged up as brief comparisons during the analysis. Conclusions will summarise the arguments.

## What is a small business?

It is crucial to define 'small business'. SME and small business are terms that are used interchangeably in policy discussion and debates to distinguish them from large firms. The importance of defining 'small business' lies in the fact that once an enterprise is classified as a 'small business', it benefits from specific policies and programmes geared towards small businesses. A small business also qualifies for government assistance, state aid or loans (for example, in the UK through the 'Funding for Lending' scheme), which are not generally available to large firms or companies that can borrow widely on a secured or unsecured basis from banks. However, surprisingly, there is no universal definition of a small business. The difficulty with providing a universal definition of small business can be attributed to a number of factors. Every economy has different levels of development. While it is understandable that international organisations' definition of small business works for their aim at providing financial support to underprivileged areas and sectors (as small businesses in those economies are relatively much smaller or more modest in size and turnover), the same definition generally does not suit the domestic markets of economically developed nations. In addition to the annual turnover and the number of employees, the business culture, the business sector that they operate in and the economic contribution of the SME in its home market are altogether decisive factors as to what should be defined as an SME.[13]

The EU has redefined[14] the scope of definition of small businesses in order to cover them under a single terminology.[15] Article 2, paragraph 1 of Commission Recommendation 2003/361/EC defines SMEs as follows:[16]

13 An independent formula for defining SMEs has been provided as follows: 'An SME is a formal enterprise with annual turnover, in US dollar terms, of between 10 and 1,000 times the *mean* per capita gross national income, at *purchasing power parity*, of the country in which it operates'. See T Gibson and HJ Van Der Vaart, 'Defining SMEs: A Less Imperfect Way of Defining Small and Medium Sized Enterprises in Developing Countries' (Brookings Global Economy and Development, September 2008).

14 For the introduction of a new definition of SME in the European Union see <http://ec.europa.eu/enterprise/enterprise_policy/sme_definition/sme_user_guide.pdf> accessed 5 September 2015.

15 For the significance of SMEs in European contract law, see MW Hesselink, 'SMEs in European Contract Law' (Briefing Note, Directorate General Internal Policies, Policy Department C Citizens Rights and Constitutional Affairs, IP/C/Juri/FWC/2007-211; PE378.300, June 2007).

16 Commission Recommendation 2003/361/EC of 6 May 2003 concerning the definition of micro, small and medium-sized enterprises (OJ 2003 L124/36). The first definition of SME was adopted

> enterprises which employ fewer than 250 persons and which have an annual turnover not exceeding EUR 50 million, and/or an annual balance sheet total not exceeding EUR 43 million.

According to this definition, number of employees and either turnover or balance sheet total are the two decisive factors in determining whether a company is qualified to be an SME. The European Commission's 'The New SME Definition User Guide and Model Declaration' discusses the grounds for adopting a new definition. These grounds aim at mitigating small businesses' vulnerability to market changes. They include: update of staff and financial thresholds to enable small businesses to retain their SME status; promotion of micro enterprises; improving access to capital by facilitating equity capital through government schemes, regional funds and venture capital companies; promotion of innovation and access to research and development; and prevention of abuse of small business status. This new definition may help small businesses to be considered as companies, which may assist them to obtain financing in the company level rather than partners' personal creditworthiness.[17]

Under the International Finance Corporation (IFC) frame SMEs are defined 'as registered businesses with less than 300 employees'.[18] While the IFC definition is basic, the working definition also indicates that the total annual sales or assets of an SME should not be more than $15 million.[19] While in the UK, in the early 1970s, the Bolton Committee[20] attempted to define small firms, the definition received criticism for being complex.[21] Under section 382(3) of the Companies Act 2006, a company qualifies to be a small company if two or more

in 1996 by the European Commission. Commission Recommendation 96/280/EC of 3 April 1996 concerning the definition of small and medium-sized enterprises (OJ L107/4).

17 'An Action Plan to improve access to finance for SMEs' (SEC(2011) 1427 final) COM(2011) 870 Final; 'Framework for the next generation of innovative financial instruments – the EU Equity and Debt Platforms' COM(2011) 662. A recent study in 2012 showed that there was no need for a major revision of the SME definition. See 'Final Report on Evaluation of the SME Definition' (September 2012) <file://tower7/home39/naka1/Downloads/executive-summary-evaluation-sme-definition_en.pdf> accessed 20 January 2016.

18 International Finance Corporation, 'Interpretation Note on Small and Medium Sized Enterprises and Environmental and Social Risk Management' (1 January 2012) 1 <http://www.ifc.org/wps/wcm/connect/de7d92804a29ffe9ae04af8969adcc27/InterpretationNote_SME_2012.pdf?MOD=AJPERES> accessed 20 November 2015). But cf International Finance Corporation, 'SMEs Small and Medium Enterprises' (2011) 5(1) *Telling Our Story* 3, where SMEs were defined as registered businesses with fewer than 250 employees.

19 International Finance Corporation, 'Interpretation Note' (n 18) 1.

20 JE Bolton, 'Report of the Committee of Enquiry on small firms' (*Bolton Report*) (Cmnd 4811) (HMSO, 1971). The definition suggested that small businesses had a small share in the market, managed by owners, and were independent. Additionally, the report qualified the definition by suggesting its economic contribution over time, its size and contribution to sectors and its comparison to other countries' small firms. The definition was used in a number of surveys in the 1970s. See e.g. Committee to Review the Functioning of Financial Institutions, 'Studies of Small Firms Financing Research Report No. 3' (1979).

21 The definition provided by the Bolton Committee was criticised on the grounds that the monetary indicators used in the definition are prone to change over time due to currency fluctuations, differ-

of the following conditions are met: its turnover is not more than £6.5 million; its balance sheet total is not more than £3.26 million; its number of employees is not more than 50. Additionally, according to the section 465(3) of the Companies Act 2006, a company qualifies to be a medium-sized company if two or more of the following conditions are met: its annual turnover is £25.9 million or less; the balance sheet is £12.9 million or less; the number of employees is 250 or less. Nevertheless, the definition of an SME in the UK adopted by the Department of Business, Innovation and Skills (BIS), in which the number of employees is the decisive factor, seems to define an SME as a business with fewer than 250 employees (0–249 employees).[22] In the United States, a firm is an SME if it has fewer than 500 employees. It must be noted, however, that different revenue indicators are applicable for different sectors.[23] By comparison, in Australia a small business is a business employing fewer than 15 employees.[24]

Thus, it can be argued that a simple, straightforward small business definition is not possible. Definitions differ according to the size and the strength of the economy of a country, the significance of the business sector and the contribution of the small business to that economy. For the purposes of the analysis here a small business is not defined by any absolute threshold in terms of turnover or employment but relatively as a firm small in staff and revenue compared to its product competitors, with the future potential to contribute to job creation, economic growth and export, and maintaining social renewal and mobility in the society, but being vulnerable to the withdrawal of external finance in a downturn. These types of organisations can be either partnerships or small companies engaged in export and import or manufacturing.

ent criteria for different sectors make the definition unnecessarily complex. See generally D Storey, *Understanding the Small Business Sector* (International Thomson Business Press, 1994).

22 This is the definition adopted by the Department for Business, Innovation and Skills: see 'Business Population Estimates for the UK and Regions 2013' (Department for Business, Innovation and Skills, 2013). There is also a definition prepared by the Law Commission to deal with non-negotiated unfair contract terms with small businesses. Section 27 of the draft Bill defines a 'small business' as follows:

> (1) 'Small business' means a person in whose business the number of employees does not exceed (a) nine, or (b) where the Secretary of State specifies by order another number for the purposes of this section, that number. (2) But a person is not a small business if adding the number of employees in his business to the number of employees in any other business of his, or in any business of an associated person, gives a total exceeding the number which for the time being applies for the purposes of subsection (1).

See the Law Commission and the Scottish Law Commission (Law Com No 292) (Scot Law Com No 199), 'Unfair Terms in Contracts Report on a Reference under Section 3(1)(e) of the Law Commissions Act 1965' (Cm 6464, 2005).

23 See 'Small and Medium-Sized Enterprise: Overview of participation in US Exports' (Investigation No 332–508, United States International Trade Commission Publication No 4125, January 2010) 1–3. Revenue threshold does not apply to manufacturing and non-export services firms; but for exporting services firms the threshold revenue is $7 to $25 million. For farms it is $250,000. See also <http://www.sba.gov/content/summary-size-standards-industry> accessed 20 September 2014.

24 Fair Work Act 2009, s 23.

## Defining 'vulnerability'

The word 'vulnerable' is defined as something 'that may be wounded; susceptible to injury, exposed to damage by weapon, criticism, etc'.[25] Robert Goodin suggests that '"vulnerability" is essentially a matter of being under the threat of harm [and] protecting the vulnerable is primarily a matter of forestalling threatened harms'.[26] Arguably, the 'susceptibility to injury' can be further extended in the context of SMEs to damages caused by the inability to access financial markets or external finance or to raise finance in general to increase resources to be able to survive in the face of market volatilities and financial crisis. The damage caused by the inability to access finance may include going bankrupt or out of business, not being able to expand resources or business (while it is accepted that not all businesses would prefer to expand business but rather prefer to stay as small businesses) and, on a more general basis, not being able to create employment.

Vulnerability within the context of small businesses' access to finance may be defined as inability to borrow or expand business, or, in the general perspective, continue to trade. It is clear that small businesses lack both power and entitlements,[27] which makes them vulnerable compared to financial institutions and larger firms. In that context, the effects of SMEs' limited or no access to finance and their inability to join in or influence effectively the decision-making process in terms of growth policies expose two specific areas of vulnerability. These are loss of business and loss of opportunity to efficiently influence socio-economic policies. The former includes two particular points. First, the loss may be internal, revealing problems of financing and insolvency issues. Second, it may be external, revealing problems of expansion for further investment. The latter directly influences concepts such as social renewal, social mobility and social cohesion.[28]

## Why are small businesses important?

The answer to this question depends on factors such as how developed the economy of that home market is, how the home market perceives the SME's sector, and how crucial is the type of sector in which the SME is operating to the economy of the home market.

It can be argued that globally SMEs are key players in economic development

25 The *Concise Oxford English Dictionary* (7th edn, Oxford University Press, 1983) 1205.

26 RE Goodin, *Protecting the Vulnerable: A Reanalysis of our Social Responsibilities* (University of Chicago Press, 1985) 110.

27 For reasons of poverty and lack of entitlements, see I Christoplos and J Farrington, 'The Issues' in I Christoplos and J Farrington (eds), *Poverty, Vulnerability, and Agricultural Extension* (Oxford University Press, 2004) 1, 3.

28 For the significant numbers of SMEs, see IFC (n 7) and Federation of Small Businesses (n 8).

and innovation.[29] They have an impact on job creation,[30] income[31] and growth in all economies.[32] They have also become internationalised due to their export of goods and services to overseas markets. The performance of SMEs has also been linked to the macro-economic performance of EU member states.[33] For all those reasons, SMEs have been widely publicised as the 'engines for growth'. It has also been argued that small businesses are instrumental in maintaining social mobility, social cohesion and social justice.[34] Social mobility occurs when the members of society move between different socio-economic layers in the society as a result of obtaining better legal, economic and political rights. It is argued that small businesses assist the process of social mobility by providing employment, entrepreneurship and business ownership and opportunities. Further, the creation of more SMEs may also assist social justice by closing gender inequality (by providing opportunities for entrepreneurship) and financing gaps caused by the financial crisis.[35]

29 K Morgan, 'The Learning Region: Institutions, Innovation and Regional Renewal' (1997) 31 *Regional Studies* 491, 492 et seq.

30 SMEs contribute to 67% of full-time and permanent employment worldwide and 85% to net employment growth. For SMEs' contribution to job creation, see e.g. J De Kok, P Vroonhof, W Verhoeven, N Timmermans, T Kwaak, J Snijders and F Westhof, 'Do SMEs create more and better jobs?' (EIM Business and Policy Research, November 2011); M Ayyagari, A Demirgüç-Kunt and V Maksimovic, 'Small vs. Young Firms Across the World – Contribution to Employment, Job Creation, and Growth' (Policy Research Working Paper No 5631, the World Bank Development Research Group, 2011).

31 According to studies SMEs contribute significantly to GDP between 15% in low income countries and more than 50% in high income countries. See e.g. M Ayyagari, T Beck and A Demirguc-Kunt, 'Small and Medium Enterprises Across the Globe' (World Bank Group, 2005) <http://siteresources.worldbank.org/DEC/Resources/84797-1114437274304/SME_globe.pdf> accessed 5 September 2015.

32 For more on these matters and the work of the International Finance Corporation (IFC) generally, see e.g. IFC, 'Telling Our Story: SMEs Small and Medium Enterprises' (volume 5, issue 1, IFC, 2011). See also generally OECD Centre for Entrepreneurship, SMEs and Local Development (n 7)). See <http://www.fsb.org.uk/stats> accessed 5 September 2015. According to the Federation and Small Business statistics (figures obtained from the Department of Business, Innovation and Skills), at the start of 2013 in the UK there were 4.9 million small businesses employing 24.3 million people and small businesses accounted for 59.3% of private sector employment.

33 See C Guglielmetti, 'Introduction' in B Dallago and C Guglielmetti (eds), *The Consequences of the International Crisis for European SMEs* (Routledge, 2012) 1.

34 See IFC, 'Strengthening Access to Finance for Women-owned SMEs in Developing Countries' (October 2011); IFC, 'Removing Barriers to Economic Inclusion Measuring Gender Parity in 141 Countries' (Women, Business and the Law, The World Bank and the International Finance Corporation, 2012); G Shapps, 'Small businesses can lead Britain back to prosperity', *The Guardian* (28 December 2013).

35 IFC, 'Strengthening Access to Finance' (n 34) 6, where it is noted 'because financing is an important means by which to pursue growth opportunities, addressing women entrepreneurs' specific needs in accessing finance must be part of the development agenda'.

## Vulnerability and resilience

In the aftermath of the financial crisis, small businesses have shown both *vulnerability* and *resilience* to the effects of the crisis. Their vulnerability is a result of 'intrinsic weaknesses of [small businesses] in facing external shocks'.[36] These weaknesses may be exemplified, from a corporate governance perspective, by weak knowledge of business or financial skills and lack of managerial skills that may be decisive during times of crisis. Smallbone et al. define vulnerability of small businesses as being 'highly susceptible to external shocks such as recession because of a number of size-related characteristics'.[37] These include limited internal resources compared to larger firms, limited line of products and customer base and less bargaining power[38] as well as the tendency, mainly, to rely on the bank credit rather than other financing patterns. Some small businesses have also shown 'resilience'[39] that reflects the small businesses' 'flexibility and capacity to adjust to external circumstances'.[40] Resilience, thus, suggests the ability to adjust or adapt to market volatilities or recover fast from the effects of systemic failure of financial markets. In the context of access to finance, for a small business, resilience may mean the existence of alternative financing arrangements (be it retained profits or non-bank financing) other than bank credit (which may be sparse at times of financial crisis) and the ability to obtain finance which enables the small business to continue its trading. Adaptation seems to be the crucial point when it comes to possible legal and financial reactions to the predicted global financial and economic crisis.

The volatility of markets as well as the impact of deregulation on access to finance have encouraged general wariness and led to market failure. Countering this problem might be described as a form of social renewal, at least in contexts where people have been, historically, pro-market. It is fair to say that law is 'a vehicle for social change'.[41] Its responsiveness to social and business needs is necessary. Nonet and Selznick note that '[a responsive law] perceives social pressures as sources of knowledge and opportunities for self-correction'.[42] In the

36 Guglielmetti (n 33) 13; and generally D Smallbone, J Kitching and M Xheneti, 'Vulnerable or Resilient? SMEs and the Economic Crisis in the UK' in B Dallago and C Guglielmetti (eds), *The Consequences of the International Crisis for European SMEs* (Routledge, 2012) 109 et seq.

37 D Smallbone, D Deakins, M Battisti and J Kitching, 'Small Business responses to a major economic downturn: Empirical perspectives from New Zealand and the United Kingdom' (2012) 30 *International Small Business Journal* 754, 760.

38 Ibid 760.

39 'Resilience', in the context of small businesses and access to finance, is defined as 'the process of adapting well in the face of adversity and the survivability of SMEs during recession'. See L Price, D Rae and V Cini, 'SME perceptions of and responses to the recession' (2013) 20(3) *Journal of Small Business and Enterprise Development* 484, 485.

40 See B Dallago and C Guglielmetti (eds), *The Consequences of the International Crisis for European SMEs* (Routledge, 2012) 13 and generally Smallbone, Kitching and Xheneti (n 36).

41 R Wacks, *Philosophy of Law: A Very Short Introduction* (Oxford University Press, 2006) xii.

42 P Nonet and P Selznick, *Law and Society in Transition Toward Responsive Law* (Harper Torchbooks, 1954) 77.

wake of the financial crisis, small businesses' vulnerability to access to finance and changes in the market is evident. In this context, while it may be regarded as a matter of contractual freedom, arguably, the law, by being responsive to social changes, should protect the vulnerable small businesses against stronger lenders with better bargaining positions.[43] Similar arguments can be made in favour of lenders who are disadvantaged in their dealings with small businesses due to the asymmetric information. The use and availability of collateral or clear information about the financial strength of the borrower (i.e. small business) encourages lending and reduces the financial vulnerability of lenders.[44]

## Some philosophical perspectives

Rule of law has been regarded as the cause of a just society as well as growth.[45] It has been argued that rule of law, and clearly defined and enforceable property rights, are conditions of economic growth that complement societal development.[46] Economic growth (development) has been defined by Joseph Schumpeter as follows:

> Development in our sense is a distinct phenomenon, entirely foreign to what may be observed in the circular flow or in the tendency to equilibrium. It is spontaneous and discontinuous change in the channels of the flow, disturbance of equilibrium, which forever alters and displaces the equilibrium state previously existing.[47]

Economic development/growth is a type of progress that occurs through the collective efforts of individuals who are entrepreneurs. A Rawlsian view will suggest that for this type of progress, be it economic or socio-legal, there is a need to have a *well-ordered society* that is:

> designed to advance the good of its members and effectively regulated by a public conception of justice. Thus it is a society in which everyone accepts and knows that the others accept the same principles of justice, and the basic social institutions satisfy and are known to satisfy these principles.[48]

43 See below for further arguments on bargain and contract.

44 B Carruthers and L Ariovich, *Money and Credit: A Sociological Approach* (Polity Press, 2010) 90. This is particularly true in the case of investment crowdfunding.

45 T Bingham, *The Rule of Law* (Penguin, 2011) 38–9; citing 'Economics and the Rule of Law: Order in the Jungle', *The Economist* (13 March 2008) 95–7.

46 DC North, 'The Paradox of the West' 1 <http://www.archipielagolibertad.org/upload/files/007%20Estado%20de%20derecho/7.1%20Derecho,%20ley,%20instituciones/0025%20North-%20The%20paradox%20of%20the%20west.pdf> accessed 15 September 2015.

47 J Schumpeter, *The Theory of Economic Development: An Inquiry into Profits, Capital, Credit, Interest and the Business Cycle* (translated by Redvers Opie, first published 1934, Oxford University Press, 1961) 64.

48 J Rawls, *A Theory of Justice* (Oxford University Press, 1978) 453–4.

Well-ordered society is part of Rawls' background assumptions and a political conception of justice. Rawls considers the 'idea of society' within the conception of justice 'as a fair system of social cooperation over time from one generation to the next'.[49] Rawls' central 'idea of society' is supported by the idea of citizens who are considered as free and equal, and the idea of well-ordered society which is 'governed by principles of justice'.[50] Rawls applies these principles to the 'basic structure' that is the society's political and legal institutions, which are governed by principles of justice.[51] In the well-ordered society institutions prevent vulnerabilities through principles of justice. As a result 'reciprocity' and 'a social minimum of primary goods' are secured. It has been argued that '[i]t is not crucial that all citizens have equal economic wealth, but it is important that citizens have a sufficient level of reciprocity'.[52] Thus, reciprocity is understood as:

> a relation between citizens expressed by principles of justice that regulate a social world in which all who are engaged in cooperation and do their part as the rules and procedures require are to benefit in an appropriate way as assessed by a suitable benchmark of comparison.[53]

When this line of thought is applied to vulnerability and the access to finance framework, the following may be argued. The *good*, here, can be argued as the increase in income levels, contribution to economic growth and the increase in social mobility and entrepreneurship and closing the gender inequality gap as a result of small businesses' access to finance. The Bank of England's *Finance for Small Firms* report noted that:

> [a] strong relationship between small firms and finance providers is an essential ingredient for promoting enterprise and growth. To innovate and expand, small firms depend upon reliable access to external finance. Ensuring that there is efficient intermediation of funds to small firms, based on a good understanding of risks and returns, is thus an important public policy objective.[54]

*Justice* is a more difficult one to argue as it must create equilibrium for both the lenders and small businesses as borrowers. The position of lenders and small businesses is analogous to a mutual vulnerability and responsibility relationship.[55] If small businesses are vulnerable to financial crisis and market volatilities, then

49 J Rawls, *Justice as Fairness: A Restatement* (Harvard University Press, 2001) 5.

50 Ibid 5.

51 Ibid 10.

52 T Brooks, 'Reciprocity as Mutual Recognition' (2012) 21 *The Good Society* 21, 26.

53 Rawls (n 49) 49.

54 Bank of England, 'Finance for Small Firms – An Eleventh Report' (Bank of England, April 2004) 1.

55 For a discussion of system of rights and mutual vulnerability and responsibility, see e.g. RM Unger, 'The Critical Legal Studies Movement' (1983) 96 *Harvard Law Review* 561, 597 et seq.

the state or the individuals who have the responsibility to protect them, need to take steps to prevent small businesses from being negatively affected from financial crisis and market failures. This is based on the idea that small businesses are important to economic growth and job creation. Thus, it is in the interest of the state to protect and enable them to access finance to achieve the results beneficial for the whole economy. An extrapolation from this argument is that there could be instances when the state might encourage 'strategic forbearance' by lenders. In other words, promoting access to finance for SMEs in a downturn might be accomplished not only through proactive schemes, but also by encouraging banks to re-write existing loan contracts.

Facilitating small businesses' access to finance may create jobs[56] and this may lead to less dependency on public sector jobs or benefits. Less dependency on public sector jobs and benefits and creation of employment may renew confidence in the markets and the financial system by regenerating the economy of a country.[57] Small businesses' ability to access finance and to have protection from vulnerability during financial crises and market changes work towards social well-being, financial inclusion and social mobility whereby people improve their socio-economic levels through their entrepreneurships and contribute to the overall growth.[58] Rising income and confidence in financial markets could have a positive impact on social renewal. It may be argued that lenders that are, say, under the Funding for Lending scheme, have the responsibility to protect the vulnerable (i.e. those small businesses that are in financial difficulty).[59] Thus, it is important and a public good to support SMEs, as this contributes to economic growth and social renewal. Lenders in this category are being funded by the state

56 See n 30.

57 Obviously there are other methods to renew confidence in markets and one of them is the ability of 'markets to demonstrate that they are more competent to regulate themselves either collectively or through bilateral contracting arrangements': see J Black, 'Rebuilding the Credibility of Markets and Regulators' (2009) 3(1) *Law and Financial Markets Review* 1.

58 On Social Cohesion, see e.g. F-B Wietzke and C McLeod, 'Jobs, Well-Being and Social Cohesion Evidence from Value and Perception Surveys' (Background Paper to the 2013 World Development Report, World Bank Group 2013) 2 <https://openknowledge.worldbank.org/bitstream/handle/10986/12138/WDR2013_bp_Jobs_Wellbeing_SocialCohesion.pdf?sequence=1> accessed 5 September 2015, noting that:

> jobs can contribute to social cohesion through their effects on personal wellbeing, identities, and political and social preferences. Individuals who perceive that they are paid fairly and not disadvantaged in their search for jobs are less likely to disengage from the political and social institutions of their communities. Likewise, workers who feel that their job prospects depend at least partially on the overall performance of a nation's economy may sense a vested interest in the political and economic institutions of their country. This interdependence of interest can align personal with societal preferences and contribute to a stronger sense of national identity and fewer conflicts within the labour market.

59 See e.g. 29 November 2013 letter to CEOs on the 'Treatment of small and Medium sized enterprise (SME) customers' from Clive Adamson, Director of Supervision of the Financial Conduct Authority (FCA) <http://www.fca.org.uk/static/fca/documents/letter-ceo-tomlinson-report.pdf> accessed 20 September 2015.

under the scheme so the state has the responsibility towards SMEs that they are funded accordingly. However, lenders have their own vulnerabilities as they are constrained by inter-bank lending and the Basel III Capital Adequacy requirements. From this perspective it is also safe to argue that the state has responsibility towards lenders, too. But these are two strong opposite positions. On the one hand, it is important to support (by establishing the necessary infrastructure) and finance SMEs to reduce their vulnerability (a moral good to further their interest); and, on the other hand, it is important to protect the interests of lenders in order to make them resilient in the face of future financial crisis. Goodin suggests that:

> [w]hom we should favour depends . . . upon the relative vulnerability of each party to us. We must determine: (1) how strongly that party's interests would be affected by our alternative actions and choices; and (2) whether or not he would be able to find other sources of assistance/protection if we failed him.[60]

His argument, with which one can concur, is that 'protecting the vulnerable is . . . an argument for aiding those in dire need'.[61] From this perspective, it would be safe to argue that failure to protect small businesses would adversely affect their contribution to economic development and social renewal. Following from that it is the external financing that small businesses need most at times of crisis and it is the banks, with the support of the state, that assist small businesses to access credit. Without their assistance at times of recession and financial crisis, it is not possible for small businesses to find alternative sources to contribute to economic growth, job creation and social renewal.

Small businesses' failure also has a clear impact on individuals to whom the state has responsibility. This can be posited as the responsibility of the state to establish a financial and legal framework that understands the barriers to access to finance, and either addresses those barriers or enables small businesses to negotiate them. In terms of individual vulnerability it has been argued that:

> . . . consideration of vulnerability brings societal institutions, in addition to the state and individual, into the discussion and under scrutiny. Vulnerability is posited as the characteristic that positions us in relation to each other as human beings and also suggests a relationship of responsibility between state and individual. The nature of human vulnerability forms the basis for a claim that the state must be more responsive to that vulnerability. It fulfils that responsibility primarily through the establishment and support of societal institutions.[62]

60 Goodin (n 26) 119.
61 Goodin (n 26) 111.
62 M Fineman, 'The Vulnerable subject and the Responsive State' (2010) 60 *Emory Law Journal* 251, 255–6.

The responsibility of the state is to protect small businesses and to prevent their failure. When the role of small businesses in economic growth is taken into account, the duty of the state to protect vulnerable small businesses will have an impact on the macroeconomic level. Their protection and prevention from becoming bankrupt will have a positive impact on the social level as well. Therefore, it can be argued that the state has both a positive duty (i.e. to take preventive measures to protect businesses from the effect of financial crisis and market changes) and a negative duty (i.e. not to take decisions that may lead to the bankruptcy of small businesses, which may cause failure of the economy).[63] The positive and negative duties can both be compiled under a concept of 'pragmatic duty' of the state. It may be argued that as small businesses account for over 90 per cent of the world economy there seems to be a relation of mutual reliance between the state and the small business sector[64] and that it is sensible for the state to protect the vulnerable party from incurring further loss.

## Some responses to reduce vulnerability to access to funding

Financial crises and their ensuing market complications tend to cause a number of problems that affect small businesses' access to finance. These include delays in payments to small businesses and lack of demand for goods and services, which cause a decrease in working capital and liquidity for small businesses to expand business, and the increase in their insolvencies, which is an indication of their lack of access to short-term finance (such as bank lending).[65] Small businesses have begun to prefer short-term finance as a result of financial crisis-related insolvencies and banks' reluctance to extend long-term finance. It can be argued, however, that banks' perception of small businesses' ability to repay (whether they are high or low risk debtors), their forecasts as to the aftermath of financial crisis, and the banks' ability to access finance (their capital and liquidity positions as required by the Basel Capital Adequacy Requirements and the problems caused by inter-bank lending) can be regarded as decisive factors in banks' decisions to lend to small businesses. Banks prefer to lend where the debtor can provide full collateral that has the ability to mitigate the effect of the debtor's default. Nevertheless, access to long-term finance could enable small businesses to spread their payments to a wider timeframe and avoid defaults.

In the aftermath of the 2008 financial crisis, steps have been taken to deal with the above highlighted challenges by introducing, for example, the Enterprise Finance Guarantee (EFG) scheme. This loan guarantee scheme, which is now run by the British Business Bank,[66] '[is] delivered via participating Lenders and aimed at supporting the availability of working capital and investment funding

63 For further discussion on positive and negative duties, see Goodin (n 26) 22 et seq.

64 For the relationship between mutual reliance and vulnerability, see Unger (n 55) 600.

65 OECD Centre for Entrepreneurship, SMEs and Local Development (n 7) 6–8.

66 British Business Bank <http://british-business-bank.co.uk/ourpartners/enterprise-finance-guarantee/> accessed 20 November 2015.

for small and medium sized businesses in the UK'.[67] Moreover, the Bank of England's introduction of Funding for Lending Scheme (FLS) in July 2012 aimed to reduce the financial vulnerabilities of small businesses. This scheme intends to promote lending to small business by banks and building societies that borrow from the Bank of England at relatively lower rates than market rates. The FLS was extended for a further two years on 30 November 2015.[68] However, while credit conditions have improved with the introduction of the FLS, the same cannot be argued for SMEs, the credit supply to which has been low.[69] It can be argued that banks that have been de-mutualised have social duties to lend to small businesses.[70] While, from the perspective of banks, the relationship between banks and small businesses can be regarded as a private one (as bargain and contract), through the FLS, it is argued, this becomes a regulated contractual relationship. The understanding under the FLS is to facilitate lending to small businesses whereby the banks and building societies are funded for an extended period by the Bank of England in line with their lending performance.[71] The argument then follows that the state then has the responsibility to make sure that SMEs are funded accordingly in order to be able to contribute to the economy. The UK government's 'Plan for Growth'[72] document provided a number of strategies that would assist small businesses' access to finance and contribution to economic growth.[73] Alternative financing platforms, which act as intermediaries between investors and small businesses, facilitate opportunities for funding. As an

67 <http://www.fsb.org.uk/policy/assets/efg.pdf> accessed 20 September 2015. For the list of participating lenders, see <http://webarchive.nationalarchives.gov.uk/+/bis.gov.uk/policies/enterprise-and-business-support/access-to-finance/enterprise-finance-guarantee/efg-questions-and-answers> accessed 25 April 2016. Small businesses in their Principles of Small Business Banking requested that all banks dealing with small businesses should apply for European Investment Bank Credit, along with the Enterprise Finance Guarantee Scheme. See <http://www.fsb.org.uk/documents/bankingprinciples/> accessed 20 January 2014.

68 Bank of England <http://www.bankofengland.co.uk/publications/Pages/news/2015/096.aspx> accessed 1 December 2015.

69 Bank of England and HM Treasury Funding for Lending Scheme 2015, Q3, Usage and Lending Data, News Release 2 December 2013. See <http://www.bankofengland.co.uk/publications/Pages/fls/q315.aspx> accessed 8 December 2015 where it is stated that the '[i]mprovements in credit conditions over the past few years in part reflect developments in bank funding spreads; despite a slight rise in some measures over the past few months, they remain significantly lower than at the time of the launch of the FLS in 2012'.

70 See e.g. Sir Andrew Large, 'RBS Independent Lending Review' (25 November 2013) <http://www.independentlendingreview.co.uk/RBS_ILR_Full_Report.pdf> accessed 15 September 2015; Lawrence Tomlinson, 'Banks' Lending Practices: Treatment of Businesses in Distress' <http://tomlinsonreport.com/docs/tomlinsonReport.pdf> accessed 15 September 2015.

71 See <http://www.bankofengland.co.uk/markets/Pages/FLS/default.aspx> accessed 15 September 2015.

72 HM Treasury, 'The Plan for Growth' (Department for Business, Innovation and Skills and HM Treasury, March 2011).

73 These include: minimising of regulatory burdens; assisting small businesses to access finance; reducing fixed costs for SMEs; enabling SMEs to access public sector procurement; encouraging innovation and exporting; enabling access to apprenticeships; setting up new enterprise zones; and making it easier for SMEs to get planning consents: ibid 26–7.

example, the Funding Circle[74] is part of the UK government's Business Finance Partnership scheme and has been operating since 2010. Lending under the Funding Circle or similar alternative financing platforms eliminates intermediaries and allows small businesses to borrow directly from investors where the lender spreads the risk by lending to multiple creditworthy borrowers and the borrower borrows from multiple lenders to obtain a low interest rate. The types of funding relevant are either loan-based crowdfunding (loans) or investment-based crowdfunding (equity based).

Private law also offers a number of solutions to small businesses' problems in accessing funding. These can be particularly found in the law of secured transactions. First, the Small Business, Enterprise and Employment Act 2015, section 1 (Business Contract Terms (Restrictions on Assignment of Receivables) Regulations 2015) nullifies clauses that ban assignment of receivables. Overriding non-assignment clauses enable the effectiveness of assignments made notwithstanding a non-assignment clause. This legislative intervention will provide an option for SMEs to use invoice discounting and factoring financing methods. It is submitted that due to the weak bargaining powers of small businesses (compared to large businesses and banks), it does not seem possible to enable this nullification via contractual methods. Thus, it is necessary to regulate this field via legislative intervention. The significant advantage of factoring and invoice factoring is that receivables owed to the small business are sold (outright assignment) to a factoring company. The factoring company pays a discounted amount in return, rather than collateralising these receivables. In other words, in collateralisation the financier takes the assets as security to satisfy the claims of creditors. If the receivables are collateralised the title stays with the small business and, in the case of bankruptcy, receivables will become part of the bankrupt small business' estate. The credit risk, thus, stays with the small business. This is a significant point in the decision of credit supplied by the factoring company, which is based on the value of the small business' receivables rather than the creditworthiness of the small business.[75] This is also the case with many international legislative instruments including the United Nations Convention on the Assignment of Receivables in International Trade, the UNCITRAL Legislative Guide on Secured Transactions and the UNCITRAL draft Model Law on Secured Transactions Law.

A second method is relevant to the priority competition between an asset based financier and an earlier secured creditor who has taken security interests over the present and future assets of the small business. A small business' main collateral, generally, is its receivables. Small businesses borrow on a secured basis, unlike large firms that borrow on an unsecured basis.[76] In some cases, where the small

74 <https://www.fundingcircle.com/> accessed 20 September 2015.

75 L Klapper, 'The Role of Factoring for Financing Small and Medium Enterprises' (Policy Research Working Paper No 3593, World Bank, 2005); see also O Akseli, 'Vulnerability and Access to Low Cost Credit' in M Kenny and J Devenney (eds), *Consumer Credit, Debt and Investment in Europe* (Cambridge University Press, 2012) 15. See also <http://www.publications.parliament.uk/pa/cm201415/cmpublic/smallbusiness/memo/sb76.htm> accessed 20 November 2015).

76 Law Commission Report on Company Security Interests (Law Com No 296, 2005) para 1.2.

business is not in the form of a company it may not be able to grant a charge over its inventory. One alternative to bank financing for small business is to utilise asset based financing. This is also called the ***purchase money security interest*** where the debtor is given value by the asset based financier to acquire rights in or the use of collateral and the value is used for that purpose. Recognising the priority of an asset based financier against a prior security right with an after acquired property clause might enable small businesses to have better access to asset based finance. That is to say that enabling businesses to have access to competing financing options is said to reduce the cost of credit.[77] The issue arises when a small business borrows from a lender who takes a charge over the present and after acquired property of the small business before an asset based financier lends for the purposes of purchasing a specific property, or supplies equipment to the same small business. If the small business is unable to obtain additional financing from the secured creditor, a priority conflict may occur. The general rule under English law, although there are exceptions, on priorities between non-possessory security interests, is that the security interests created first in time obtains priority,[78] whereas if the super-priority position of the asset based financier was recognised, the priority would be based on the type of the security right rather than the time of registration. Unless a subordination agreement is agreed upon between the secured creditor and the asset based financier, the latter might not be willing to extend credit. This could be a problem particularly for small businesses that are new to the market (and which thus have no credible credit history and present information asymmetry problems) or too small to be able to provide additional collateral. For this reason, it could assist small business to have access to competing financiers, if the super-priority position of the asset based financier was recognised. Previous law reform initiatives on secured transactions law have offered justifications that the asset based financier should be granted a super-priority status.[79] A super-priority position is offered to the asset based financier under Uniform Commercial Code Article 9-324 as well as under the UNCITRAL Legislative Guide on Secured Transactions recommendations 178–180.[80]

A third method might be to enable non-bank lenders to have better access to the credit history of small businesses. This will perhaps enable non-bank lenders to better evaluate the creditworthiness of a particular small business. Lenders share data among themselves about the borrower's credit information. However, this information is not readily available to non-bank lenders. Having clear information about the creditworthiness of the borrower enables lenders to make better

77 See e.g. UNCITRAL Legislative Guide on Secured Transactions, para 52, at 20, which states that 'Open competition among all potential credit providers is an effective way of reducing the cost of credit'.

78 See H Beale, M Bridge, L Gullifer and E Lomnicka, *The Law of Security and Title-Based Financing* (2nd edn, Oxford University Press, 2012) 464 et seq.

79 See e.g. The Law Commission, 'Registration of Security Interests: Company Charges and Property other than Land a Consultation Paper' (Law Com CP No 164, 2004) para 4.159.

80 UNCITRAL Legislative Guide on Secured Transactions, para 123, at 352.

informed lending decisions. This will also mitigate the risks of information asymmetry and increase competition among lenders.[81] One way to enable transparency particularly related to unincorporated businesses is to remove barriers presented by the Bills of Sale Acts (the Bills of Sale Act 1878 and the 1882 Amendment Act). The registration under the current regime is not electronic. The registration system needs to be transparent and accessible by third parties. The Bills of Sale Acts exclude incorporated businesses from their scope as security interests over the assets of these businesses are registrable under the Companies Act 2006, Part 25. Thus only individuals and ordinary partnerships are covered by the Bills of Sale Acts. However, the secured transactions law should be comprehensive and include all business and individuals under one comprehensive legislation and registration scheme.[82] This would enable a transparent and fully electronic system that provides notice to third parties (and, inter alia, non-bank lenders) about the credit information of the small businesses that are unincorporated. There is currently a limited Bills of Sale Act reform initiative.[83] However, the initiative does not intend to establish a notice filing registration system. It rather seeks to simplify the current registration requirements with the High Court. While there are justified legitimate reasons (such as the need to harmonise law reform initiatives with the Secured Transactions Law Reform project and the City of London Law Society draft Code on Secured Transactions) not to embark upon or suggest a notice filing system, it would have been better if there had been a comprehensive contribution to the debate on notice filing system. Nevertheless, the reform on this front will enable small businesses whose wealth mainly lies in goods to have simplified procedures to employ the Bills of Sale Act rather than resorting to unsecured borrowing.

## Conclusions

The preceding paragraphs have argued that small businesses are vulnerable to financial crises and market changes. Their vulnerability is linked to their difficulty in accessing external finance mainly through commercial loans (bank loans). The protection of small businesses will produce consequences that are for the benefit of the whole economy. Failing to protect them during crisis times may be interpreted as failing to promote economic welfare as small businesses are crucial to economic growth.[84] Economic growth is generated by the banking system's ability to produce money through leverage and financing of businesses.[85]

81 See Bank of England, 'Should the Availability of Credit Data be Improved?' (a Discussion Paper, Bank of England, May 2014) 5.

82 See e.g. UNCITRAL Legislative Guide on Secured Transactions, which applies to all individuals and businesses. Paragraph 50, at 20 states that 'the law should apply to all types of debtor (that is, legal and natural persons, including consumers)'.

83 <http://www.lawcom.gov.uk/project/bills-of-sale/> accessed 20 November 2015.

84 Goodin (n 26) 14 suggests that '[t]he point of protecting the vulnerable is . . . that in doing so we produce good consequences (i.e., promote the welfare of the vulnerable people we are protecting)'.

85 D Bholat, 'Money, Bank Debt and Business Cycles: Between economic development and finan-

It can be argued that there are a number of methods to address the problem of the small business' limited access to finance as discussed in this chapter. One of these methods can be found within the private law processes offered by secured transactions law. These are, first, nullifying clauses that ban assignment of receivables to the extent that these prevent the small business' access to factoring and invoice discounting practices. This has been effectively achieved by the Small Business Enterprise and Employment Act 2015, section 1. Second, as part of the general reform activities of secured transactions law, the law could offer super-priority position to the later in time asset based financier against the earlier security interest holder with an after acquired property clause. Third, in order to prevent the effects of information asymmetry, security interests over unincorporated businesses should be registrable. This would also eliminate the need to incorporate to access finance.

Another method can be found in the regulation of alternative finance practices. Particularly, investment-crowdfunding needs to be tightly regulated in order to prevent the effects of information asymmetry. Protecting investors by increasing transparency in the information offered by small businesses will increase investor confidence and eliminate the effects of information asymmetry.

Finally, it can be posited that supporting and protecting the vulnerable leads to greater resilience in the future. Resilience may be achieved at both socio-economic (positive social renewal, better life conditions, social mobility and cohesion, sustainable economic growth) and legal levels (ability of small businesses to access finance on a systematic basis, the ability to absorb financial shocks and fewer insolvencies).

cial crises' in O Akseli (ed.), *Availability of Credit and Secured Transactions in a Time of Crisis* (Cambridge University Press, 2013) 11, 16 et seq.

# 8 Conclusion

## The lessons to be learned from the now told stories of the 2008 financial crisis

*Abdul Karim Aldohni*

The 2008 financial crisis shares some common characteristics with previous financial crises: first and foremost, they all involved, one way or another, the same destabilising factor that is debt. As thoroughly demonstrated in Chapter 2, historically there was a shift in the way in which debt was approached and understood. Debt was transformed from a legal relationship between debtor and creditor to a tradable commodity. This shift has not only distinguished debt from the other ways of acquiring purchasing power and the other forms of contractual obligations but has also made it a systemic threat and a major source of financial instability.

Further, the International Monetary Fund (IMF) in its April 2009 report, 'World Economic Outlook: Crisis and Recovery', identified a number of common elements between the Great Depression and the 2008 global financial crisis. The report referred particularly to the high risk and short-term profit-driven model of banking that dominated the sector before the Great Depression and in the run-up to the 2008 financial crisis.[1] In addition, they both resulted in a major regulatory paradigm shift to which restrictive measures, prudence and risk aversion were central. This can be seen clearly in the UK through the substantial regulatory reforms that have taken place since 2008 and the creation of the two new separate financial authorities for prudential regulation and conduct of business. In other words, it is a common occurrence that the explicit effect of any crisis has always been regulatory in nature.

On the other hand, what distinguishes the 2008 crisis from the previous ones, in the UK context, is its implicit manifestations in the financial market. The unfolding events of the 2008 crisis have reshaped the landscape of the UK financial market and impacted its relationship with some important aspects of the business sector, which makes the 2008 financial crash unique in that sense. The book advanced this argument through pursuing two threads: the first concerns the rising financial trends that have become a recognised component of the UK financial market and its practices; while the second's focus is the strain that the 2008 financial crisis put on some of the older financial trends and on some important aspects of the business sector.

1 International Monetary Fund, 'World Economic Outlook: Crisis and Recovery' (April 2009) 106 <http://www.imf.org/external/pubs/ft/weo/2009/01/index.htm> accessed 9 October 2014.

As demonstrated in Chapters 3, 4 and 5 of this book, the UK financial market post 2008 experienced the rise of new financial trends, which varied in their nature. First, there are some relatively new market participants, such as peer-to-peer lending platforms, that emerged just a few years before 2008; however, the 2008 crisis was a turning point for their business. Second, there are some long-existing market participants, for instance high cost short term credit providers, which, with the help of digital technology and the increased demand for credit, have proliferated and become a recognisable source of credit. Finally, there are some new financial instruments, for instance contingent convertible capital instruments (Cocos), which were invented after 2008 and have been increasingly used by banks since.

The increased prominence of peer-to-peer lending platforms in the UK financial market can be considered as an implicit effect of the 2008 financial crisis. By combining loan-level data analysis and empirical research, Chapter 3 provided a snapshot of the peer-to-peer lending sector in the UK market, charting its significant growth from nothing before the crisis to over £500 million in cumulative gross lending as of May 2013. In this regard, peer-to-peer lending platforms were found to be a positive financial innovation, which is endogenous by nature although it has been greatly helped by the new conditions imposed by the 2008 crisis. Peer-to-peer lending platforms have a number of features that have drawn borrowers into them, such as data transparency, financial return, and empowerment as they give investors control over how their money is used.

It is, therefore, suggested in Chapter 3 that this particular implicit effect of the crisis may have a long-lasting effect on the banking sector. Two possible key impacts have been identified in this respect: first, banks reducing their interest rates on unsecured lending in order to compete with peer-to-peer lenders, which eventually would adversely affect their profitability; second, banks readjusting their distribution channels towards more internet- and mobile-based channels.

On the other hand, it is difficult to consider high cost short term credit providers as a positive new financial innovation since they have long existed in the UK market. And, as demonstrated in Chapter 4, they prey on the vulnerable using extortionate rates and irresponsible lending practices to fuel their business. Therefore, although they provide a service to those who cannot access mainstream credit at the best of times, let alone during the time of a credit crunch, their cost is excessive and their practices are exploitive, which makes their input far from positive.

It is important to note that their long existence in the UK market does not change the fact that their new found status as a rising trend in the UK can be primarily attributed to the crisis. Since 2008 this sector has managed to proliferate at a significant scale, widening its client base through the use of digital technologies and filling the credit gap brought about by the 2008 crisis. As argued in Chapter 4, the rise of this financial trend post 2008 in the UK market has had adverse effects on the consumer side of the business considering the ineffective legislative protection available to high cost short term credit consumers.

Finally, Cocos are a clear example of post 2008 financial innovation for two reasons. First, they are designed to address the shortcomings of other types of convertible bonds, which were uncovered by the 2008 crisis. Second, they have been increasingly used by banks in order to comply with the new capital requirements of Basel III, more specifically to boost their Tier I capital, which is part of the regulatory change brought about by the 2008 financial crash. As Chapter 5 argued, these instruments have many positives to offer, such as encouraging better market transparency, improving banks' resilience, and eventually protecting taxpayers' money. However, Cocos are still risky and highly complex instruments whose design is far from perfect and raises certain concerns among which is the effectiveness of the trigger indicator and pricing. Some of these concerns and more have materialised recently (February 2016) and led to a sharp fall in trading in Cocos.

Further, in the UK, the large stake that UK banks have in the issuance of Cocos in addition to the risk and complicated nature of these instruments have made the FCA intervene and restrict the sale of Cocos to retail investors.

Despite the difference in their influence on the UK financial market, where some have been more positive than others, these rising trends have a key feature in common: they all owe their significance in the UK financial market to the new conditions imposed by the 2008 financial crisis. In other words, they might be described as the implicit effects of the crisis, yet the trigger for their growth or emergence is directly linked to the 2008 crisis, whether this trigger was the shortage of credit supply or the regulatory reforms of post 2008.

With regard to the second thread that this book has pursued, it is suggested that the crisis has also challenged some of the old practices in the UK financial market. For instance, the essence of the ethical finance sector has been put to the test by the 2008 financial crisis. As argued in Chapter 6, the unfolding events of the 2008 crisis exposed a contaminated business culture that is fuelled by selfish pursuit of personal gains and unaccountability. The uncovering of the ethical deficit in the financial market led to questioning the immunity of ethical financial institutions to this problem and whether they can be part of the solution. Chapter 6 demonstrated that while ethical financial institutions were more equipped to deal with the problem of selfish pursuit of personal gains, they were not so in relation to the problem of unaccountability. The scandal of the Co-operative Bank in 2013 showed that the bank lacked the required mechanisms to hold its individuals accountable for fulfilling the long-term commitments of their institution.

Further, the crisis has also put a strain on the relationship between the financial market and the business sector, more specifically small and medium-sized enterprises (SMEs). As demonstrated in Chapter 7, SMEs are most vulnerable at times of financial crisis yet at the same time they are essential to economic recovery and growth. In this regard, SMEs account for 58 per cent of employment in the UK; nevertheless their access to finance has significantly decreased since 2008. In the wake of the crisis, when making their lending decisions to businesses UK banks have primarily relied on business size, profitability and the ability to provide satisfactory collateral. Since it is this type of criteria that almost all SMEs would find very difficult to satisfy, they are faced with a credit supply problem. As argued in

Chapter 7, the state intervention to support SMEs is essential and can be justified not only on economic but also social grounds, given the important role that these institutions play in social and economic progression and the extensive challenge that the crisis brought to their very existence.

## Reflections on the implicit effects of the 2008 crisis on the UK financial market

Having considered the implicit effects that the crisis of 2008 had on the UK financial market it can be suggested that with regard to the market's prospect it is not all doom and gloom. Some of the rising trends of post 2008 represent positive financial innovations.

Peer-to-peer lending platforms are a good example of this type of financial innovation as they represent a new source of finance that is transparent and capable of generating financial return to its investors. Another positive to add to peer-to-peer lending platforms is that they have a social aspect to their business. In other words, investors have a real sense of connection to where their money will end up. This is important as it helps introduce less commodified and more relational understanding of debt. Finally, some of the peer-to-peer lending platforms in the UK, such as Funding Circle, are being used by SMEs as an alternative source of finance. This makes this relatively new financial innovation a part of the solution to deal with the strain that the crisis put on the relationship between the UK financial market and the business sector.

Cocos are also an innovative financial instrument that helps banks improve their resilience and can also be used as an additional regulatory compliance mechanism. However, this positive outlook of this rising trend should be accepted with caution considering the concerns raised with regard to the design of these instruments, more specifically their pricing and trigger mechanism. The recent sharp fall in trading in Cocos (February 2016) is a clear indication of the seriousness of these concerns and the need for a careful reassessment of this new financial innovation.

On the other hand, there is no doubt that some of the implicit effects of the 2008 crisis have damaged some aspects of the UK financial market, for example the credibility of ethical finance. In this regard it can be suggested that the crisis may have undermined the ethical finance sector in the short run. However, in the long run the crisis has helped the ethical finance sector reflect on its weaknesses and has given it the opportunity to address them, which may eventually allow this sector to play a role in changing the contaminated culture of the financial business.

Finally, it comes as no surprise that the financial authorities in the UK were quick in responding to the crisis, yet the same cannot be said about its implicit effects. This can be seen in their delayed response to the problem of high cost short term credit. High cost short term credit providers were running wild until very recently when some restrictions were imposed on their lending practices, including a cap on the credit cost. Further, there is certainly room for more regulatory involvement with regard to some of the identified implicit effects. For instance, peer-to-peer lending appears to be a success story, but the regulator should continue to ensure that these platforms are making prudent lending decisions in order to avoid another financial crash in the future. In addition, the financial authorities can be more innovative with their use of secured transactions law in order to ease the credit supply problem for SMEs.

# Index

For Product Safety Concerns and Information please contact our
EU representative GPSR@taylorandfrancis.com Taylor & Francis
Verlag GmbH, Kaufingerstraße 24, 80331 München, Germany